# GETTING
# GLOBALIZATION
# RIGHT

A project of the
Latin American Program
of the Woodrow Wilson International
Center for Scholars

# GETTING GLOBALIZATION RIGHT

## The Dilemmas of Inequality

edited by

Joseph S. Tulchin
Gary Bland

LYNNE
RIENNER
PUBLISHERS

BOULDER
LONDON

Published in the United States of America in 2005 by
Lynne Rienner Publishers, Inc.
1800 30th Street, Boulder, Colorado 80301
www.rienner.com

and in the United Kingdom by
Lynne Rienner Publishers, Inc.
3 Henrietta Street, Covent Garden, London WC2E 8LU

**Library of Congress Cataloging-in-Publication Data**
Getting globalization right: the dilemmas of inequality / edited by
Joseph S. Tulchin and Gary Bland.
   Includes bibliographical references and index.
   ISBN 1-58826-346-0 (hardcover: alk. paper)
   ISBN 1-58826-322-3 (pb: alk. Paper)
1. Democracy. 2. Globalization. 3. Equality.
I. Tulchin, Joseph S., 1939– II. Bland, Gary.
JC423.G376 2005
303.48'2—dc22

                           2004029653

**British Cataloguing in Publication Data**
A Cataloguing in Publication record for this book
is available from the British Library.

Printed and bound in the United States of America

 The paper used in this publication meets the requirements
of the American National Standard for Permanence of
Paper for Printed Library Materials Z39.48-1992.

5  4  3  2  1

# Contents

# Tables and Figures

## Tables

## Figures

# Acknowledgments

The editors would like to thank former Latin American Program associate Meg Ruthenburg and current program members Trisha Fields, Cristina Jimenez, and Alana Parker of the Woodrow Wilson Center for their help in various stages of the publication of this book. We also are grateful to our colleague Kent Hughes for his advice and encouragement at every step of the project. A debt of gratitude also goes to Elizabeth Bryan for her help in the organization of the workshop that led to the book.

# 1

# Introduction:
# Getting Globalization Right

*Joseph S. Tulchin and Gary Bland*

When the Soviet Union collapsed suddenly, it brought to an end a period marked by a confrontation between two different systems of governance, two different systems of international and economic organization. Since one of the two systems had "won" the conflict, it seemed logical to a number of observers that the next stage in history would be dominated by the rules, values, and modes of production of that system. For a very brief period, at the beginning of the 1990s, it was assumed that the international community was about to enter a period of peaceful governance in which differences, tensions, and the like would be resolved within the framework of one or another of existing multilateral organizations. That assumption quickly proved excessively optimistic. Nationalists, especially in the United States, were unwilling to cede sovereignty or authority to international institutions. On the other hand, internationalists were reluctant to have those organizations, especially the United Nations or, in the Western Hemisphere, the Organization of American States (OAS), serve as the arbiters of global governance because certain individual nations, such as the United States, were thought to exercise too much influence over them. Both the UN and the OAS were created in response to the Cold War, and the great powers had designed them to protect their interests as the leaders of the international community. Until the end of the Cold War, there was little sense of community outside the great power competition.

Throughout the debate following the end of the Cold War, most took for granted that there was an international community and that it was being drawn together by a process known as globalization. Early on, globalization seemed to be a politically neutral phenomenon—natural and inexorable—that brought almost entirely positive outcomes in its wake, as it tied peoples and nations closer together through increasing and increasingly rapid exchange of information, capital, goods, people, and services. The only difficulty appeared to be one of attaining access to the benefits, espe-

1

cially consumer goods and information technologies, of a new world order. The only policy questions appeared to be how quickly nations could open their economies to trade and flows of capital within the global economy and how quickly they could open themselves to the newest modes of communication and thereby become more globalized.

Following more than a decade of scholarship on the topic and a series of events—from regional economic crises to street riots—we can see that globalization is both controversial and complex. Globalization has its critics (Stiglitz 2002a). It also has its staunch supporters.[1] What it does not yet have is a set of prescriptions for public policies to deal with the problems globalization is perceived to create or to maximize the benefits it is supposed to deliver. The antiglobalization forces remain just that, opposed to something that is hard to define and whose proponents are not always easy to identify (George 2002; Weiss 1997).

The principal dilemma provoked by globalization is inequality. There are unequal benefits from the process. There is unequal distribution of goods, services, and cultural values. Most disquieting, there is rising inequality among nations and within nations that appears to result, at least in the short term, from certain facets of the process itself, particularly market opening and the sacrifices imposed on developing countries so that they might enjoy the benefits of access to certain goods and services controlled by richer, more developed nations.[2] The Internet may be free, but only to those with telephones, fast connections, and computers—and the software to run all of them. In the question of trade and investment, there is a clear "race to the bottom" where cheaper and cheaper labor costs drive the market, where low wages do not appear to bring benefits to workers in many countries, and where increasing numbers of jobs are being lost in countries where wages are relatively high. This is true even between developing countries, so that increasing trade and investment flows by themselves may conflict with the rights of working people and create social and political tensions within developing countries. In other words, we now understand that globalization is not a process independent of politics; that market opening—whether in the richest countries or the poorest—involves political decisions and that there will be winners and losers in each case.

The backlash to globalization that has emerged over the past few years is centered on a single concept—getting globalization right, in the sense of making its benefits more available and making them more equitable between countries and within countries. This book is an inquiry into one facet of getting globalization right: how globalization is linked to inequality within emerging or relatively new democracies. We offer a series of detailed case studies of Brazil, Mexico, the Philippines, South Africa, South Korea, Spain, and Turkey in which we ask the same set of questions and that we use as the basis for a series of proposals for policies to alleviate inequality. We focus on democracies because we believe that any discussion of policy decisions cannot occur within a vacuum. That is, the state does certain things because its constituents want those things done. If the state does those things badly, someone is (or should be) accountable for those deficiencies and there are processes, such as elections, through which people can express their satisfaction or displeasure. In other words, we begin with the assumption that getting globalization right is a process, a political process, in which nations or groups of nations make decisions as to how to deal with the forces of globalization. In this volume we want to see whether nations or groups of nations are helpless in the face of globalization or whether they have some capacity to deal with these forces.

Understanding the complexity of globalization begins with the recognition that there is no consensus on what it means. Generally, globalization is considered to be the emergence and thickening on a world scale of networks of connections in the realms of the economic, political, social, and cultural (Keohane 2001: 1). Globalization is viewed variously, for example, as a kind of natural occurrence resulting from relatively rapid global economic and other changes in recent years, the continuation of an historical process that began centuries ago, and/or an intense penetration of national life by all kinds of international networks (Held 1995). It surely entails networks of all kinds, from international organizations and associations, financial markets, security systems, and nongovernmental associations to new political thought, ethnic revival, religious movements, and advocacy for environmental protection. But, as has been shown, networks by themselves are not necessarily democratic or equitable (Cohen 2004).

In this volume, we seek to take on the controversial, much analyzed question of globalization and social inequality. Rather than looking to measure the impact of globalization on poverty levels, however, we more broadly examine how democracies have or have not been able to deal with the persistence or growth of inequity. Through a diverse series of case studies of new or consolidating democracies, we look to address a central dilemma: How do democratic countries successfully face the powerful combination of increasing globalization pressures, deepening problems of income distribution, and the absence of clear policy options to deal with the dilemma? Economically, globalization provides a prescription for growth and prosperity based on market competition, labor flexibility, free trade, and capital flows.[3] Politically, effective and responsive democracy is the watchword worldwide. The demand for formally representative government and accountability to the citizenry has never been more widespread than it is today. And yet, as our case studies make plain, the demands of economic and political globalization frequently place opposing pressures on new democracies. It is also important to note that, although we take a political-economy approach to global integration, other facets of globalization occasionally intrude, particularly mass communication and information technology (Castells 2002).

## To Globalize or Not to Globalize?—A False Choice

Given the polemics that quickly surround a discussion of globalization, a point made by Simon Schwartzman in Chapter 6 bears repeating here. Simply stated, the globalization debate is too often presented for rhetorical purposes as a choice between two clearly definable alternatives. The reality is radically different: an array of policy choices are involved and decision-makers face pressures from all quarters to select an option that appears best given the available information. Developing countries do not have the luxury of simply opting either for international integration (which will bring new markets and growth or, depending on your perspective, raise the risk of increased poverty) or national self-sufficiency (which will either promote economic development and equity or risk stunting economic growth, again, depending on your perspective). All countries already experience some degree of integration with the world economy, and the impact of deepening or reducing such integration is not easy to determine in advance under any circumstances. Moreover, the key questions appear to be the terms under which developing nations are able to negotiate their incremental integration into the international community and the autonomy each of them might have from exogenous and endogenous forces to formulate policies that effectively mitigate the possible negative consequences for their citizens of additional integration.

There certainly is evidence that international integration, taken to mean increased participation in world trade, has benefited all parties under the appropriate circumstances, which include good social and economic policies (Dollar and Kraay 2002: 27). In Chapter 8, Oliver-Alonso and Vallés provide a consummate example of a case—Spain—in which the policies and context for global integration can have a dramatically positive impact. Yang and Moon, on the other hand, demonstrate in Chapter 4, the case of South Korea, that a poorly designed and implemented labor market reform leads to personal economic insecurity and increased inequity under conditions of increasing globalization. Other scholars have similarly argued that some poor countries have changed their policies to exploit globalization and gained the most from it, while others, especially those who were too isolated from the world, have lost the most (Lindert and Williamson 2001). Some in the media have argued that singling out globalization as the cause of inequality within nations is a difficult case to make; other factors, they note, are important as well (Henwood 2003: 3).

The starting point for this volume is that the response to globalization is a political process involving relations between nation-states and relations within nation-states. To understand how nations cope with globalization we must take into account the context in which a nation or group of nations operates, as well as the internal constituencies for national policies. Winners and losers in the globalization process are determined as much by state capacity and by the capacity of political actors within states as by economic forces. From this perspective, globalization itself is a political process. As Ulrich Beck (2000: 1) has put it, "Globalization means politicization." Having said that, however, we should recognize some of the arguments made by others in the debate over globalization, especially those arguments that may be taken to criticize globalization and acknowledge the importance of political processes.

At the beginning of the 1990s, the consensus among economists was that increasing trade and investment was beneficial to all participants in the international community, just as it was assumed that sustained economic growth was the best way to reduce poverty (Morley 1995). More recently, concern for the poor and for the globalization losers in the short term, has produced a more nuanced approach. Trade liberalization can be a good way to reduce poverty, but only if it is accompanied by appropriate policies: "Certainly, the evidence suggests that with care, trade liberalization can be an important component of a 'pro-poor' development strategy" (Winters, McCulloch, and McKay 2004: 108). A number of authors have suggested that capital flows also can be harmful and might require improved modes of regulation, either by the receiving nation or by international agencies such as the International Monetary Fund (Stiglitz 2004). Ten years earlier, on December 14, 1993, David Felix of Washington University made the same suggestion in a Wilson Center seminar titled "Capital Markets in Developing Countries." A number of studies by Dani Rodrik and others have emphasized the link between effective "pro-poor" policies and domestic institutions and political processes. Rodrik also has alluded to the need for more effective international governance, a point made often in the literature on international relations by Robert Keohane and others (Rodrik 1997; Keohane 2001). Nancy Birdsall and her colleagues at the Center for Global Development have published a number of studies of the links between globalization and social policy and how to ensure that the benefits of globalization reach the poor in developing countries (Birdsall 2002).

One of the most specific proposals made to ameliorate the pernicious effects of globalization in developing countries has to do with the need to protect working people. These proposals call for better rules in the international community to protect working people, and insist on the need for international labor standards. One of the more prominent advocates of new policy is Oxfam, which—to the dismay of antiglobalists—sees world trade as a potential engine for growth and poverty reduction. The problem is the unfair rules by which the poorest nations are forced to play. Industrialized countries such as the United States and those in Europe are able to institute agricultural subsidies and other protectionist measures that are treated as taboo for serious free-market economies in the developing world. Oxfam argues not only for a series of trade measures including the removal of such barriers, but also has called for the adoption of policies that directly or indirectly serve to redistribute wealth to the poor. Economic growth by itself cannot reduce poverty. Directed social, educational, and health programs are also required if low-income populations are to contribute to the economy, develop skills, and earn higher income (Watkins 2004).[4]

## Chapter Summaries

As noted, this volume brings together a group of case studies in an effort to examine globalization and its impact on inequality around the world. Indeed, the seven cases—South Africa, Turkey, South Korea, the Philippines, Brazil, Mexico, and Spain—cover four continents and readily allow for a diverse set of perspectives. Yet, in many ways the observations and arguments made are similar enough to lend support to the notion that globalization is indeed a process of interstate homogenization.

In Chapter 2, Steven Friedman of the Centre for Policy Studies in Johannesburg examines the case of South Africa. He provides a detailed review of the rise of the African National Congress (ANC) from a national liberation movement to the leader of a governing alliance based on identity politics. Emphasizing the predominance of domestic influences, Friedman adds that the South African adjustment to globalization may largely be an expression of the workings of a diversity of interests gathered under the ANC banner. Most importantly, the pro-poor elements of the ANC alliance have been out of touch with the preferences of the poor since 1994, leaving them without a voice in the policy debate on issues addressing inequality. To resolve the problem, Friedman calls for a deepening of representative democracy through a redesign of democratic institutions, improvements in international donor programs, and a commitment to opening up the debates on policy.

In Chapter 3, E. Fuat Keyman of Koç University addresses the growth of poverty and inequality in Turkey, which he sees as a direct result of globalization. The focal point of his analysis is the February 2001 financial crisis and the dramatic impact it had on Turkish national politics. The crisis forced the issue of distributive justice onto the policy agenda, notably during the November 2002 elections. It became clear to all political actors that if Turkey was to become modern and prosperous, economic stability had to be accompanied by social progress. Otherwise, any economic adjustment program would lack the legitimacy needed to survive. In other words, good governance, Keyman adds, must be replaced by democratic governance.

Jae-jin Yang and Chung-in Moon of Yonsei University assess the South Korean case in Chapter 4. Their analysis focuses largely on the labor market and the impact of globalization on the welfare of workers. During the authoritarian era, South Koreans accepted a "social contract" with the state that promised economic growth and increased income in exchange for restrictions on social policy. With the 1997 economic crisis, however, that contract was shattered, and the government's response was to combine neoliberal economic reform with a stronger social-welfare system. The new welfare system has not, however, been able to resolve the predicament of nonregular workers, whose numbers have increased dramatically. These workers, whose rates of social insurance coverage are low, are seen as the great victims of globalization.

In Chapter 5, Aprodicio Laquian of the University of British Columbia describes how a longstanding and unwavering Filipino commitment to liberal democracy may be limiting the country's economic and social progress in a globalizing world. More than any of the authors, he details the historical roots of globalization, and he traces the evolution there of liberal democracy and elaborates on its key characteristics—compulsory education, a strong civil society, and a free media. Laquian points out that the Philippines needs to overcome a number of structural and institutional factors, especially the problem of corruption, if it is to achieve greater growth and equality within its liberal democratic system. Selective interventions in the market must also be instituted, however, including environmental and labor regulations, protection of the welfare and rights of indigenous populations, and effective social safety nets for the benefit of the poor.

In Chapter 6, Simon Schwartzman, now an independent researcher in Brazil, begins with an examination of the conceptual linkage between the dependency theory of the past and globalization, then takes a historical view of Brazil's reentry into the global world. He provides a thorough examination of the social question, which has long been recognized as a severe problem in the country. Equity, the education system, employment, and traditionally marginalized sectors (minority races, children) are all given detailed treatment. Brazil now recognizes, Schwartzman writes, that the reduction of poverty and inequity are not a limitation on economic growth but, rather, an important instrument in bringing the Brazilian economy to new levels of economic performance. Ultimately, he concludes, the battle for economic progress and social equity will be won on the domestic front.

Chapter 7, authored by Ilán Bizberg of the Colegio de México, addresses the case of Mexico. Bizberg takes a close look at the politics of the new economic model in his country. This model was imposed by an authoritarian regime, he argues, absent any kind of societal consensus. So the model lacks the "regulatory mechanisms that ensure social cohesion";

instead, minimal social cohesion is being provided through social assistance to the poorest sectors. Moreover, Bizberg argues that since most of the nonrepresentative institutions that adopted this economic model remain in place today, even with the election of Vicente Fox, Mexico will therefore find it difficult to overcome its economic limitations, especially low salary levels and a failure to promote indigenous technological development.

In Chapter 8, Josep Oliver-Alonso and Josep Vallés, both professors at the Autonomous University of Barcelona, examine the lessons of the Spanish experience with globalization over the last twenty-five years of the twentieth century. In contrast with the other cases in this volume, that experience proved to be highly favorable. The authors view globalization and the social and political transformations that constitute democratization as part of the same process. Globalization began at the end of the 1950s and has been strongly related to the country's entry into the European Union in 1986. A democratic system was a prerequisite for achieving EU membership. Meanwhile, a strong public-sector role in reducing inequality provided for the legitimization of the system. In essence, Spanish workers accepted a social contract in which they moderated their wage claims, thus helping ensure global economic competitiveness, in exchange for extensive social investments in education, health, and other sectors. Social and political instability was replaced by a "virtuous circle" of stable democracy, economic growth, and a reduction in inequality.

Are there lessons to be learned about globalization? Certainly. But they vary across cases and through time. What the experiences of all of these countries suggest, however, is that to mitigate the potential damages globalization might cause, particularly increasing poverty and inequality, it is necessary to have a government sensitive to the needs of its people and that the government must have at its disposal effective institutions that allow for the effective, efficient execution of public policies. It helps, as in the Spanish case, to have a supportive and nurturing external environment and a propitious moment in time. However, even in the best of times and the best of circumstances, it is necessary to face the effects of globalization deliberately and in a manner that enhances the democratic qualities of society. Access and inclusion are the keys to successful public policy in softening the negative effects of globalization. This is probably what economists mean when they say, "this rule is true, all other things being equal."

### Notes

1. For example, Stiglitz's own colleague, Jagdish N. Bhagwati (2003), and Thomas Friedman (2000). The A.T. Kearney Company produces an annual index that measures how "globalized" nations are and concludes that the most globalized benefit the most. See *Foreign Policy* (2004).

2. For a critical viewpoint of the globalization process and its impact on inequality, see Castels (2001).

3. The World Bank maintains a website devoted to studies of how to get globalization right: http://www1.worldbank.org/economicpolicy/globalization. It is a wealth of information that focuses mainly on economic issues and takes a positive position, although many of the papers posted on the site criticize the process and provide evidence of failures of the globalization process.

4. See also Tonelson (2002). Rodrik (2002a) has proposed better labor rules also; and Barbara Stallings (forthcoming) is engaged in a comparative study of labor standards and globalization in different developing nations.

# 2

# South Africa: Globalization and the Politics of Redistribution

*Steven Friedman*

South Africa's transition to democracy is sometimes cited as a model of the resolution of identity conflicts. It may yet prove to have an added significance—it may show that the chain of causation proposed by conventional understandings of globalization are only as weak as their strongest link.

To present the case less cryptically, South Africa appears, at first sight, as a particularly strong exemplar of conventional globalization wisdom; so closely does the evidence seem to fit the theory that the society's experience might have been scripted for textbooks presenting current mainstream understandings of the influence of global markets on states. But a more thorough analysis demonstrates that, on the contrary, the real significance of the South African story lies in the way in which it undermines the conventional wisdom. On closer inspection, South Africa demands a fundamental rethinking of many current notions of globalization.

In this chapter, I analyze the development of macroeconomic and social policy in postapartheid South Africa against the background of conventional understandings of globalization. I argue that, despite the apparently inexorable logic of this "adaptation" to "global realities," failure to launch an effective assault on inequality lies in domestic factors to which globalization, understood more as the increased diffusion of ideas and information than as an economic force, has added some nuances but has rarely if ever been a decisive influence. Three related factors—the domestic policy elite's desire to refute racial prejudice by emulating Northern societies, the particular contours of the society's identity politics, and structural changes in the labor market—combine to ensure a context that, while reasonably favorable to the survival of formal democracy, is inhospitable to an effective egalitarian politics. I suggest that the antidote lies not in a concerted attempt to adjust to or to withstand exogenous shocks but in the strengthening of domestic representative democracy and a deepening of associational life. The analysis begins with a brief discussion of the conventional notion of globalization and its relation to South Africa's transition.

## Cross-Country Comparisons

How does this analysis of the South African reality relate to the other country studies in this book?

There are strong parallels between the analysis proposed above and the Mexican study in Chapter 7. While specifics obviously differ significantly, both illustrate the extent to which the nature and choices of domestic elites determine social policy outcomes under current conditions. And both stress the need for a new government relationship with society—or key actors within it—if inequality is to be effectively addressed.

There are also important similarities to the Brazilian study in Chapter 6, and not only in its conclusion that "ultimately, it is in the domestic front that the battle for economic progress and social equity will be won or lost." Its conclusion that the key constraint to greater equality lies in the "governments' inability to redirect social spending and to implement better social policies" applies just as emphatically in the South African case. And in South Africa as in Brazil, inefficient and at times regressive social spending has far more to do with the uneven distribution of access to official policy, and decisionmaking, than it does with technically inadequate choices. The notion that there is some sort of politically neutral "technical" solution to the problem of inequality is in any event called into question by the sharp differences in approach between specialists in both societies—the division between contending ideological positions and their attendant proposed solutions is found in both countries and in both, inevitably, the argument is settled by who is politically dominant.

To suggest that many South Africans lack effective access to the political process is not to say that South African democracy is a sham. Rather, there are distinct parallels with the Philippines study's argument that considerable democratic enthusiasm has produced a democracy that, for all its flaws, operates relatively well—but which has failed to offer substantial and sustainable increases in living standards for the poor. There are certainly important differences. In contrast to the Philippines, the electoral dominance of South Africa's governing party and its cause, the predominance of identity politics (which may prompt citizens to support representatives of "their" social group regardless of probity or performance), places constraints on democratic vigor that do not appear to apply in the Philippines. Capacity to participate in politics may be more unevenly distributed in South Africa: poverty, physical distance from political decisionmakers, and language (English is the *lingua franca* of politics, but the home language of less than 10 percent of the population, many of whom are rendered largely voiceless by a lack of English proficiency) may exclude many from politics in South Africa. But the democratic enthusiasm described in the Philippines study is found in abundant measure: high levels of participation in general elections, a vigorous public debate, and the independence of the media are testimony to this. That democracy has been unable to offer many of the newly enfranchised a route out of poverty has to do not with a failure of the system—although I would argue that details of South African democracy are open to improvement—as with the reality that most citizens lack the resources to imprint their voice on the social policy debate.

If the Philippines study illustrates the dangers of simplistic judgments on democracy—in South Africa as well as that country—then the Korean study in Chapter 4 shows the dangers of equally sweeping categorizations of economic policy. Like the Kim Dae Jung government, South Africa's ruling party has a strong egalitarian tradition and labor support base but has embarked on reforms that threaten organized workers and other sections of its constituency with a proclaimed interest in egalitarianism. But in both the shift has been accompanied by an attempt to balance neoliberal reforms with measures that seek to compensate sections of the governing-party constituency. The details differ—while our Korean study shows that labor market reform has been the government priority, in South Africa the governing African National Congress (ANC) has been inclined to leave legislated labor rights largely intact. The ANC also arguably has a more complex balancing act to negotiate given that it must be seen to be tackling racial inequality, rejection of which is the "glue" that unites its diverse constituency, and that this may cause it to take the black poor more seriously than a reforming elite unencumbered by a history of racial domination might otherwise do. But in both, social spending has been seen by the governing party as a means of softening the blow of economic reform and in both, it will be argued here, the increasing shift toward informal work has proved the Achilles' heel of attempts to address poverty. But, while the Korean attempt has been undermined by the technical difficulties of relying on a social-security net dependent on formal wages in a context of growing informalization, I argue that the South African problem is primarily political since increasing informality has deprived the poor of a voice in social and economic policy.

The contention that there are political "virtuous cycles" that can erode poverty and produce much more egalitarian outcomes—despite the purported constraints that globalization is said to place on states—is demonstrated by the Spanish case in Chapter 8, where "democratic legitimacy, economic growth and redistribution of income through the public sector" have achieved rising living standards and greater social equality despite an opening to the world economy that, in much contemporary analysis, is said to doom egalitarian ventures. In Spain, the chapter shows, openness has produced greater equality because it has been accompanied by "a public responsibility for the reduction of social and economic inequalities." This in turn was made possible by arrangements that are said by many to be increasingly ineffective under current conditions—a social contract in which workers accept reductions in real wages in exchange for a "compensatory social salary," increased public spending in education, health, pensions, and unemployment benefits—and which are clearly made possible by the greater possibility for free interest-group bargaining that democracy brings. Through the agency of "an active public sector in social policies," Spain has achieved a "virtuous circle" of stable democracy, economic growth, and inequality reduction. If further evidence were needed that individual states do have considerable latitude to address inequality even as they participate in the international economy—and that considerable scope does still exist for effective redistributive public policy—the Spanish case serves as an important example.

In South Africa, too, there is no evidence that the opening to the world economy that occurred after apartheid-induced siege ended in the 1990s has hampered attempts to address poverty and inequality. Attempts have been made to generate a workable social contract and to ensure that social benefits are extended to the poor. That they have been far more successful in Spain may owe much not only to the greater coherence of interest-based politics in the European country, but also the greater strength and access to political decisions of interests with a stake in reduced inequality, conditions that do not exist in a country such as South Africa, where access and strength, like material goods, are bestowed to some in far greater abundance than others.

While this chapter may differ from others in this collection in the importance—or lack of it—it assigns to globalization's effect on state capacity, it derives from all of them important congruences with the South African case. All, in differing ways, offer insights that demonstrate the importance of politics in general, and its democratic variant in particular, in entrenching or reducing inequality. The central contention of this chapter—that effective action against inequality is a consequence of a thus far elusive deepening and broadening of democratic politics—finds much to sustain it in the other studies, even while it recognizes the specificity of each.

## South Africa: A Profile

Before beginning the analysis, it may be useful to offer a brief sketch, supported by statistical data, of the South African economy and some of its social implications. Greater detail is provided by Tables 2.1–2.5.

South Africa is a middle-income country with a gross domestic product (GDP) of US$153.024 billion.[1] Per capita GDP is US$3,368—an increase

**Table 2.1    Free but Unequal: Inequality and Poverty by Race**

| Race | Gini Coefficient | Headcount Index (percentage of households living in poverty[a]) |
|------|------------------|---------------------------------------------------------|
| Black African | 0.53[b] | 38.22 |
| Colored[c] | 0.49 | 21.51 |
| Asian | 0.48 | 3.73 |
| White | 0.49 | 3.03 |
| Total | 0.603 | 32.02 |

*Source:* Poswell (2002: 14).

*Notes:* a. Poverty is defined as US$126 per household per month in 1995 real terms.

b. The figure cited for the black African Gini coefficient is considered low by specialists who insist that it is equal to or greater than the national coefficient.

c. The term "colored" denotes people of mixed race or of Malay ancestry.

**Table 2.2    The Growth of Informality: Formal and Informal Sector Employment**

| Year | Formal Employment | Percentage Change | Informal Employment | Percentage Change |
|------|-------------------|-------------------|---------------------|-------------------|
| 1996 | 8,291,000 | — | 996,000 | — |
| 1997 | 8,111,000 | −2.17 | 1,136,000 | 14.06 |
| 1998 | 8,074,000 | −0.46 | 1,316,000 | 15.85 |
| 1999 | 8,462,000 | 4.81 | 1,907,000 | 44.91 |
| 1996–1999 increase | 171,000 | 2.06 | 911,000 | 91.4 |

*Source:* Bhorat (2003: 4).

**Table 2.3    The Legacy of the Past: Employment Creation By Race 1995–1999**

| Race | Jobs created | Percentage change | Employment absorption rate |
|------|--------------|-------------------|----------------------------|
| Black African | 612,146 | 9.94 | 25.07 |
| Colored | 178,515 | 15.95 | 69.17 |
| Asian | 43,607 | 12.37 | 49.25 |
| White | 119,799 | 6.22 | 70.36 |
| Total | 971,504 | 10.17 | 32.59 |

*Source:* Bhorat (2003: 11).

of 4.5 percent since 1995 (South African Reserve Bank 2003: S-153). Inequality is particularly acute and the Gini coefficient is estimated at 0.603, either the highest in the world or second behind Brazil (Poswell 2002: 14) (See Table 2.1). Poverty is also significant—32 percent of all

**Table 2.4   The Wage and Salary Share: Compensation of Employees, 1995–2002**

| Year | Amount in US$millions ($1 = R7.18) | Percentage of GDP |
|------|-----------------------------------|-------------------|
| 2002 | 69,337 | 51.4 |
| 2001 | 63,846 | 52.7 |
| 2000 | 59,186 | 53.9 |
| 1999 | 55,294 | 55.8 |
| 1998 | 51,759 | 56.3 |
| 1997 | 47,363 | 55.3 |
| 1996 | 42,913 | 55.4 |
| 1995 | 38,255 | 55.8 |

*Sources:* South African Reserve Bank, *Quarterly Bulletin,* September 2003, "Statistical Tables: National Income and Production Accounts of South Africa" (preliminary and subject to revision), p. S-110; South African Reserve Bank, *Quarterly Bulletin,* September 2003, "Statistical Tables: National Accounts: Ratios of Selected Date at Current Prices," p. S-154.

**Table 2.5   Government Priorities: Consolidated Government Spending on Selected Areas, 1995–2000 (as a percentage of total)**

| Year | Education | Health | Social security and welfare | Housing and community services | Defense | Public order and safety |
|------|-----------|--------|-----------------------------|-------------------------------|---------|-------------------------|
| 2000 | 20.2 | 9.7 | 11.3 | 2.8 | 4.5 | 9.7 |
| 1999 | 20.6 | 10.1 | 11.1 | 3.0 | 4.9 | 10.0 |
| 1998 | 21.3 | 10.3 | 11.0 | 3.4 | 5.1 | 9.1 |
| 1997 | 22.0 | 9.9 | 9.8 | 2.8 | 6.0 | 9.1 |
| 1996 | 21.2 | 9.5 | 9.6 | 4.0 | 6.7 | 9.0 |
| 1995 | 20.4 | 9.1 | 9.2 | 3.4 | 6.7 | 8.8 |

*Source:* South African Reserve Bank, *Quarterly Bulletin,* September 2003, "Statistical Tables: Total Expenditure—Consolidated General Government: Functional Classification: Percentage," p. S-80.

households are estimated to be living in poverty, which in this case is defined as US$126 per household per month in 1995 real terms. While poverty has a marked racial dimension, inequality within racial groups is substantial: this ensures that social inequality cannot be reduced purely by addressing racial disparities since a purely racial approach to inequality will benefit only the upper echelons of the black majority. However, race remains a key factor in discussions of poverty and inequality not only because the country's history ensures that progress in addressing racial socioeconomic disparities is a key test of progress toward a nonracial society, but also because race still shapes access to resources and opportunities in a variety of ways. Thus, while a sustained campaign to enhance black access to capital and to management and professional posts continues—and achieves significant successes in some areas—racial access to jobs remains highly differentiated (see Table 2.3).

Conventional economic indicators suggest an economy in much better shape than that of many other countries in the South—this is the result of a macroeconomic stabilization policy pursued since 1996. Growth has been modest—a 3 percent increase in GDP in 2002 has been followed by 2 percent growth in the first half of 2003 (South African Reserve Bank 2003: 5); but, while this is only marginally above the estimated population growth rate, the fact that it was recorded at all during a difficult period for the world economy does suggest that the economy has become relatively inured to external turbulence. Foreign debt in 2002 was US$32.788 billion, some 21 percent of GDP—the amount has declined slightly since democracy's advent when it stood at US$35.355 billion in 1995 (p. S-104). Government loan debt, which was 38.9 percent of GDP in June 2003, is only 18.7 percent foreign (pp. 59–60), the legacy of the late apartheid period when international sanctions forced the government to rely on domestic borrowing. Total gold and foreign exchange reserves stood at US$19 billion at end July (Mboweni 2003: 65–67). Inflation has tended to remain low compared to many other Southern economies: although it is negatively affected by the volatility of the currency, which prompted a sharp rise in 2002, consumer inflation was 6.6 percent in July 2003.

Evidence that stabilization has been largely effective is a government deficit before borrowing and debt repayment of 1.8 percent of GDP in April-June 2003—while this is an increase on the corresponding quarter of the previous fiscal year, the ratio is far lower than those recorded during the last years of apartheid. National government revenue as a ratio of GDP decreased from 24.6 percent in the April-June quarter of 2002 to 23.5 percent in the April-June quarter of the current fiscal year (South African Reserve Bank 2003: 57). And, despite the emphasis on fiscal discipline since 1996, social spending remains high as a proportion of the budget. Table 2.5 lists key items of social spending, as well as expenditure on defense and policing. The social spending items listed in the table are only a portion of the amounts budgeted for social purposes.

In the view of some, these "sound economic fundamentals" do not generate a sustainable growth path because domestic savings remain inadequate to sustain investment—gross savings were 16.1 percent of GDP in 2002, compared to 22.7 percent in 1998 (South African Reserve Bank 2003: S-154)—and investment levels, both foreign and domestic, remain inadequate. However, for our purposes, a far more important point is that the current growth path sharply limits the welfare effects of prudent financial management.

A key constraint is an inability to halt increasing unemployment, particularly among people who lack skills. In the first five years after democracy was established, about 1 million jobs have been created (see Table 2.3). But unemployment has continued to rise—from 29.24 percent of the economically active population in 1995 to 35.85 percent in 1999 (Poswell 2002: 2)—for two reasons. First, the rate of job creation is not, as Table 2.3 shows, sufficient to absorb new entrants to the labor market. Second, the jobs that are being created are overwhelmingly among the more qualified, thus excluding unskilled entrants or economically active people with traditional factory floor skills. Thus, between 1995 and 1999, managerial jobs increased 36.66 percent and those for professionals 71.62 percent. At the same time operator jobs—an area of factory floor employment that has been a key job creator in earlier periods—declined by 2.12 percent and elementary jobs—for unskilled people—by 13.7 percent (Bhorat 2003: 2). Employment in the financial and business services sector grew by 61 percent over the five years—close to double the 31.2 percent needed to stabilize unemployment (p. 5). But manufacturing job creation was poor—in 2003, for example, year on year manufacturing output measured in mid-year declined by 1.5 percent compared to the previous year (South African Reserve Bank 2003: 5)—and another key factor was a sharp reduction in public service jobs: 145,000 were shed between 1995 and 1999 but, even here, jobs were created for managers and professionals while unskilled workers were shed (Bhorat 2003: 2, 6, 9, 10, 13). This trend has a substantial effect on inequality: new jobs are being created for those who have access to qualifications, while those who do not—both the unskilled or semiskilled poor and those with factory floor skills who lose jobs—are unable to participate in the formal job market. Since access to skills has been segmented racially, this also, as Table 2.3 shows, has racial implications since black or "colored" (mixed-race or Malay) new entrants to the labor market are not being absorbed to the same degree as Asians and whites.

A further significant implication that is key to our analysis is the growth of informality. While Table 2.4 shows that wages and salaries continue to account for more than half of GDP, Table 2.2 demonstrates the strong shift toward informality—if the unemployed are added to those listed in the table, then the proportion of people outside of formal employment rises to some 46 percent of the economically active population in 1999.[2] This suggests that formal employees may already constitute a minority of the economically active population, although the scholarly consensus does continue to suggest that formal employees remain a majority. But even if the consensus is accurate, if current trends continue they will not remain a majority for long.

Since this background suggests that inequality has a significant structural base, it places a substantial burden on government action to redress inequality: even a much more robust growth rate would not have substantial job creation effects as long as the mismatch between jobs and the skills of the poor continue. As Table 2.5 indicates and as noted above, government expenditure does show a desire to address this challenge, not only because social spending is a priority but because education, a key to closing the mismatch between skills and labor demands, is a priority. It will be argued below, however, that the quality of government spending rather than its quantity may be a significant block to progress and that the constraints to better-quality spending are primarily political. I now turn to the analysis that seeks to demonstrate this argument.

## Globalization and "The Retreat from Equality"

Prevailing orthodoxy sees in globalization an economic process that imposes an inexorable constraint on the freedom of movement of the democratic state.

The term has become pervasive: "Politicians and scholars, active citizens and passive spectators . . . all invoke its omnipresence and omnipotence when trying to make sense of the multitude of uncertainties which surround them" (Schmitter 1999: 973). It may be used, depending on the perspective of the user, as a bogeyman to scare childlike interventionist states away from violating the new laissez-faire natural order, or as a left-wing expletive to explain any and every frustration of the socialist project. But, across the political spectrum, all are agreed both that it exists, and that it has sharply narrowed the options of states, precluding vigorous redistributive experiments.

The chief feature of globalization is said to be the increasing power of the global marketplace over individual states. Large flows of capital, goods, and services over international borders, it is claimed, force states either to comply with the preferences of those whose resources decide the fate of currencies and the growth prospects of economies or to face poverty and stagnation.[3] For better or worse, Leviathan is now at best a servant of the Invisible Hand: whatever the preferences of voters, winning elections now is said to be not a mandate to select and implement a policy program of the electorate's choice, but a certificate qualifying the bearer to implement the reforms required by those who decide the destination of footloose global capital. A brief examination of South Africa's recent history would seem to vindicate the theory.

### The Identity of Class Compromise

For decades before South Africa achieved democracy in 1994, it was assumed that the end of racial domination would also bring a robust redistributive experiment. The first reason for this expectation lay in the country's political history. A vigorous attempt to use the state to redistribute resources is no novelty—on the contrary, just such an endeavor had been essential to the white welfare state that apartheid created.

From the 1920s, a nationalist alliance between Afrikaner intellectuals, professionals, farmers, and workers sought not only to constrain the power of English-speaking business and to suppress the black majority more harshly: it also used welfare measures to fight acute white poverty. Successive versions of the Industrial Conciliation Act, a labor law introduced in 1924, also extended statutorily recognized bargaining rights to nonblack workers. This largely successful exercise in class compromise and cross-class alliance suggested that a broad coalition between social strata can make significant redistributive gains—inequality in white society was substantially reduced by state action underpinned by white social consensus. But the difference between this and some other social-democratic or welfare states was that it was racially exclusive: severe intrawhite class conflict in the early twentieth century was defused by the fact that whites could make common cause against a black majority and monopolize power and resources at its expense.

The white welfare state could be generous because its benefits were extended to only about a fifth of the population—and business resentment at conceding prerogatives and resources to a government run by an alien linguistic and cultural group (as noted above, business was largely English-speaking, the government was from 1924 mainly an Afrikaans preserve) was leavened by access to cheap labor and, except for periodic resurgences of black union activity, a quiescent work force. The result was a substantial incentive for compromise within the white group, whose outcome produced widespread and substantial white affluence and, for decades, the highest recorded level of inequality in the world, much of it racially based.

The spur was the existence of a common racial Other that could be denied entitlements and used as a plentiful source of labor for the white economy. For Afrikaner business, government control was not experienced as a constraint, for it was imposed by an ethnic alliance of which it was an important member and it received substantial benefits in the form of ethnic preference—for its English-speaking counterparts, it had elements of a classic class compromise in the sense that the constraints imposed by ethnic patronage were, at least initially, outweighed by the benefits: during the 1960s, extremely high growth rates—among the healthiest in the world—were recorded. While English-speaking business may have seen the approach as an economically inefficient exercise in ethnic patronage, the considerable compensations ensured that it bestowed legitimacy on the arrangement by meticulously meeting its tax obligations (Lieberman 2000; Lieberman 2001: 515–555).

For decades, therefore, white interests derived material benefit from racial domination; this made generous social protection for whites the subject of a fairly stable consensus in white society. While it was to come under some pressure from the consequences of the 1973 oil shock, skilled labor shortages and then unrest in the mid-1970s, it proved fairly resilient and a significant measure of white protection remained when racial domination was replaced by nonracial democracy in the 1990s. But it was perhaps inevitable that inequality within the white group would grow as apartheid, and the racial protectionism it enforced, eroded—as, indeed it did (see McGrath and Whiteford 1994: 47–50). Nevertheless, the white welfare state provided a material standard to which the black-led liberation movements aspired—and seemed to suggest that vigorous state action backed by a social coalition could launch an effective assault against inequality.

### From Freedom Charter to Investment Code?

There was also a strong redistributive flavor to the resistance politics that sought to overthrow apartheid.

During the early 1950s, the ANC, the dominant vehicle of black opposition to racial domination, formed a cross-racial alliance with socialists and Marxists, as well as with antiapartheid organizations representing activists of other races.[4] The credo of the Congress Alliance, as it came to be known, was the Freedom Charter, which appeared to commit the alliance to a vigorous redistributive policy when and if it gained power (Suttner and Cronin 1985). While the charter was open to nationalist, social-democratic, and socialist interpretations, its stated commitment to, among other measures, the nationalization of mines and "monopoly industries" was emblematic of an approach that seemed to promise that majority rule would inevitably entail a vigorous redistributive program.

In 1994, as the alliance, now recast as a coalition between the ANC, the Congress of South African Trade Unions, and the South African Communist Party, entered the first universal franchise elections, its key manifesto was the Reconstruction and Development Programme (RDP) which promised an ambitious attempt to rein in privilege and address poverty (African National Congress 1994). Besides an ambitious set of development policy goals, the RDP also promised redistributive intervention in the market and society.[5] While the debate had moved on, and nationalization was not proposed by the RDP, it seemed to confirm the egalitarian impulse of the ANC and its allies.

The decades-old expectation that majority rule would bring a concerted egalitarian agenda was heightened by the reality that the ANC alliance's apparent commitment to address inequality seemed less like a free policy choice than an acknowledgment of political and social necessity. As noted above, by the time the negotiation period of the early 1990s began, South

Africa was said to hold the dubious distinction of most unequal society in the world. Equally important, the poor were almost exclusively black. This seemed certain to ensure that, in contrast to many new democracies whose citizens appeared content to accept a democratization that left inequality undisturbed,[6] the clear correlation between continued relative deprivation and racial domination would ensure that the latter's political demise would inexorably create pressure for its social and economic equivalent. The notion that people whose poverty could so clearly be ascribed to racial sub-jugation would value a "freedom" in which they remained poor seemed unlikely. The new economic and political elite's interest in government intervention to address racial privilege in business, the professions, and the academy also seemed to ensure that an assertive defense of the free market would enjoy little political purchase once white rule ended.

The postapartheid reality confounded these expectations. Even before the 1994 election and the birth of the RDP, there were signs of shifting eco-nomic thinking within the ANC. When Nelson Mandela was released from prison amid world acclaim in 1990, he repaired to a rally in Cape Town where he reiterated the Freedom Charter's commitment to nationalization as a "fundamental policy" of the ANC. Only three years later, he returned from a tour of Germany, which included intensive discussion with business, to declare that privatization was now fundamental policy. This switch was less dramatic or unexpected than it might seem—it followed a series of engagements with businesses, domestic but, more importantly, international (since the latter were assumed not to have been tainted by enjoying the ben-efits of minority rule), which produced significant changes in ANC policy as its Department of Economic Policy urged adaptations to prevailing eco-nomic thinking.[7] The development of the RDP reflected some of the ten-sions between policy technicians and activists. The original document is thus less unambiguous than it seems: it often "fudges" differences within the ANC by paying obeisance to economic pragmatism as well as assertive egalitarianism. The government white paper released in 1995 that turned it into official policy suggested that the economic specialists had made further gains as the interventionist features of the program were further diluted.

After the 1994 election installed the ANC at the head of a multiparty government, the influence of the economic policymakers grew significant-ly, partly as engagement with (particularly international) business increased, and partly as the RDP faced severe implementation challenges (Rapoo 1996) that ironically ensured a fall in social spending in the first year of popularly elected administration (Kabemba 2000). The result was not a renewed effort to implement it, but a significant change in course: the adoption in 1996 of the Growth, Employment, and Redistribution (GEAR) strategy (Department of Finance 1996), which has been repeatedly denounced by the left of the governing alliance as a neoliberal departure from the redistributive impulses of the RDP,[8] and has consequently been seen as a reflection of the triumph of business policy influence over the government. GEAR has been contested since its introduction by the ANC's labor ally, the Congress of South African Trade Unions (COSATU), as well as by a range of activists within the governing party's camp, but neither the unions' political connections nor resorts to mass public protest have secured any significant changes in policy. To complete a familiar picture, income inequality has, according to official statistics, widened significantly after an initial postapartheid period when it appeared to have narrowed slightly. [9]

The transition from Freedom Charter to RDP to GEAR, from commitment to nationalization to market-friendly dedication to deficit reduction, privatization, and export orientation, seemed to offer a textbook illustration of globalization's power. A redistributive alliance, impelled to intervene in markets not only by policy preference but by political realities and backed, arguably, by a moral capital unavailable to other new democracies (since inequality is so clearly a consequence of racial domination), found itself seemingly powerless before the strength of world markets and the harsh choices they impose. The conformity with textbooks was seemingly enhanced by government sensitivity to international business opinion: thus president Thabo Mbeki has established an investment council comprised of international business people who advise him on policy and some analyses claim that his government is more open to the influence of foreign business than domestic civil society. Exposed at international forums to an inexorable logic that forced a choice between adaptation or stagnation, the ANC was compelled to bend the knee to economic constraints that restricted it in a way in which white power could not. So, at any rate, ran the conventional wisdom on both sides of the divide. Reality was rather different.

### Mistaken Identity?

Despite its rhetoric, the alliance that fought apartheid was never built on an interest-based opposition to inequality. Like the "class compromise" that underpinned the apartheid economy, the resistance to the system was based essentially on identity politics.

The resistance that began—formally—with the launch of the South African National Native Congress, later the African National Congress, in 1912 was not necessarily racially exclusive in its composition or the society it sought to achieve; on the contrary, a strong strain adopted nonracialism as a strategy as well as a goal. But inevitably, since black people were both the demographic majority and the victims of institutionalized racism, mainly black people were mobilized against the system. And, in contrast to the hopes of socialists who stressed class mobilization, the major resistance movements sought to mobilize and speak for all black people, rather than particular classes within black society. The dominant liberation movement, the ANC, was thus a multiclass agglomeration united behind a common rejection of minority rule.

This unity was, however, not achieved by negotiated interest compromises: rather, the ANC's "glue" was a common identity; interest differences were ignored as it sought to portray itself not merely as one among many parties but as the sole voice of black society (Shubane 1997). Indeed, it presented itself not as a political party, but as *the* (rather than *a*) national liberation movement. Thus, when the prospect of winning power began to prompt it to devise detailed policy (Simkins 1988), it generally sought to do this by gliding over interest differences, often seeking to include competing perspectives in the same policy statement, rather than by encouraging their clear expression by competing interests. The resultant policy was often vague and general, leaving considerable latitude for interpretation to its implementers when the ANC became the government in 1994.

As noted earlier, class-based parties and interests have played a key role in the alliance that the ANC leads. Before it was banned in 1960, the South African Communist Party (SACP)[10] was an ally, as was the South African Congress of Trade Unions (SACTU). The resurgence of black trade unionism in the 1970s also prompted the formation of the COSATU (Friedman 1987; Baskin 1991) in the mid-1980s, which again later became a formal ANC ally. But while this may have had some effect on ANC rhetoric, it was never enough to steer it away from its role as an articulator of identity toward a more overtly class-based redistributive position—SACTU was far more a vehicle of African nationalism than of working-class interests (Friedman 1987: chap. 2), while the SACP's pursuit of socialist goals was constrained (or its recognition of the primacy of identities over interests illustrated) by its adoption of a strategy of "national democratic revolution," which held that the defeat of the white minority state would have to enjoy precedence over working-class control (Hudson 1986). As later events were to show, these groups did far more to mobilize a class constituency in support of African nationalism than to mold the latter to a class-based, egalitarian agenda.

The development of a stronger and more organized trade union movement—which was also accorded legally sanctioned bargaining rights—in the 1970s and 1980s altered this to a degree, ensuring a greater union independence and propensity to stress worker interests rather than broad identity concerns. This has had its concrete effect in union opposition to liberalized economic policy after 1996, which has repeatedly prompted public conflict between the governing party and its trade union ally. But the initial hope of left intellectuals and some unionists that this would produce an independent working-class party or politics distinct from that of the ANC was dashed: while the need for working-class political independence was a watchword of the largest union federation in the early 1980s,[11] identity politics proved far stronger than the labor strategists who sought a class-based politics expected, and by the mid-1980s the largest union federation had again been absorbed into the nationalist ambit—many unionists who once extolled independent working-class politics later held office as ANC representatives or government officials.

The struggle against apartheid reconciled different political traditions. For some in the trade unions and Communist Party, even when the system of racial oppression ended, blacks would not be free until liberated from an economic slavery imposed by the market. In contrast, the nationalist tradition emphasized the racial dimension: inequality was seen to be more the product of racism than the market economy—the problem was not the economic system but that its control had been monopolized by a racial minority. Nor is this the only cleavage within the ANC—the rise of a black African professional class, has, for example, produced an articulate middle-class feminism that clashes with the patriarchy of traditional leadership, also represented in the alliance. There are, albeit in vastly different contexts, echoes of the alliance within the dominant group under white rule, providing material and symbolic inducements for economic elites to accept fairly high levels of social provision for and protection of the poor if they share an identity with the affluent. But the importance of identity politics meant also that socioeconomic differences within racial groups, most notably the black African majority, were always less politically salient than identity bonds.

These observations have been confirmed since 1994: while income inequality within racial groups has continued to widen (McGrath and Whiteford 1994), identity remained the salient determinant of political party support, ensuring continued high levels of ANC support despite repeated claims that its base was shrinking as black hopes of rapid economic advance were disappointed (Friedman 1999a). Certainly, the claims of disenchantment often oversimplified or simply distorted reality; much of post-1994 South African reality has been analyzed through a template, assiduously used by many journalists and public commentators, that assumes that all black-led governments, having purported to liberate their compatriots from subjugation, then proceed to disappoint or oppress them or both. In reality, the assertion that black people are deeply disillusioned is gainsaid both by research evidence showing that expectations of economic change are far more modest and pragmatic than conventional wisdom claims (Charney 1995) and by the reality that public goods have been distributed to significant sections of the population. However, the fact that, despite this, income inequality has widened since 1994 but neither the social unrest nor the drop in governing party support that this trend was expected to produce[12] have occurred testifies to the power of the politics of identity over that of material interest.

This has several implications for our theme. The first is to note that the post-1994 "retreat from redistribution" may be largely illusory since, rhetoric to the contrary notwithstanding, there was never a dominant redistributive program in the ANC from which to retreat. There were egalitarian impulses—there still are—among sections of the ANC alliance. But the chief goal of the movement was not to address social inequality; it was, rather, to tackle its racial equivalent. While this does not preclude action against poverty, it does potentially subordinate it to other goals, such as ensuring enhanced black access to the professions. And, where the goal of promoting a black business or professional class conflicted with or was seen to conflict with the interests of the poor, the inevitable reality that organizational resources are disproportionately concentrated in the hands of the more affluent classes ensured that their interests would predominate. Thus a subsidy program that aims, among other goals, to provide black people with seed capital to buy farmland has been revised to provide more generous subsidies to persons buying larger tracts—while officials continue to protest that the poor have not been abandoned (Mayende 2000), subsidies for the landless poor will, in effect, be reduced by the stipulation that they contribute in cash or kind if they want financial aid. And a stated reason for the change is an intention to promote the growth of a black commercial farming class (Schmitz 2000: 7–9; Centre for Policy Studies 2000). This owes far less to globalization than to the diversity of interests gathered under the ANC's broad identity-grounded banner.

The second follows from this: what appears to be an inevitable adjustment to globalization may largely be an expression of the workings of identity politics. While emulation of Northern models is a common desire among Southern elites (O'Donnell 1996), in South Africa the desire for global competitiveness and "world class status" takes on a particular flavor. Postapartheid politics have been underpinned by a theme often not stated overtly, but which is pervasive: whites expect a black government to fail and the leaders of that government are well aware that they do.[13] It is, therefore, a key preoccupation of much of the new governing elite to demolish these assumptions by demonstrating that black people can govern an industrialized society. This, rather than concern for democratic depth, is considered likely to show whites that assumptions of black inferiority are myths.

A further consequence is that, ironically, the government can only dispel the myths by demonstrating competence *on white terms*: How else to prove to the white skeptics that race is no guide to competence than to succeed at those endeavors that whites are considered to hold dear? Rather

than stress South Africa's actual and potential contribution to conflict resolution through bargained compromises, or, as in the early period of the
Mandela administration, its interest in entrenching human rights in an
unlikely setting, emphasis increasingly falls on aspiring to techniques and
outcomes that are assumed to characterize "winning societies"—without, in
many cases, acknowledgment that resolving conflicts and respecting rights
are in many cases a precondition to "winning," not an incidental by-product
(Rodrik 1999). In a paradox that would no doubt have intrigued Frantz
Fanon, many in the new black elite believe that they can only demolish race
prejudice by embracing one of its cornerstones: the belief that there is a
"white" and a "black" way of doing things and that the former is superior
(at least in the minds of whites) to the latter. In many cases, the assumptions about what whites value may be as stereotyped as suburban myths
about what blacks are good at; but myths and generalizations can, of
course, shape actions even if they lack empirical foundations.

It is this dynamic that produces an obsession among the new elite with
demonstrating that postapartheid South Africa is capable of "world class
standards."[14] Whether the subject at hand is constitutional design, public
management systems, or inventing new technologies, the elite, regardless
of race or political allegiance, is obsessed with achieving "world class" status. Many whites, imbued with deep forebodings of the consequences of
majority rule in Africa, are concerned to maintain the standards of Western
Europe and North America to which they were accustomed under
apartheid. They therefore measure the new society's progress not against
its capacity to include the once excluded, but its ability to offer as
amenable a home as the Northern countries to which whites with the will
and resources emigrate. It is against these standards, therefore, that the
black elite must measure itself if it wants to persuade these whites that they
are as well off under a largely black government in Africa as under a largely white one in Australia, Canada, or the United States. The result, crucial
for the argument of this chapter, is an enthusiastic willingness to imbibe
fashionable theories of public and economic management from Western
capitals, not because, as in some other parts of the South, the World Bank
and the IMF insist on it, but because domestic intergroup dynamics dictate
it. To this must be added, as suggested earlier, a tendency to see foreign
business as a more appropriate source of direct cooperation than its local
white equivalent since it is not tainted by having been white and South
African during the time of legislated race privilege. It is this dynamic,
rather than a clear strategic need to obey the will of international business,
that explains the current administration's enthusiasm for ascertaining and
acting on foreign business opinion.

This argument does not deny that international influences played a role
in shaping GEAR. To challenge the globalization hypothesis is not to deny

that policymakers are influenced across national boundaries; it is, rather, to argue against the claim that the influence now operates in a way that denies choices to Southern states and renders them passive policy-takers rather than -makers. This analysis also acknowledges that ideas and influences now cross borders more easily and that this helps to shape policy choices. The issue is whether these influences are absorbed because there is no alternative or because domestic elites in the South are particularly receptive to them—this analysis argues that, where international influences are persuasive, this lies not in the workings of an ineluctable Invisible Hand but in domestic dynamics that ensure a willing ear to these ideas and influences. Since the South African analysis clearly cannot be applied to other Southern countries, investigation would be needed in their cases to determine why these ideas enjoy influence—below, I will suggest that changes in production technology may help explain the influence of current economic orthodoxies in many countries of the South. But the South African case is a useful guide to the degree to which international influences take root because domestic realities allow them to do so. The *volte face* dictated by globalization turns out to be far more a continuation of decades-old trends than a radical change of direction. And to the extent that the dictates of the global marketplace have been embraced to an unexpected degree, the cause is less the unavoidable dictates of globalization than the peculiar way in which domestic identity politics provides the governing alliance with strong incentives to emulate Northern economic policy and governance models where these do not conflict with core government priorities.

### (Mis)Understanding the Problem

This analysis enables us to dispense with those understandings of South Africa's transition that draw a sharp distinction between the redistributive coalition of the pre-1994 period and the neoliberal government that assumed office when majority rule was achieved. This holds true whether the shift is seen as an inevitable realignment to global realities, or if, as a brand of left analysis claims, it is explained as the avoidable consequence of a misguided preference by the postapartheid elite.[15]

Because the governing alliance is an identity-based coalition, it inevitably includes a range of interests and classes—it is a vehicle for a rising business and professional elite concerned to claim a greater share of opportunities as much as for the poor seeking a redistribution of wealth. This was so throughout its history—even when social differentiation between black people was largely flattened out by white domination's restrictions on black upward mobility, the ANC leadership consisted largely of a professional elite; many of the campaigns conducted by the ANC when it was a legal organization in the 1950s, for example, betrayed strong elite preoccupations.[16] Indeed, it was precisely because the commitment to redistribution within the ANC camp has always been obliged to take a back seat to identity concerns that the trade union movement, in the year before the 1994 election, sought to assemble a coalition behind the RDP in the express hope that this would bind a government elected by universal franchise to an egalitarian agenda (Gotz 2000). And it was also this that, as noted above, ensured that the RDP itself contained significant concessions to a more "market friendly" perspective.

## Misreading the "Retreat"

That said, the ANC remains a multiclass and multi-interest alliance, part of whose constituency includes organized workers and the poor. This explains why the "lurch to neo-liberalism" is more qualified than much public rhetoric would claim.

GEAR's language is far less neoliberal than conventional portrayals suggest. Its references to "Washington consensus" desiderata such as privatization and the deregulation of the labor market are either vague or premised on negotiated compromises between business, labor, and government. The only issue on which it is uncompromisingly neoliberal is deficit reduction—not surprisingly, since the document is seen by several analysts as a hasty attempt to construct an intellectual edifice for budget cuts designed to counter the buffeting of the currency, the rand (Friedman and Chipkin 2001). The claim that the change was a response to events in world currency markets would seem to confirm the role of globalization, as conventionally understood, in the drama. However, the travails of the rand seem to have been prompted primarily by domestic identity politics—more specifically, the appointment of the country's first black finance minister, which worried domestic white business, whose concern was reflected both in its economic behavior and, presumably, in the perspectives it shared with foreign business people: the "response to globalization" turns out again to be in reality an acting out of a domestic drama.[17]

Government actions since 1996 have tended to confirm that GEAR was largely an attempt to justify deficit reduction. First, while privatization remains government policy, its progress has been limited, much to the chagrin of some business commentators, largely because of resistance within the alliance, particularly among the trade unions.[18] A fairly generous set of legislated rights for trade unions and workers remains in place, besides repeated complaints by business that the labor market is too rigid. A stated government desire to relax labor market regulation[19] has produced only minor changes, which have been negotiated with labor as well as business.[20] Exchange control remains in force, despite some concessions to demands for liberalization. The government has also remained committed to racial redistribution and has been willing to intervene in the market to achieve it.

Certainly, the direction on all of these issues except racial equalization (which, as implied above, is a fundamental ANC alliance goal) leans toward liberalization—hence the heated resistance of the trade unions and their allies. But the pace of change is slow and the South African version of the change is not always orthodox—a key requirement to qualify for ownership of privatized assets is the presence of a black-owned company in the bidding consortium. With the possible exception of exchange control, on which government technical specialists are said to harbor reservations, the block to speedier change is negotiation with the trade unions or the need to retain the support of other sections of the alliance who oppose market liberalization.

More unequivocally, the government continues to implement a reasonably generous set of social programs—some two-thirds of the national budget is devoted to social spending and, according to the minister of finance, 57 percent of its spending is allocated to the poorest 40 percent, under 9 percent to the wealthiest 20 percent (Manuel 2000). The allocation of funds to the nine provinces is bound by a formula that gives preference to those with higher poverty indices and social backlogs, despite the substantially lower absorptive capacity in poorer provinces. The money is used to fund a range of social programs committed to enhancing access to water, electricity, shelter, and primary health care. These are accompanied by initiatives, such as a proposed law to transfer legal title to mining land from private firms to the state, which intervene in the market, or measures, such as a change guaranteeing an allocation of 6,000 liters of free water per month (Department of Water Affairs and Forestry 2001), which are clearly redistributive (and are also opposed by the World Bank) (Kihato and Schmitz 2002).

The evidence, therefore, suggests a rather more complicated picture than that portrayed by conventional analysis. It seems more appropriate to see the postapartheid government's economic and social policy through the prism of the political balance of power and influence within the governing alliance than as a capitulation to the global marketplace. Viewed in this way, one of the most significant features is the degree to which, despite the farm subsidy example cited above, the postapartheid elite has not pursued a straightforward attempt to deracialize the market economy without addressing the distribution of its output. The actual trajectory of policy, rather than that which appears in much of the public rhetoric, suggests that diversity within the alliance ensures that redistributive and labor-friendly strands will remain.

This is surely further evidence that current government policy is a result of domestic interest politics, not the dictates of the global market. It may well be that the remarkable feature of ANC alliance politics and their redistributive impacts—positive and negative—is not the sharp break between 1996 and the movement's history, but their sameness.

## A Voice for the Poor?

A second, more plausible, left explanation, offered by Hein Marais, of the "change of tack" after 1994 thus acknowledges the degree to which the ANC alliance has always been diverse and blames the outcome not on globalization or even the elite's misguided perception of it but on the consequence of a political battle for "hegemony" that the ANC left has, at least for now, lost (Marais 1998).

His analysis therefore moves beyond those that see the new government's assumption of office as some sort of rupture and that assume a uniformity to the alliance and its policy agenda before 1994, which flies in the face of the evidence. It notes the presence within the governing coalition of interests who would see egalitarianism purely in racial terms—who would hold that sufficient equality is achieved when there is no correspondence between social inequality and race—as well as a set of organizations and perspectives that favor sharp reductions in social inequality within race groups and in poverty levels and would therefore see racial egalitarianism as a necessary but not sufficient feature of a just society. It is the latter, COSATU and a range of nongovernmental organizations, many of whom belong to the South African National NGO Coalition, which this strain of analysis sees as the standard-bearers of an egalitarian agenda and whose failure to win control over the policy program is said to explain widening inequality.

This explanation is also, albeit from a different perspective, consistent with an analysis that sees successful redistributive social policy under democratic conditions as, at least in part, the outcome of a capacity by those with an interest in egalitarian outcomes to assemble a winning political coalition capable of framing and implementing (a task that also requires securing the consent of the affluent) a social policy program favorable to the poor.[21] The diagnosis that a winning pro-poor coalition has not been assembled in South Africa is clearly accurate—and equally importantly, this account accurately locates the lack of progress in addressing inequality in the failure of the poor to gain access to the policy agenda. It is also open to significant objections that help to illuminate the nature of inequality in postapartheid South Africa.

First, it is useful to slightly rephrase Marais's question to fit the concerns of our analysis. The history sketched above noted that an earlier brand of identity politics—that which created the apartheid coalition that underpinned white minority rule—had offered significant gains to the white organized workers and nonunionized poor who supported it. In that context, then, identity politics produced a "class coalition" of a sort that helped to almost eliminate white poverty. Why, given its history, has the victory of the ANC's identity-based, multiclass politics not produced similar outcomes?

Marais's explanation tends to attribute this purely to strategic failures on the left: by implication, had the ANC's egalitarian wing adopted a more appropriate strategy it might have won the battle and ensured steady reductions in inequality. However, while much of his critique of left strategy is hard to fault, the analysis fails to understand the extent to which the outcome was a result of structural factors that would have constrained options even if the left had adopted an optimal strategy. Perhaps the most telling point here is that there is no guarantee that a left victory in this debate would have led to any greater say in social policy for the poor.

The left critique at least partly misdiagnoses the reason for the society's poor record in addressing inequality since 1994. Because deficit reduction has been a key pillar of GEAR, it is repeatedly argued that the poor are being starved of badly needed services by ideologically generated fiscal stinginess. The spending figures quoted above should give cause for pause. So too should the fact that a common problem in postapartheid government has been the failure of some key development departments to spend their annual budgets.[22] And, at present, the "standard" image of the cash-denuded Southern state in the era of globalization is, in the South African case, contradicted by the fact that, largely as a result of more efficient tax collection,[23] the 2003–2004 budget distributes revenue that exceeded expectations by some R18 billion (Manuel 2002).

All of this suggests that the chief obstacle to effective action against inequality is not controls on public spending but a failure to spend the government budget effectively. Further examination invites the conclusion that this failure is significantly linked to a mismatch between the needs and preferences of the poor on the one hand and the mainstream postapartheid policy agenda on the other. And, crucially for this analysis, those sections of the governing alliance who seek to champion the interests of the poor show no greater understanding of their preferences than the ANC politicians and government officials who are said to have turned their backs on poor people.

One illustration is provided by housing policy. During the early 1990s, this provided something of a model for negotiated policymaking between all social interests. It was one of a dozen social and economic forums established during the political negotiation period—its participants included important sections of the ANC's pro-poor interests and one of its focuses was a lengthy negotiation between them and business on ways to ensure that mortgage finance reached the poor, but none of the participants questioned the assumption behind this, that is, that mortgage finance was a resource that the poor desired (Tomlinson 1997). Research, however, suggests that several years were spent seeking ways of offering poor people something they did not want. Far from seeking mortgages, poor people who participated in nationwide focus group interviews insisted that they associated this form of housing finance with evictions and therefore were anxious to avoid mortgage commitments (Tomlinson 1996). (The perception was largely based on experience—when home ownership was first opened to black people in the cities in the mid-1980s, housing was "oversold" and many of the purchasers proved unable to meet their obligations.)

A further example of the gap is experience with social pensions since 1994. These pensions, paid by the fiscus to people who pass a means test, are—admittedly in the absence of more generous alternatives—the most effective current instrument for poverty alleviation: while they are ostensibly meant for the elderly, they are used for many other purposes and, in many poor households and regions, operate as a form of general income support.[24] And yet, not only did pension increases between 1994 and 2001 fail to keep pace with inflation, but government representatives continued to assume that they serve the aged only (Manuel 1999).[25]

Real pension cuts encountered little or no opposition from those interests usually pressing for redistribution such as the unions, civic organizations, and NGOs. The fact that neither public representatives nor those sections of civil society who campaign against poverty seem aware of the role that pensions play in the household budgets of many of the poor indicates the degree to which grass-roots social life and experience is not filtering through to the elite—and, therefore, the extent to which the poor remain without effective representation.

There are some signs of change in the mainstream policy debate. First, COSATU has launched a campaign for a basic income grant, which would entail expanding the notion, underpinning social pensions, of cash transfers as a means of redressing poverty. This does suggest that analyses that claim that the unions represent a "labor aristocracy" whose interests are in conflict with those of the poor—research finds that the income gap between the employed and unemployed is far sharper than disparities among the employed (South African Labour and Development Research Unit 1994)—and which is concerned only with the immediate interests of the employed are misplaced. COSATU is, it appears, willing to take up the concerns of the poor when it becomes aware of them. But this does not suggest that the unions are now responding to the voices of the poor; the change seems to have been prompted more by the influence of academic work (much of which was made available to a government investigation into an income grant) on union policymakers than by a deeper base among the poor. Second, the government has identified pensions and other welfare grants as general antipoverty instruments rather than support for the aged alone (Mbeki 2002). However, in a budget year in which, as noted above, a considerable surplus is available, the increases in pensions offered as an antipoverty measure (Manuel 2002) are only slightly above the inflation rate, suggesting that, at this stage at least, the shift is more symbolic than real.

These examples suggest that the pro-poor elements of the ANC alliance have been, since 1994, out of touch with the preferences of the poor and that the latter have therefore been without a voice in the policy debate on questions that influence inequality (rather than on identity issues). And that, while the balance of power within the ANC alliance ensures that a purely market-oriented agenda will not be pursued by the governing alliance, it is not sufficiently tilted toward the poor to ensure that social policy accurately reflects what they want. The result is ineffective policy (in which housing subsidies are, for example, used to finance dwellings that their recipients sell to more affluent buyers [Tomlinson 1997] because they prefer cash to the housing that is offered or electrification programs are based on inaccurate diagnosis of the consumption patterns of the poor [White et al. 2000]); whether the funds that current policy makes available for fighting poverty would be enough if the poor were accurately heard is not yet clear. At present, what is evident is that the money available is being spent far less effectively than it could be, either because its design does not respond to the needs of the poor or because the lack of a voice for the poor means that there is no effective citizen pressure to ensure effective implementation.

It should be stressed here that the term "the poor" is in important respects an oversimplification since, within this broad social category, there are subgroups whose needs are likely to differ sufficiently to ensure that social policy interventions would need to be tailored to them—gender differences are important, as are those between persons who enjoy South African citizenship or residence on the one hand, undocumented or "illegal" migrants on the other. But this serves only to strengthen the argument: the fact that a variety of groups with very differing experience are referred to by a single catch-all term, "the poor," may be itself ample illustration of their lack of voice. In the case of migrants, this is an outcome of policy that illustrates continued resistance by states to the flow of people across their borders[26] despite claims that our world is becoming increasingly "borderless." In the case of citizens, it is the outcome of a political system rendered impermeable by organizational issues to which this analysis will return.

It is also perhaps worth noting here that the left—or, to be more precise, activist groups that believe that intervention in markets is necessary—is not as impotent as Marais's analysis may imply. Thus, in 2001, a loose alliance of South African activists led by the Treatment Action Campaign—

which seeks affordable medication for persons suffering from HIV/AIDS—succeeded in pressing international pharmaceutical companies to drop a lawsuit seeking the overturning of legislation allowing the import of cheaper drugs.[27] The firms have also subsequently offered to cut their prices significantly.

It is unclear how sustainable this campaign's success is likely to be since domestic political considerations have intervened to persuade the government not to accept with alacrity the drugs offered at reduced prices. But the implications for understandings of globalization are profound. The campaign was certainly evidence that something we might call "globalization" is indeed at work—but it seems to operate rather differently to the presumptions of conventional wisdom.

A key feature of the campaign was the degree to which the South African activists were supported by like-minded individuals and organizations in other countries, particularly in the North. It seems likely that this was a significant feature in the companies' retreat: the firms may well have decided that the embarrassment they would suffer in their primary Northern markets—and in their corporate "home countries"—imposed costs that outweighed the benefits of continuing to pursue their action. This suggests that ideas and information do indeed cross borders today as never before—to the extent that citizens of Southern countries enjoy access to contemporary communications technology, so are they able to form alliances with colleagues whose Northern location may substantially increase their bargaining power. But the incident also suggests that the presumed power of multinational companies in the current global environment may have been overstated—they are not impervious to moral pressure. And ironically, that to which they may be susceptible, that is, embarrassment at home, may be largely a result of intellectual and cultural globalization.[28] The campaign seems to add weight to the proposition that the real novelty in the current global environment may not be the oft-cited capital flows as much as the increased ease with which information flows across borders. This may, as we are repeatedly told by some contemporary scholars,[29] make possible new forms of collective action that seek to hold businesses and governments to account.

This does not mean that the power of activists now exceeds that of corporations. It is easy to imagine issues less peripheral to company priorities than offering to cut the price of medicines that are said by activists to have already yielded a handsome return on research and development costs in markets in which most people cannot pay the full cost. But it would be hard to imagine an example that illustrates most clearly the strength of the globalization of information—and the weakness of globalization theories that claim that a key effect is to render citizens in the South powerless to regulate the behavior of multinational companies. The example may also illustrate that egalitarians retain significant influence on the policy agenda and that the chief obstacle to their effectiveness may be their tenuous links with the poor.

## The Power of the Informal

This analysis may also, by implication, have helped us to answer the question posed at the outset: Why has postapartheid democracy failed to generate a cross-class coalition able to ensure narrowing inequality indices? And the answer may lie less in tactical misreadings than in the very different circumstances in which the task would now need to be attempted.

In South Africa, as in many other economies, there is, as noted above, a clear trend to informalization that, on the available evidence, seems set to endure.[30] As suggested above, this is a consequence not of globalization but of changes in production technology that enable firms to produce more with less workers; this has ensured a decline in traditional mass-production job opportunities (Epsing-Andersen 1996). Thus, as noted above, a key trend over the past decade has been creation of jobs for skilled people only (Bhorat and Cassim 1999).[31] The result is to heighten the international trend and to ensure that the poor are working in informal settings, not formal workplaces.

This, as this author has argued elsewhere (Friedman 2001), seems a far more plausible explanation for the decline in egalitarian politics than the oft-cited impact of globalization. In some analyses, the two are treated as one—changing production technology is said to be a feature of globalization. The result is to blur two distinct phenomena and thus to confuse analysis. The globalization argument rests on the assumption that states now have reduced options because power has shifted from these political units elsewhere—to multinational corporations or international investment funds or multilateral governance institutions, or all three. The argument advanced here suggests that states retain the latitude to formulate and implement egalitarian social and economic policy but that the political coalitions that might prompt them to do so are currently absent because the preconditions that previously sustained these alliances are now lacking.

What has changed is that the chief ingredient of the earlier success of democratic egalitarianism—and, arguably, one of the reasons for the white South African trajectory—is no longer available to anything like the same degree as it was when egalitarianism could command majority support. Then, the poor were primarily engaged in wage labor in mass-production workplaces. They were, therefore, easier to organize because they were concentrated in sites of production and integrated into a formal economic environment in which they possessed considerable bargaining power, derived from their ability to withhold labor. Now the poor are dispersed and lack bargaining power. There is also some evidence that informality may enhance the propensity to operate outside the norms of the democratic polity. There is, for example, reported evidence of the decline of manufacturing industry prompting complicity in a gang-controlled drugs industry or in other forms of criminal behavior. Informality is also fertile ground for the exercise of unaccountable power.[32] While there are cases around the globe in which trade unions are seeking to organize people working in informal settings,[33] the obstacles are formidable—both the South African union movement and its allies have yet to overcome them.

The failure of the franchise to produce egalitarian outcomes may, therefore, have far less to do with strategic miscalculations on the left than with structural changes that social analyses have yet to fully understand. The identity-based class compromise available after 1994 may be far less favorable to the poor and far more compatible with growing inequality because the trend toward informal employment deprives the poor of an organized voice. And poor progress against poverty and inequality may be primarily a result of the reality that policies are framed without a full understanding of preferences and needs among the poor and implemented without active monitoring by those whom they are intended to benefit.

One point may need to be added to the analysis before we turn to proposed remedies. While the organization of the poor is an essential prerequisite to an effective egalitarian politics (one capable not only of framing and implementing a social policy agenda, but of also ensuring that it does, indeed, reduce inequality), it is not the only requirement. In a market economy, a crucial part of this endeavor would need to be a willingness by the affluent to contribute to inequality's reduction—it is arguably the failure of populist governments in Latin America to secure this which prompted the "boom and bust" economics associated with populism and, when the perceived burden on the affluent became too great, its attendant coups.[34] Under apartheid, it was, as I have argued earlier, the advantages to be accrued from uniting against a racial "Other" that secured compliance. In principle, we should expect it to be far more difficult under majority rule as long as the affluent remain largely white and thus both unavailable for identity-based alliances with the political elite and, if one study is to be believed, lacking in the sort of "social consciousness" that might prompt them to accept a responsibility for poverty (Kalati and Manor n.d.). There is, however, some evidence that securing the cooperation of the affluent is possible in principle (Lieberman 2001; Friedman and Chipkin 2001), suggesting that this question is at least worth exploring.

Until an effective coalition that gives voice to the poor is mobilized, this question will perforce remain of secondary importance. But, given its significance to a coherent strategy for reduced inequality, the issue will be addressed in this chapter's policy recommendations.

## Conclusions: The Realm of the Possible?

This analysis has sought to argue that globalization, if it is understood as the impact of cross-national markets on states rather than the increased diffusion of ideas across states' borders, is not significant in providing or constraining opportunities for turning the political rights that apartheid's end conferred on most South Africans into a "social citizenship" in which greater freedom will also mean reduced inequality.[35] Rather, the tendency for postapartheid democracy to produce widening inequality is a consequence of domestic considerations that have been accentuated and influenced, but not created, by the intellectual fashions that produce current global orthodoxy.

South Africa is not the only country in which the nature of globalization has been misread. In other places, too, the failure of governments to pursue successful egalitarian policies cannot be attributed to new constraints imposed by the movement of goods and capital across borders (Friedman 2002).[36] If this is what is meant by "globalization," it is not new and, just as it was possible for states to pursue egalitarian policies during earlier phases of globalization, so is it now. The constraints have tended to lie, rather, in the degree to which notions of governance that are inimical to egalitarianism have become dominant. And this in turn is a consequence not only of the greater ease at which, given advances in communications technology, fashionable ideas can be disseminated across the globe, but also of the absence of a counterweight, an organized voice for the poor.

What, then, can be done to halt the trend toward greater inequality in this new democracy?

The first and perhaps most important recommendation is that every attempt be made to address the root cause of the problem—the lack of a political voice for the poor. In South Africa, this proposal needs to be made with some caution and great clarity lest it produce a "cure" that serves to reproduce the ailment. Over the past decade, the suggestion that weaker groups need greater access to decisionmaking has produced a propensity to attempt to simulate representative democracy by establishing "participatory processes" alongside (after 1994) the formal institutions of democratic representation. Originally, the most popular vehicle was the forum, a parallel body comprising those citizens' associations with a presumed interest in development.[37] Currently, "public participation" processes are in vogue.

The flaw in this approach may be evident to readers who have been following this analysis. If the poor indeed lack a voice because they remain unorganized, then special vehicles for the voicing of "community perspectives," for example, forums and "public participation" exercises, are likely to provide a platform for anyone *except* the poor. The notion that weaker groups who find it difficult to organize will gain greater access to the polity through forums or participation mechanisms is deeply flawed—the resources required for these mechanisms are invariably found among organized groups, not the unorganized poor. Far from offering the poor a way into democratic processes, these vehicles are likely to work as instruments of exclusion. This is hardly a surprise: corporatist or quasi-corporatist institutions invariably recognize and reward organization—for those who lack the capital required for organization, pluralism, the free exercise of political "voice" by making demands on the authorities is a far more plausible source of power (Cawson 1986).

Opportunities for access for the poor will, therefore, be much enhanced if democratic representative institutions become more accessible. The problem is not that representative democracy has failed but that it has not yet been tried. On one level, recipes are inappropriate here: the problem may lie not in grand institutional design but in building a political culture in which elected representatives are ready to take the trouble to find out what constituents want and to champion these causes. In South Africa, a closed-list proportional representation system in national and provincial elections creates severe disincentives to effective representation, but even in local government, where a constituency system operates alongside a party list, the dominance of parties and the effect of their internal discipline ensures that opportunities for representation for the poor are reduced. Ironically, the power of identity politics probably means that parties could afford to relax discipline: precisely because party loyalties are shaped by identity questions, public representatives would need no prompting to vote the party line on identity questions—nor would they be inclined to decamp to a rival if they differed publicly with their parties on questions of socioeconomic interest. At present, there are no signs of a break with party discipline in legislative forums. The issue may, however, gain salience if the delicate balance between interests that is currently ANC policy were to tilt more firmly toward the new professional and business elite or (far less likely) the poor, enhancing the incentives for "losers" to take independent positions.

Despite these constraints to effective representation, its centrality in any attempt to address widening inequality needs to be stressed since its importance is not acknowledged by the current conventional wisdom on inequality reduction in South Africa. A community of interest between the political preoccupations of the current ANC leadership and fashionable governance theories among aid donors has provided support for a view that sees inequality reduction as a technical task whose antidote lies in enhanced administrative and policymaking capacity in the executive arm of government, and most particularly in the public service.[38] By contrast, this analysis insists that more effective democratic representation for the poor is the sine qua non of effective action against inequality because, without it, policy is likely to misunderstand the nature of the problem and implementation is, without the active participation of the intended beneficiaries, likely to be ineffective. The gap between policy and grass-roots reality on the one hand, and between intention and implementation on the other, that has constrained social and development policy can be closed only by deeper and more vigorous representation. Only when South African government preoccupations and donor programs see the strengthening of representative institutions—legislatures—as a priority at least equal to that of enhancing bureaucratic effectiveness are opportunities for more effective action against inequality likely to open.

It is also worth questioning whether the current South African government's stress on centralization—on concentrating powers and functions in national government[39]—is appropriate to an egalitarian agenda. A history in which formal decentralization, most notably through ethnically defined black "homelands," was used by the apartheid system as an instrument of racial domination has created a strong assumption among many in the governing party that centralization is the only feasible route to redistribution.[40] But, if it is accepted that a voice for the poor is an essential ingredient of effective action against inequality, then it may well be that the accessibility of institutions to the grass-roots poor is a crucial test of appropriateness to an egalitarian agenda. Local institutions may offer a better prospect of access than centralized channels. This is certainly not axiomatic, and local institutions are vulnerable to capture by local elites (Mamdani 1995; Gotz 1997). But they are more physically accessible to the grass roots and may be the sphere of democratic governance in which the voice of the poor, at least initially, is most likely to be heard.

Elected representatives are, however, not the only actors in the democratic system with the capacity to open up or constrain opportunities for the poor to influence the agenda. Officials, too, can exclude or include, depending on the strategies they use to test grass-roots development preferences. In place of the current reliance on contrived and exclusionary "public participation" processes, two changes of attitude may be required. The first is the recognition that democratic government's primary task is to inform citizens of their choices. This sounds straightforward, but in reality would require a significant change in how government operates. First, it presupposes a capacity to communicate with people at the grass roots. Second, it assumes sufficient restraint to explain technical options in ways that allow citizens to select between costs and benefits, rather than the more common approach in which the specialist or official "informs" in ways that predetermine the response by stressing the favorable aspects of the preferred choice and the negatives of the alternative. But, while this is difficult, it is hardly impossible. If the myriad "capacity-building" projects in the public service were to focus on the skills and resources needed to perform this task, the prospects of more effective action against inequality would be greatly enhanced.

The second requirement proposes a change of attitude that may require significant adjustments, but which is clearly within the capacity of government: that is, if citizens choose to respond to the information by making demands on government, it will respond appropriately, not necessarily by acceding to their demand (for it is the prerogative of elected government, rather than particular interests, to make policy) but by allowing them full access to the policy debate. This may again seem trite. In reality, however, a key rationale for forums and "participation processes" is often that they reduce the state-citizen relationship to one that is subject to convenient administrative control. But citizens often need to express their preferences in ways that are not administratively convenient [41]; public officials who take seriously their mandate to serve the citizenry may, therefore, need to adjust to the poor's way of expressing themselves rather than straightjacketing the expression of social policy choices into channels that may ensure bureaucratic convenience at the expense of public voice. A greater openness to the voice of the poor, however it is expressed, may be essential if government action against inequality is to have its intended effect.

It could be argued that the approach proposed here is naïve because it insists on a culture change as a prerequisite for effective representation and that it therefore ignores the difficulty of achieving the recommended change. One response is to note that to propose a solution is not to insist that it can be implemented swiftly or easily—indeed, it could be argued that policy debates that assume that an approach is impractical unless it can be implemented through a recipe that promises instant results may be leading us away from progress because they obstruct the development of longer-term strategies that may be more appropriate interventions than short-term tinkering. If the only solution to a problem is one that will take a long time, then an effective intervention will be that which seeks to build the preconditions for the required solution over time, not one that leads away from it by a misconceived stress on the immediate. Indeed, where "public participation" exercises spring from an attempt to broaden participation rather than to ensure bureaucratic convenience or favored access for the few, they could be a symptom of precisely this attempt to rely on a short-term device to simulate that which can be created only by a longer-term intervention.

However, another response could note that the change of culture suggested here is feasible in the short term and that there are interventions that might assist it. At present, for example, the incentives for legislators in the African National Congress to act in the manner suggested here are slim, the disincentives substantial. Strengthening a connection with voters might anger the party leadership, ensuring that representatives are not retained on the party list or reawarded nomination as candidates in local government: some ANC activists and local representatives have been expelled for disloyalty (Heller and Ntlokonkulu 2001). But the ANC approach that is currently dominant stems from only one of its political cultures, that which emerged when it operated in exile. Internal resistance was premised, partly rhetorically and partly in practice, on a culture that could be interpreted to support the approach proposed here.[42] And, even within current conditions, some legislators do seek a closer connection with their voters—without losing their seats. On intervention, it was noted earlier that much democracy support in postapartheid South Africa has been devoted to strengthening the executive branch rather than to encouraging legislators to represent constituents, and equipping them to do so (Friedman et al. 1998). This has been underpinned by a donor approach that has tended to give priority to administrative competence as a key to the success of new democracies, rather than representative depth (Friedman forthcoming). A change in this approach is hardly a Utopian prospect. If we combine to a degree this point with the plea for a longer-term perspective proposed above, we could argue that an approach by donors and promoters of democracy that sought to strengthen a culture open to deeper and more vigorous representation by offering moral and financial support to efforts to broaden and deepen representative democracy is most likely to ensure a democracy able to deal effectively with its social policy challenges, even if the results would initially be modest and the measures of success incremental.

Nor is institutional design irrelevant to this change: the argument presented here merely insists that it cannot on its own produce the desired effect and that institutional arrangements that are grafted onto a hostile political dynamic are likely to make no difference or to produce perverse consequences. But it is nevertheless important to stress that there are arrangements that make the required changes more possible, and those that make them less so. Thus a degree of constituency representation that nevertheless continues to produce proportional electoral outcomes in national, provincial, and local legislatures offers the poor options that the current system is more likely to foreclose. A further issue is the nature and size of local government, the site at which the voice of the poor is most likely to be heard because it is the only one in which constituencies are likely to be small enough to ensure that representatives are accessible to people with very limited resources. Local government needs enough power to exercise real choices if local voices are to make a practical impact. On size, the current emphasis is on large municipalities—a choice motivated, again, by a stress on administrative and technical criteria such as economies of scale. A second level of municipal government was abolished in 2000 because multiple local structures of representation are said to complicate governance, obstruct redistribution, and consume resources wastefully. In reality, the introduction of a borough system below the metropolitan or district level, creating elected representatives with constituencies small enough to allow accessibility to the poor, would enrich governance by making it more representative, would not hamper redistribution because resources are largely allocated at the metropolitan level, and would require very minor expenditure, as these would be representative rather than administrative units. Finally, here, governments, the local sphere in particular, could establish committees that could hold regular hearings in poor areas. None of these innovations are certain to produce an effective voice for the poor; but they would do much to make it possible.

It must also be stressed that the openness of democratic institutions can, at best, make access by the poor to decisions possible—it cannot guarantee it in the absence of effective organization. As long as the poor remain unorganized, so will the promise of a fuller political citizenship capable of producing its social equivalent remain elusive. This is a challenge not for the state but for those interests and activists who purport to champion the poor. To insist that the poor's lack of voice is a result of structural factors is not to assert that it is inevitable and unchangeable—this analysis has noted the attempts by unions in other parts of the world to organize the unemployed and informally employed. Current trends in South Africa—in particular COSATU's embrace of a basic income grant campaign—do suggest that the union movement may increasingly perceive an interest in organizing people in informal settings. There are also embryonic signs of a reassessment among civil-society organizations who seek a mass constituency: its chief features are a view that the government's declining propensity to include them in policy discussion is primarily a symptom of their own tendency to substitute political connections for organization and that their influence is likely to depend more on their ability to develop a mobilized constituency, and on effective use of the rights to participate bestowed by the constitution, than on a place at the official policy table.[43] Much intellectual interest is also currently focused on grass-roots action by the poor, either through the South African National Civic Organisation (Heller and Ntlokonkulu 2001) or as a result of the efforts of other activists.[44] It is far too early to claim that this is a significant trend—fashion among the intelligentsia is rarely an accurate guide to grass-roots sentiment. Nor is it appropriate to dismiss it without empirical investigation. Whether the agents turn out to be unions, their retrenched members who have both organizational resources and a motive for organizing the unemployed,[45] or activists imbued with ideological zeal, there is little prospect of an effective egalitarian agenda unless the poor themselves acquire sufficient organization to imprint their concerns onto the policy debate.

This analysis has, however, suggested that an attempt to organize the informally employed will take activists and social analysis into uncharted waters since too little is known about the associations, networks, and power relations that govern informality. We know from experience in development negotiations that informal power holders are often not those figures who present themselves to official negotiation forums—evidence is provided in the negative by the fact that agreements made in these discussions are often not honored by those on behalf of whom they are made. Evidence from other sub-Saharan African societies[46] and from South Africa (Gotz 1997) suggests that this is likely to be explained by the role of power holders who do not operate within the norms of democratic politics and who are strong enough to veto decisions that threaten their interests.. But visible organization among the informally employed is also evident: fieldwork in the coastal city of Durban, for example, has noted the existence of formal associations of women street traders who negotiate with the local government for sites.[47] Whether they are likely to become sources of egalitarian claims on the state is a question for further research and analysis. They do, however, appear to confirm the complexity of informal organization. If a democratic path that can also ensure reduced inequality is to be found, scholars and activists will need to learn far more about informal associational life and the challenges it poses—or opportunities it offers—to democratic organization aimed at securing appropriate policies and programs.

It is also worth noting that democratic egalitarian organization, if it is to succeed in South Africa (and, conceivably, elsewhere in sub-Saharan Africa), is likely to take a different course to that in the North. Traditionally, the vehicle for redistributive social policy has been a political party that, by forming alliances with other parties, assembles a winning electoral coalition (Przeworski 1987). In South Africa, however, the primacy of identities in shaping electoral choices, which seems set to endure for a generation or more, suggests that, if contests over social policy are to occur, battle is likely to be joined within identity-based political parties since the political and symbolic costs of leaving parties with strong "liberation" credentials derived from their role in the achievement of freedom is likely to be too high. This means that a key egalitarian challenge is the interpretation of identities in egalitarian ways. In South Africa, this is certainly possible: the nationalist paradigm of the ANC does not necessarily exclude the poor, and does not mandate a preoccupation with the business and professional classes alone. It is possible that the pro-poor camp could exploit this space to build relations with the unemployed in support of a redistributive agenda. This position would be consistent with a tradition of African nationalism exemplified by the Freedom Charter. The development of an identity-based democratic egalitarianism is thus a crucial challenge for attempts to narrow inequality in postapartheid South Africa.

Finally, there may be cause for those social actors concerned to pursue an egalitarian agenda to devote far more attention to the circumstances under which the affluent may be persuaded to contribute to egalitarian social policy—not only by making their tax contributions but by continuing to invest in economies as vigorous attempts to redress poverty proceed. The findings may well invite some discussion not only of egalitarian tactics but also of social policy design.

The white affluent, for example, may be more amenable to contributing toward equity than current rhetoric on both sides of the racial divide suggests. This possibility is illustrated by a focus group exercise conducted not long after the new order began, in which relatively affluent non-black African respondents were asked whether they would be willing to pay more per unit for water than black people to make amends for apartheid. Participants cited a host of black sins to show why they felt this to be unfair. Not long afterward, the same group was asked whether they felt it fair that people who consumed more water should pay more for a unit than those who used less.[48] Unhesitatingly, they agreed to an option that is more egalitarian than the first (because it excludes the possibility that affluent black people would benefit at the expense of the poor).

Besides the obvious point that race is not the automatic indicator of inequality that some suggest, the policy lesson is that appeals to egalitarianism framed in universal terms, rather than the language of racial retribution, win wide support. Not long after the exercise was held, it was (inadvertently?) tested: the minister of water affairs introduced a differential tariff that charged more for greater use—but justified it on grounds not of racial recompense, but the need to save a scarce resource. There was no protest, a sharp contrast to the rebellions that have followed increases in municipal property taxes for suburban households (which have included public refusal to pay by businesses and individuals). During the 2000 local election campaign, the promise of a free initial allocation of water to each household, another redistributive measure framed in universal terms—and offering a small benefit to the well-heeled—was endorsed by the white-led official opposition and has elicited little, if any, rate-payer resistance. Similarly, a "transition levy" imposed on all taxpayers just after 1994 prompted little dissent because it was framed as a common national contribution to the costs of achieving (the common good of) democracy. But an approach that seeks to win support for redistributive measures by appealing to universal values would, at least to a degree, require a change of approach by government and opposition as the ethos of reconciliation of the immediate post-1994 period has given way to a more adversarial politics.[49]

If the experience of Northern welfare states is a guide, the design of aspects of social policy could play an important role in building egalitarian consensus. "Social democratic" welfare states, which have extended benefits universally, have tended to win broader social support—for the obvious reason that the middle classes are beneficiaries and therefore have a stake in their survival (Epsing-Andersen 1990). It has therefore been suggested that universal cash transfers—available in principle to every citizen—could be used to provide income support to the poor. Initially, the prospect of suburbanites receiving cash grants from the state seemed bizarre, but the idea that they should receive a small initial allocation of free water or a basic income grant has implemented a similar principle.

This approach would defuse resistance because it would be symbolically unifying. The water tariff seems to support this point. It is not economically feasible to offer entitlements sufficiently generous to give the middle class a tangible stake in the changes. Thus, while all citizens are entitled to use the public school system, attempts to retain the middle class within it have had limited success. An even stronger trend seems evident in use of public hospitals—again, open in principle to all. This limits the strategy's applicability and ensures also that the benefits extended to the middle class are hardly ample enough to prompt any mobilization in defense of redistributive measures were their survival to be threatened. Resource constraints ensure, therefore, that the social policy approach proposed here can reduce resistance by the affluent, but cannot create a middle-class interest in preserving the new entitlements. This does not, however, mean that pessimism about solidaristic social policy is appropriate. If the limits of the possible are policies that, because they are universal even if of no great benefit to the middle classes, will not be opposed, and there is concrete evidence that this opens new areas for social policy, then egalitarian strategy needs to take this into account rather than hankering for an unattainable cross-class solidarity.

In sum, globalization, to the extent that it influences prospects for democratic egalitarianism in South Africa, merely builds on domestic trends—the chief constraints and opportunities exist largely independently of it, even if its intellectual and cultural manifestation accentuate existing trends and provide handy political weapons to partisans on both sides of the racial and social divide. Turning the political rights gained on apartheid's demise into reduced inequality requires primarily an agenda designed to address a set of endogenous political and intellectual challenges, which has been tentatively sketched here. Other societies, too, may find that the constraints on egalitarianism are primarily to be found within, the obvious inequities in the international system (and the likelihood that egalitarian Southern governments would need to challenge discriminatory Northern tariff regimes, for example) notwithstanding. Thorough democratization remains a necessary condition of an effective attempt to reverse both international and domestic inequality.

## Notes

1. South African Reserve Bank (2003: S-110), preliminary and subject to revision. The calculation is in market prices. All US$ amounts are calculated at an exchange rate of 7.18 rand to the dollar.

2. These are my own calculations based on data from Bhorat (2003) and Poswell (2002).

3. See, for example, Ohmae (1990; 1996) and Strange (1996). This prognosis has also been endorsed by no less an international icon than Vaclav Havel (1999: 4–6). For a critique, see Krugman (1998).

4. One of several identity categorizations under apartheid divided the population into black (African), "coloured" (or mulatto and Malay), Indian, and white. The ANC formed an alliance with the South African Coloured People's Organisation, South African Indian Congress, and the (white) South African Congress of Democrats. See Roux (1964). The extent of support that the minority organizations enjoyed among their identity groups is unclear.

5. For a discussion of the RDP and its attempted implementation, see Rapoo (1996).

6. See, for example, Perreira, Maravall, and Przeworski ( 1993) and Haggard and Kaufman (1995).

7. For an account and analysis of the process see Kentridge (1993).

8. See, for example, Michie and Padayachee (1998) and Habib and Padayachee (2000).

9. Statistics South Africa (2000) places the Gini coefficient at around 0.80, but this figure enjoys little credibility among specialists. The figure used in this analysis, close to 0.60, is far closer to the scholarly norm. On general inequality trends, see van den Bergh and Bhorat (1999).

10. Operating since 1950 (when the SACP was banned) largely through the Congress of Democrats, a white, legal organization formally allied to the ANC (Roux 1964).

11. The Federation of South African Trade Unions (FOSATU), which later merged into COSATU (Friedman 1987).

12. For a popular version of these expectations, see Venter (1997).

13. The attitude is by no means restricted to South African whites. A (white) mining executive tells of visiting fund managers in North America and Western Europe in an attempt to raise investment capital. His and his colleagues' pitch consisted largely of references to healthy economic fundamentals and progress in resolving conflicts. In many cases, the appeal was not persuasive. "But you have a black government," many of his audiences responded. Discussion, senior mining executive, 1995.

14. For a discussion of this dynamic in an urban setting, see Friedman (2001b: 31–68).

15. For the latter, see Bond (2000).

16. For example, the ANC's campaign against the forced removal of black people from the Sophiatown township failed to take into account that many residents were open to the apartheid authorities' spurious claims that they would be moved to a better place because they were being charged exorbitant rents by local landlords (Friedman 1987).

17. There is also some evidence that GEAR was partly a response to implementation problems that beset the RDP, again an endogenous constraint (Rapoo 1996).

18. See, for example, Kihato (2001).

19. See interview with finance minister Trevor Manuel, *Sunday Independent* (Johannesburg). 9 January 2000.

20. See, for example, Mdlalana (2000).

21. For an elaboration of the argument, see Friedman (2001a). For its intellectual inspirations, see Esping-Andersen (1990) and Przeworski (1987).

22. In the last budget year, the minister of finance requested parliamentary approval for R2.2 billion in "roll overs" (a process in which money is carried forward to the next budget year) for unspent money (Manuel 2001).

23. See, for example, figures provided in South African Revenue Service (2001).

24. See, for example, May et al. (1998).

25. See also remarks by Nelson Mandela quoted by this author in *Business Day*, 1 March 1999.

26. For some possible effects on South African social policy, see Simkins (1996).

27. See Steven Friedman, "Corporations Are Not All-Powerful," *Mail and Guardian* (Johannesburg), 12 April, 2001.

28. This argument is elaborated in Friedman (2002: 13–40).

29. See, for example, Melucci (1996).

30. See Friedman and Chipkin (2001) for views of social policy specialists consulted by the Centre for Policy Studies.

31. For the general mismatch between skills levels and job opportunities, see Abedian (2001). For current detailed data, see Poswell (2002).

32. In the South African context, many shack settlements "began with an emphasis on participation and ended up with a shacklord" (Mamdani 1995: 295). See also White (1993).

33. See comments by Frances Lund in Friedman and Chipkin (2001).

34. The argument interprets evidence offered in Ernesto Calvo, Juan Carlos Torre, and Mariela Szwarcberg, *The New Welfare Alliance*, cited in Friedman (2001).

35. The notion of "social citizenship" as a consequence of political rights in liberal democracies is derived from Marshall (1992).

36. For an argument insisting that this argument holds in Northern societies, see Garrett (1998).

37. For debate on forums, see Villiers (1994); for a discussion of mechanisms for civil society participation, see Humphries and Reitzes (1995).

38. See Friedman (1999b: 3–18).

39. For current trends see Rapoo (2001) and Kihato and Rapoo (2001). For a critique of current centralization policies, see Friedman and Kihato (forthcoming).

40. For a full exposition of all perspectives in this debate, see Friedman and Humphries (1993).

41. For a critique of governance approaches that seek to fit social reality to the requirements of technical and administrative manipulation, see Scott (1998).

42. On competing traditions within the ANC, see Friedman and Chipkin (2001).

43. Distilled from proceedings of discussion group on civil society in the post-1999 period convened by the Centre for Policy Studies and Friedrich-Ebert-Stiftung, Johannesburg, 2000.

44. See, for example, Centre for Civil Society, University of Natal CCS-l digest; online at: http://lists.nu.ac.za/mailman/listinfo/ccs-l.

45. Current Centre for Policy Studies research, for example, focuses on retrenched workers who lead a development forum in an informal shack settlement near Johannesburg.

46. See, for example, Simone (1995).

47. See Lund's reported findings in Friedman and Chipkin (2001).

48. Project Manzi, May 1995: focus group study of consumer responses to water delivery and payment commissioned by Rand Water (unpublished).

49. See, for example, a column by Steven Friedman in *Mail and Guardian* 25-30 August 2000.

# 3

# Turkey: Globalization, Democratic Governance, and Inequality

## E. Fuat Keyman

In this new millennium, it has become apparent that our post–Cold War world is beset by contradictions, ambiguities, and insecurities. On the one hand, the post–Cold War world has been defined by globalization, referring to the process of the worldwide widening, deepening, and speeding up of interconnectedness in societal and international affairs (Held et al. 1999; Beck 1997). It has been argued in this context that "just as postmodernism was *the* concept of the 1980s, globalization may be *the* concept of the 1990s, a key idea by which we understand the transition of human society into the third millennium" (Waters 1995: 1). What Leftwich (1993: 605) calls "a new orthodoxy dominating official Western aid policy and development thinking" has identified globalization mainly and basically as an economic phenomenon that elevates the "free market" to the status of being a universal code for economic development and growth, as well as for international peace and democratization. As Faux and Michel (2001: 109) correctly point out, "while the promoters of globalization have grudgingly acknowledged that there are costs to society, they have assumed in all cases that the costs, whatever they are, must be less than overall benefits to society, an assumption reinforced by the ideological disposition of economists to glorify free markets." Thus, globalization has been assumed to be a positive development with the potential to bring about economic prosperity, political democratization, and cultural modernization in societal and international affairs by disseminating the free-market rationality throughout the post–Cold War world.

On the other hand, however, the 1990s also witnessed the sheer magnitude of ontological insecurity, inequality, and poverty on a global scale. While both ethnic/religious wars and global terrorism have created the feeling of ontological insecurity in different parts of the post-Cold War world, inequality and poverty have become structural and systemic problems. Identity-based conflicts around the world (in Bosnia, Kosovo,

Rwanda, Chechnya, East Timor, Eritrea, Palestine, to name a few) and the deadly attacks of global terrorism have created the predatory face of globalization. Yet poverty has constituted "by far the greatest source of human misery today": in 1998, for example, "starvation and preventable diseases . . . claimed about 18 million human lives, thus causing about one-third of all human deaths" (Pogge 2001: 8). In a time when "average real incomes in the developed world are 75 times higher than in least-developed regions" (Drache and Froese 2003: 6); approximately 40 percent of the world's population face the problem of deep economic recession; "one-quarter of all human beings alive today, 1.5 billion, subsist below the international poverty line; 790 million persons are not adequately nourished; one billion are without safe water; 2.4 billion without basic sanitation; more than 880 million lack access to basic health services; about one billion are without adequate shelter and two billion without electricity; and two out of five children in the developing world are stunted, one in three is underweight and one in ten is wasted" (Pogge 2001: 7), inequality and poverty should be considered structural and systemic global problems requiring global solutions. Since inequality and poverty have risen dramatically in the 1990s (see Figure 3.1), and as Wade claims, this

**Figure 3.1    Unweighted International Inequality, 1950–1998, Measured by the Gini Coefficent**

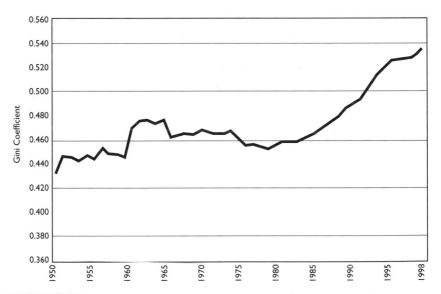

*Source:* Milanovic (2002).

dramatic rise has been clearly "outpacing all poverty reduction efforts by the international community" (in Drache and Froese 2003: 6), it would not be mistaken to suggest that today they, together with ontological insecurity, constitute one of the most significant challenges to the post–Cold War world.

Turkey does not constitute an exception in the post–Cold War world, defined by the simultaneous existence of the process of increasing interconnectedness and the problems of inequality and poverty. On the contrary, the processes of globalization have generated crucial impacts on radical changes and transformations that have occurred in Turkey since the 1980s. Indeed, globalization has been "internal" to the changing nature of Turkish modernization since the 1990s, by contributing (1) to the increasing political and ideological dominance of the neoliberal restructuring of the Turkish economy and its exposure to the world economy; (2) to the revitalization of identity politics in the form of political Islam and the "Kurdish question"; (3) to the problem of social injustice in the areas of distribution, recognition, and participation; and (4) to the emergence of civil-societal calls for democratization, all of which have determined the content, the scope, and the actors of Turkish politics in the 1990s (Kramer 2000).

Furthermore, globalization has also been beset by contradictions in Turkey. In a parallel fashion to the contradictory tendencies of the post–Cold War world, the 1990s in Turkey too, have given rise both to the modernization and liberalization of the Turkish economy in terms of its technological and organizational structure, while, at the same time, causing a dramatic increase in problems of inequality and poverty (Keyman 2000). As will be elaborated later, these problems are not limited to the economic sphere; on the contrary, they have social, cultural, political, and ethical consequences in Turkey, insofar as they have played a significant role in the emergence of identity-politics making strong claims to recognition and cultural group rights.

In this chapter, I will try to analyze the impacts of globalization on Turkey by focusing on the problem of inequality/poverty and its challenge to Turkish politics. The chapter consists of four parts. First, I will approach the problem of inequality/poverty in a theoretical fashion, in order to construct an analytical framework for my analysis of the impacts of globalization on Turkey. Such an analysis will be the focus of the second section. Third, I will deal with the 2001 financial crisis in which the problem of inequality/poverty has become so visible that it can no longer be ignored by political actors in Turkey. Fourth, I will focus on the November 2002 national election, in order to demonstrate the significance of the challenge that the problem of inequality/poverty poses to Turkish politics.

## The Problem of Inequality/Poverty:
## A Theoretical Reflection[1]

In his important study on "world-wide rising inequality," Wade argues correctly that it is difficult to pinpoint its cause (2001: 3). In analyzing inequality and poverty, one could speak of a number of causes, such as the differential population growth between poorer and richer countries, the fall in non-oil commodity prices that have a negative impact on poorer countries, the debt trap leading to devastating financial crises, or technological changes to which lower-cost developing countries are not adapting themselves. These causes have had the potential to create an increasing gap between the richer and the poorer countries, resulting in a structural and systemic problem of inequality/poverty. According to Wade (p. 4), this income polarization has also given rise to another kind of polarization in the world system: a polarization

> between a zone of peace and a zone of turmoil. On the one hand, the regions of the wealthy pole show a strengthening republican order of economic growth and liberal tolerance (except toward immigrants), with technological innovation able to substitute for depleting natural capital. On the other hand, the regions of the lower- and middle-income poles contain many states whose capacity to govern is stagnant or eroding, mainly in Africa, the Middle East, Central Asia, the former Soviet Union, and parts of East Asia.

In this pole, there is a tendency toward increasing restrictions on basic needs, going hand in hand with the problem of high unemployment.

In exploring the causes and consequences of the problems of inequality/poverty, it would be a mistake to think of the problem as a "statistical measure" or as a component of human development (Drache and Froese 2003; Pogge 2001; Beitz 2001). For this mode of thinking might result in our failure to see, either that the problem also constitutes a central/primary issue in human development that cannot be reduced to a quality of secondary importance to economic growth, or that it has social, cultural, political, and ethical components that make the realm of social justice a complex and multidimensional problem area for democratic governance. Therefore, in this chapter, I will approach the problem of inequality/poverty not as a derivative problem whose solution depends on macroeconomic stability, but as a theoretical object of inquiry that has to be analyzed in its own right and specificity. In other words, I will argue that inequality and poverty pose a serious problem to any discourse of development aimed at creating a linkage between globalization and democratic governance, insofar as they together function as a "reminder" that economic development cannot be achieved without a strong commitment to democracy and social justice. In a time when the world in which we live is increasingly defined by starvation, suffering, insecurity, and lack of access to basic capabilities, the problem of inequality/poverty can no longer be put aside, nor can it be reduced to a derivative problem. Instead, it should be conceived of as a "direct problem" for global governance (Beitz 2001: 97), which forces us to admit that neither effective governing nor a legitimate democratic order at global or national levels can be constructed without a fair distribution of wealth and income.

I will attempt to substantiate in an illustrative fashion the importance of taking the problem of inequality/poverty as a "direct problem" for democratic governance by focusing on Turkey, where the effects of globalization since the 1980s, but especially in the 1990s, have given rise to both the economic liberalization of market relations and the increasingly unjust distribution of wealth and income. In doing so, I will suggest theoretically that one could speak of two forms of inequality operating in the realm of social justice, namely those of *distribution* and *recognition*. These forms of inequality constitute separate but nevertheless interrelated problems for democratic good governance. Inequality embedded in distribution refers to the unjust distribution of wealth and income between the rich and the poor, that is, between classes, whereas inequality embedded in recognition occurs as an identity-based inequality, in which the uneven and unfair distribution of wealth and income functions as a process of "Othering," as a mode of social subordination, and a technology of exclusion of different identities from the dominant regime of industrialization in a given national site (Keyman 2001; Özbudun and Keyman 2002). In this sense, while inequality embedded in distribution constitutes a "class-based inequality," inequality embedded in recognition refers to an "identity-based inequality," as in the case of the resurgence of Islam and the "Kurdish question" in Turkey.

To explain the relationship between these forms of inequality, it is useful to draw on Fraser's diagnosis of the current state of progressive politics:

> For some time now, the forces of progressive politics have been divided into two camps. On one side stand the proponents of "redistribution." Drawing on the long tradition of egalitarian, labor, and socialist organizing, political actors aligned with this orientation seek a more just allocation of resources and goods. On the other side stand the proponents of "recognition." Drawing on newer visions of a "difference-friendly" society, they seek a world where assimilation to majority or dominant cultural norms is no longer the price of equal respect. Members of the first camp hope to redistribute wealth from the rich to the poor, from the North to the South, and from the owners to the workers. Members of the second, in contrast, seek recognition of the distinctive perspectives of ethnic, racial, and sexual minorities, as well as of gender difference. The redistribution orientation has a distinguished philosophical pedigree, as egalitarian

> redistribute claims have supplied the paradigm case for most theorizing
> about social justice for the past 150 years. The recognition orientation has
> recently attracted the interest of political philosophers, however, some of
> whom are seeking to develop a new normative paradigm that puts recog-
> nition at its center. (Fraser 2000: 95–96)

According to Fraser, in order to establish a defensible claim for political and social equality, it is necessary, if not imperative, to see the politics
of distribution and the politics of recognition not as antithetical to one
another, but as intertwined claims for fair distribution of wealth and
income. Relying on Fraser's diagnosis, I will argue that as a "theoretical
object of inquiry," as well as a "direct problem" for democratic good governance, the problem of inequality/poverty should be considered as intertwined claims to fair distribution and recognition. This consideration
allows one to analyze the problem of inequality/poverty in a given national
site by going beyond the reductionist and derivative approaches to economic growth and, as will be elaborated in detail, by seeing how claims for
social and political equality also constitute claims to recognition, both of
which operate within the realm of social justice. In this way, it becomes
possible to "transform" the existing "predatory globalization" (Falk 2000)
into democratic good governance. In what follows, I will try to analyze the
impacts of globalization on Turkey by employing a multidimensional concept of inequality/poverty.

## Globalization and Turkey[2]

Since the 1980s, and especially during the 1990s, the circular movement
between modernization and the state has been radically challenged by a
variety of societal developments in Turkey. These developments range from
the integration of the Turkish economy into the world market (economic
globalization) to the constant efforts of Turkey to gain full membership status in the European Union (political globalization); from the resurgence of
Islam and the Kurdish question to the emergence of civil-societal calls for
democratization and pluralism (cultural globalization); and from the
increasing legitimacy and governing crisis of the bureaucratic-strong state
tradition to strong liberal demands for the protection of individual and civil
rights (Keyman 2002: 85–89). Despite differences, all these societal developments have a number of commonalities; first, they are all constructed at
the intersection between the global, the regional, and the local, thereby
demanding the transformation of the nation-state in an effective and democratic governing institution; and second, they have all indicated that the
state-centric mode of Turkish modernization is no longer capable of dealing
effectively with economic, cultural, and political change.

There are a number of significant sites that have emerged from these societal developments in which globalization has played an important role and functioned as an internal variable to the changing nature of Turkish modernization since the 1980s. Four of them are worth emphasizing here. The most crucial site where the impacts of globalization on Turkish society are most visible is in economic life, the scope and the organizational structure of which has been increasingly extended beyond national and territorial borders. In fact, in the 1990s, the Turkish economy has been (1) exposed to the process of the globalization of capital and trade and (2) organized on the basis of the primacy of the global market over the domestic one, which has led economic actors to realize (3) that market relations require rational and long-term strategies and (4) that in order to be secure and successful in (globalized) economic life, it is imperative to gain organizational capabilities to produce or maintain technological improvement and strategic planning for production and investment (Öniş 2003). As a result, in the last decade we have seen the increasing importance of market liberalization as a linkage between Turkey and the globalizing world.

The recent report, prepared by Central Bank of the Republic of Turkey, on "The Impact of Globalization on the Turkish Economy" (2002), has also suggested that since the 1990s, market liberalization has been the most visible domain in which the integration of the Turkish economy into globalization has taken place. In this context, since the state has initiated a number of market-liberalization reforms, aimed at transforming the Turkish economy into a more outward-oriented economy through, first, the liberalization of the foreign trade regime and the financial sector, and then the liberalization of the capital account. In doing so, Turkey managed "both to remove quantity rationing and reduce import tariff levels. In this respect, the World Bank classified Turkey as an intensive adjuster in 1991" (Central Bank of the Republic of Turkey 2002: 10). However, the Central Bank's report also indicates that although Turkey has been successful in integrating into the world economy (see Table 3.1), the Turkish economy has not adequately benefited from this integration. The main reason for this lies both in the increasing inability of the bureaucratic-strong state to pursue long-term and structural reforms, "mainly in the areas of the banking sector, public finance, and public management during the 1990s" (p. 58), and in the vulnerability of the Turkish economy to the crisis-ridden nature of the world economy in the same period (such as the Gulf war in 1990–1991 and the Russian crisis in 1998).

The Central Bank report on the impacts of globalization on the Turkish economy summarizes the overall effect of market liberalization and integration into the world economy since the 1980s in the following way:

**Table 3.1    Main Macroeconomic Indicators of Turkey, 1970–1999**

|  | 1970–1979 | 1980–1989 | 1990–1999 |
|---|---|---|---|
| GNP per Capita (US dollars) | 1,073 | 1,502 | 2,810 |
| GNP Growth (%) | 4.8 | 4.0 | 3.9 |
| Agriculture | 1.9 | 0.7 | 1.6 |
| Industry | 6.4 | 6.0 | 4.6 |
| Trade | 7.1 | 6.1 | 5.0 |
| Financial Services | 7.6 | 2.8 | 1.9 |
| Agriculture (% of GNP) | 31.9 | 20.4 | 15.6 |
| Industry (% of GNP) | 18.0 | 23.2 | 24.8 |
| Trade (% of GNP) | 13.7 | 18.3 | 19.3 |
| Financial Services (% of GNP) | 2.1 | 2.5 | 4.4 |
| Private Consumption (% of GNP) | — | 65.4 | 67.7 |
| Gross Fixed Investment (% of GNP) | 22.9 | 21.6 | 23.8 |
| Public (% of GNP) | 7.6 | 8.9 | 6.0 |
| Private (% of GNP) | 15.3 | 12.8 | 17.8 |
| Savings (% of GNP) | 20.1 | 19.8 | 21.7 |
| Gross Fixed Investment (% change) | 7.1 | 3.6 | 2.6 |
| Public (% change) | 7.1 | 3.6 | 2.6 |
| Private (% change) | 7.0 | 3.6 | 2.6 |
| Foreign Debt Stock (% of GNP) | 10.3 | 34.9 | 42.0 |
| Short-Term (% of GNP)[a] | — | 6.5 | 9.1 |
| Medium- and Long-Term (% of GNP)[a] | — | 32.9 | 33.5 |
| Private Foreign Debt (% of GNP)[a] | — | 5.8 | 14.3 |
| Public Foreign Debt (% of GNP)[a] | — | 24.2 | 21.8 |
| Foreign Trade Deficit (% of GNP) | −4.0 | −4.4 | −6.1 |
| Foreign Trade Volume (% of GNP) | 11.0 | 24.2 | 31.7 |
| Exports/Imports (%) | 48.3 | 68.2 | 66.9 |
| Current Account (% of GNP) | −1.7 | −1.6 | −0.8 |
| Capital Inflows (% of GNP) | 3.4 | 1.8 | 1.7 |
| FDI | 0.1 | 0.2 | 0.4 |
| Portfolio | 0.0 | 0.3 | 0.5 |
| Long-Term | 3.0 | 1.2 | 0.4 |
| Short-Term | 0.2 | 0.1 | 0.3 |
| CPI (% change) | 24.1 | 51.0 | 77.4 |
| Real Effective Exchange Rate (1995=100) | 180.8 | 129.6 | 113.0 |
| US Dollar (Selling) | 16.8 | 54.0 | 73.0 |
| PSBR (% of GNP) | 6.0 | 5.0 | 9.4 |
| Consolidated Budget Balance (% of GNP) | −1.6 | −2.8 | −6.2 |
| Consolidated Budget Interest Payments (% of GNP) | 0.5 | 2.1 | 7.5 |
| Financing of Consolidated Budget (% of GNP)[b] | 2.1 | 2.7 | 6.3 |
| Foreign Debt | 0.1 | 0.0 | −0.5 |
| Domestic Debt | 0.7 | 1.6 | 5.6 |
| Central Bank | 1.1 | 0.7 | 1.0 |
| Others | 0.2 | 0.4 | 0.2 |
| Domestic Debt Stock/GNP (%) | — | 18.6 | 19.7 |
| Net Domestic Borrowing/Domestic Debt Stock (%) | — | 37.3 | 45.0 |

*Source:* Central Bank of the Republic of Turkey (2002).
*Notes:* a. Available as the same classification since 1983; b. Average of 1975 and 1979.

The balance of payment problems of the Turkish economy seem to have slightly improved during the last two decades compared to the pre-reform period (of the import-substitution industrialization). Nevertheless, this improvement has coupled with the declining long-term growth rates and with high and persistent inflation. Especially after the liberalization of the capital account at the end of 1989, the growth rate has become more volatile and the overall level of uncertainty in the economy has increased. Besides, the reform process resulted in a higher foreign indebtedness. Although in terms of per capita income there has been an improvement, this was coupled with a worsening of income distribution. (2002; 59)

Thus, one could suggest that the impact of globalization has both positive and negative consequences, in that the transformation of the Turkish economy into an outward-market economy went hand in hand with the economic crisis and a dramatic increase in the problem of inequality/poverty. (See Figure 3.2.)

The second important site has been the increasing legitimacy crisis of the strong-state tradition. The 1990s have witnessed the growing dissatisfaction in political and public discourse with the hegemonic position of the

**Figure 3.2    The Impact of Globalization on the Turkish Economy**

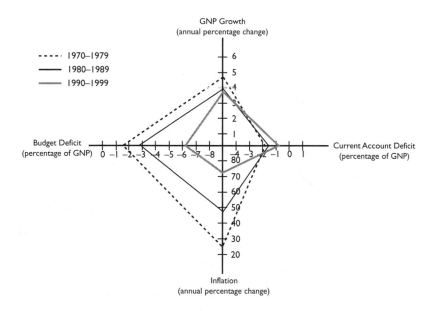

*Source:* Central Bank of the Republic of Turkey (2002).
*Note:* The larger the area of the quadrilateral, the better is the performance of the economy.

state in the political realm, due especially to "a series of political and criminal scandals" (Kramer 2000: 18), and also because of the constant attempts of the bureaucratic-strong state to impede the dynamism of economic and civil life in the name of security and stability. The result has been the emergence of a "discursive and political gap" between state-centric modernization and societal needs/demands. Thus, the strong state has become subject to the criticism that it is "too big and too independent" to adapt itself to the rapidly changing nature of societal affairs in a globalizing world, and at the same time "too small and too weak" to deal effectively with the societal needs/demands. Thus the principle of the strong state is now regarded as no longer capable of governing Turkey in a rational and legitimate manner (Heper and Keyman 1999). As we will see, the need to transform the bureaucratic-strong state into a democratic, accountable, and effective governing institution has become apparent, as Turkey faced the most devastating economic crisis of its post–World War II history on 19 February 2001.

Similarly, the 1990s also witnessed the representation crisis of the organic vision of society, whose reproduction had been secured in Turkish modernization on the basis of a secular national identity. Since the 1980s, the process of revitalizing "the language of difference" has become a significant challenge to the state-centric Turkish modernization and its attempt to accord normative primacy to the ideas of unity and homogeneity over those of difference and pluralism (Keyman 2000). The societal actors who have voiced the language of difference have become powerful actors of Turkish politics, so much so that their challenge has framed, even dominated, the scope and the content of the political during the 1990s. These actors have given rise to "the resurgence of Islam as a strong political actor," the "Kurdish question," and "the liberal claims to the protection of individual and civil rights," and have created the process of what N. Göle calls "the relative autonomization of economic activities, political groups and cultural identities," which have "shift[ed] the focus of political practice from the state to society" (Göle 2000: 33). Thus, Turkish politics have been confronted by "new societal demands, problems, and needs" (Buğra 1999) with which the bureaucratic-strong state cannot cope effectively through its organic vision of society. What is important here is the fact that the language of difference has emerged from within the underdeveloped and poor peripheral geographical regions of Turkey facing the problem of inequality/poverty, and therefore operated also as societal calls demanding for social justice in the realms of distribution and recognition. Therefore, it is no surprise that while the resurgence of Islam has found its social support and mobilization mainly in Anatolia and the poor peripheral sections of the urban centers, the Kurdish question has also operated as a regional question related directly to the southeastern part of Turkey. In this sense, the societal calls, voicing the language of difference, are also calls for the need to make the realm of social justice a central concern of Turkish politics (Özbudun and Keyman 2002).

The fourth important development of the 1990s, which challenged the state-centric Turkish modernization was the problem of inequality/poverty, indicating both the increasing gap between the rich and the poor (inequality embedded in distribution) and the increasing regional uneven development (inequality embedded in recognition). While the exposure of the Turkish economy to global capital has created economic liberalization and techno-logical development since the 1980s, the problem of inequality/poverty has also worsened, which has placed "Turkey nearer to the Latin American cases of severe inequality rather than the so-called developmental states in East and Southeast Asia" (Senses 2003: 94). Today, "Turkey is one of the 20 countries in the world that have the utmost unequal distribution of income" (Sönmez 2001). For instance, the monthly income of the richest in Turkey is 236 times more than the poorest. Furthermore, the upper-middle-class segment of the society, constituting 16 percent of the population, uses 25 percent of the gross national product (GNP), whereas the lower-income groups (lower-middle class and the poor) constitute 80 percent of the population and utilize only 42 percent of the GNP. Similar discrepancies can also be found among the geographical regions in Turkey. While Istanbul and the Marmara region is the richest in Turkey by getting 38 percent of the GNP, in the southeast, wherein the Kurdish problem has originated, the monthly income can go down to US$40, and the percentage of the utiliza-tion of the GNP is at most 4.5 percent (Sönmez 2001: 31).

As for the problem of poverty, during the 1990s we have also seen a trend toward increasing poverty in rural and urban areas in Turkey. When we employ the World Bank's extreme purchasing power parity poverty line of US$1 per person a day, and the definition of urban food poverty as "those in urban areas with equivalent consumption below the cost of a food basket" (World Bank 2003: 1), it is estimated that in 2001 2.4 percent of the population had per capita income under US$1 per day in Turkey and face the problem of extreme poverty, while around 10 million persons have per capita consumption less than US$1 per day. Women and unemployed youth constitute the most vulnerable segments of society. The World Bank report has also indicated that the problem of extreme poverty was unchanged in 2001, poverty has sharply increased, especially in urban areas, as a result of the 19 February 2001 economic crisis. There is a consensus among those who are working on the problem of poverty that the trend toward increasing poverty is most likely to continue (Senses 2003; Sönmez 2001). It can be argued in this context that coupled with the problem of inequality, poverty appears to be one of the most pressing challenges to Turkish politics.

There is a common denominator that links together all these develop-ments and challenges (market liberalization, the crisis of the bureaucratic-strong state, the representation crisis of the organic vision of society, and the problem of inequality/poverty). That is, they have created a "gap" between the bureaucratic-strong state and the rapidly changing economic/cultural relations, a gap from within which have emerged a number of strong challenges to state-centric Turkish modernization (Keyman 2000). Globalization has constituted a "historical context" for the emergence of both these gaps and all these challenges. Moreover, and more importantly, during the 1990s globalization has also been "internal" to the simultaneous emergence of market liberalization and the problem of increasing inequality/poverty in Turkey. As a result, the question of how to regulate market liberalization in a way that deals effectively with the problems taking place in the realm of social justice has remained unsolved during the 1990s.

Given the fact that the realm of social justice involves not only claims to fair distribution and poverty eradication, but also demands for recognition and participation, Turkey can no longer have stability without exploring efficient answers to the complex question of effective and democratic governance. It is the February 2001 financial crisis, with its devastating effects on Turkish society, that has created a turning point in Turkish politics, in that it yielded a strong impact on the state and political actors by forcing them to focus on the hitherto ignored question of effective and democratic governing, which in turn requires taking seriously not only the need for macroeconomic stability, but also the problem of inequality/poverty. I will focus next on this financial crisis and its consequences in Turkish politics.

## Economic Restructuring and the Problem of Inequality/Poverty

When the president of the Turkish Republic, Ahmet Necdet Sezer, "threw a copy of the Turkish constitution" to the prime minister, Bülent Ecevit, in their heated debate on the problem of corruption during the National Security Council meeting on 19 February 2001, neither of them, of course, realized that their quarrel had the potential to trigger the worst and the deepest economic crisis ever faced by Turkey in its modern history. The next morning, the *Financial Times* declared that "Turkish economy collapsed" into the biggest financial crisis of her history. The crisis negatively and very strongly affected every segment of society by giving rise to the contraction of the national economy by 9.4 percent, causing Turkey around a US$53 billion loss in its GNP, creating more than 1 million unemployed, and reducing the gross national per capita income from US$2,986 down to US$2,160. Thus, the political economy of Turkish capitalism in the 1990s, which had been organized around the clientalist and populist ties between

the government and its constituencies and which was also structurally conducive to the problems of high inflation, increasing internal and external
debts, and corruption and illegal accumulation of wealth, totally collapsed
by bringing the state to its worst legitimacy and governing crisis. As a
result, in the year 2001 Turkey witnessed not only the devaluation of
Turkish lira and the steady increase in the value of the U.S. dollar, coupled
with the declarations of bankruptcy by banks and companies, but also a
dramatic increase in layoffs, as well as in the problem of inequality/pover-
ty. All have given rise to an increasing social and moral distrust for the
bureaucratic-strong state tradition and its ineffective and undemocratic
mode of governing.

For the preparation of a strong economic program to overcome the crisis, Kemal Derviş, who had been working for many years as a World Bank
executive, was appointed as the state minister responsible for and in charge
of economic affairs. He came to Turkey as the fourth partner in the existing
coalition government formed by the Democratic Left Party, the Mother
Land Party, and the Nationalist Action Party. Over the year, under his leadership, a number of legal (constitutional) and institutional changes were
initiated in order to restructure the Turkish economy with a strong financial
sector, so that the desired macroeconomic stability could be achieved,
which is necessary for economic growth based on a free market. The economic restructuring program, prepared by Derviş and his team, consisted of
not only economic and financial measures, designed to create macroeconomic stability, but also, and more importantly, a new governing rationality
for creating a sound political-development management necessary to make
the state more efficient and accountable in the mode in which it governs
society. The aim was to "restructure the state" to achieve the elimination of
structural distortions caused by clientalism and populism, as well as the
establishment of sound macroeconomic management necessary for economic growth through the eradication of inflation and the strengthening of
the financial sector (Derviş 2001: 4). In this sense, the economic program,
financed mainly by the IMF and supported by the World Bank, was suitable
to the economic rationality, embedded in the discourse of "good governance" through a rigid structural adjustment program.

The discourse of good governance, supported by the IMF and the
World Bank, involves both stabilization and adjustment in that

> stabilization normally meant immediate devaluation and often drastic
> public expenditure cuts. This was followed by adjustment which sought to
> transform economic structures and institutions through varying doses of
> deregulation, privatization, slimming down allegedly oversized public
> bureaucracies, reducing subsidies and encouraging realistic prices to
> emerge as a stimulus to greater efficiency and productivity, especially for
> export. (Leftwich 1993: 607)

The economic program, designed to overcome the February crisis in Turkey, adopted this discourse of good governance both by giving primacy to macroeconomic stability and the free market over production in creating a sufficient ground for economic growth and by approaching the question of "restructuring the state" in terms of a neoliberal idea of the state as minimal, limited but more efficient, and "detached from its prior involvement in economic matters. Such a state would undertake basic investment in, and management of, essential physical and social infrastructure, while also monitoring and supervising the free play of market relations in an impartial, open and accountable manner" (Leftwich 1993: 607).

However, it should be pointed out that the economic program for overcoming the February crisis also had to involve the problem of distributive injustice in terms of poverty and inequality, in order to create a "well-governed, modernized and prosperous Turkey" ready to reach the level of living standards in Europe as well as in other advanced industrial societies. It has been argued that without solving the problem of distributive injustice, good governance would not lead to "democratic governance." In a country where market liberalization has gone hand in hand with the problems of inequality/poverty, uneven regional development, and the increasing gap between the rich and the poor, economic stability cannot be achieved without taking the realm of social justice seriously. In this sense, in addition to macroeconomic stability and the restructuring of the state, the need to overcome the problem of distributive injustice constituted the third leg of the economic structural-adjustment program (Derviş 2001: 3–4).

The focus on the problems of inequality and poverty was necessary for two reasons. The first is that contrary to the previous and consecutive economic crises that the Turkish economy had faced throughout the history of modern Turkey, the impact of the February crisis on society in terms of inequality and poverty was so deep and devastating that it was impossible to ignore and exclude the problem of distributive injustice from the economic program aimed at creating good governance in Turkey. In a society where the gross national income per capita is US$2,160, and this amount is reduced to US$700 in the southeast region (and in certain provinces, such as Hakkari, to around US$300), no economic program for structural adjustment can gain legitimacy and accountability without presenting itself as a reform program that is strong enough to cope effectively with inequality and poverty. The second reason concerns the international context in which poverty was recognized by the dominant international institutions as a serious problem that has to be overcome for good governance. By acknowledging the fact that in today's world, more than 2.8 billion people try to survive with less than US$2 a day, the World Bank announced in its 1999 report that the problem of poverty should be regarded as a global problem becoming increasingly capable of creating a powerful obstacle to global good governance with its negative impacts on the principles of economic liberalization and liberal democracy. This new focus on global inequality/poverty has given rise to the "post–Washington consensus" as an acceptance of the fact that the neoliberal discourse of economic growth, defined as macroeconomic stability plus free-market rules, has resulted not in global prosperity and democracy but in poverty and war, mostly in the developing world.[3]

The economic program aimed at overcoming the February crisis in Turkey was embedded in the international context characterized by the post–Washington consensus. Therefore, it employed the discourse of democratic good governance normatively and thematically both as a solution to economic crisis and as a rational and effective foundation for making Turkey "a regional economic giant in the near future" (Derviş, 2001: 9). In doing so, it also claimed that a modern and democratic Turkey requires the elimination of the problems of inequality and poverty, for socioeconomic stability cannot be achieved and maintained without creating even and equal development in terms of a just distribution of wealth and income. However, besides the discursive emphasis placed upon the need for overcoming the problem of inequality/poverty, no such real and serious effort had taken place in the 2001–2002 period of economic restructuring. Instead, the problem was deferred, as the economic program in its actual operation has privileged macroeconomic stability over production by suggesting that without a strong financial sector, economic growth cannot be achieved. It can be argued therefore that the modus vivendi of the economic program still relies on the neoliberal assumption that although good governance involves a triangular and intertwined relationship between economic rationality, political rationality, and the fair distribution of wealth and income, the desired economic growth first requires macroeconomic stability, followed by an impartial, accountable, and effective state "supervising and monitoring the free play of market relations," and lastly, coping with the problems of inequality and poverty.

It can also be argued in this sense that the economic program did not perceive inequality and poverty in a similar and parallel manner to the dominant actors of the discourse of structural adjustment, as a problem to be dealt with in its own right and specificity, but approached them as a problem whose solution should be derived directly from sound macroeconomic stability and a strong and effective free market (Bağımsız Sosyal Bilimciler İktisat Grubu 2001; Leftwich 1993). Thus, the strong economy program and its tendency to reduce the problem of inequality/poverty has been subject to strong criticism, coming from the different segments of society. On 3 November 2002, the national election day, Turkey faced the political consequences of the democratic expression of such criticism. As I will briefly analyze in what follows, the November 2002 national election can be considered a historical moment in which the problem of inequality/poverty finally struck back and placed itself in Turkish politics as a central issue that can no longer be shrugged off.

## A "Communitarian-Liberal" Response to Inequality/Poverty

On the evening of 3 November 2002, as the election results were becoming known, a political earthquake shook Turkish politics. The three governing parties that had formed the coalition government after the 1999 national election, as well as the two opposition parties, all failed to pass the 10 percent national threshhold and found themselves thrown outside parliament as the complete losers of the election. In a time when Turkey was going through its deepest economic crisis, generating the severe problems of unemployment, inequality, and poverty, the November 3rd national election resulted in the electoral punishment of both the governing parties and the opposition parties, so much so that the winner of the 1999 election, the Democratic Left Party lost almost all of its electoral support and thus its leader, Bülent Ecevit, completed his long political career with a tragic but deserved end. The other governing parties—the Nationalist Action Party and the Mother Land Party—lost more than half of their electoral support. The leaders of these parties announced their resignations. The opposition parties—the True Path Party and the Felicity Party—were also subject to electoral punishment. The election took the form of social unrest, meaning that it created a suitable platform for the democratic expression of the deep anger that Turkish people had been feeling since the 1990s toward the existing political system and its parties, whose modus vivendi was characterized by economic populism, clientalism, corruption, and democratic deficit.

The winners of the election were the Justice and Development Party (JDP) and the Republican Peoples Party (RRP). By receiving 34.2 percent of the popular vote and with the aid of the undemocratic 10 percent national treshhold, the JDP gained 66 percent of the parliamentary seats (that is, 363 of 550 seats) and constituted the single-party majority government. With its 19.4 percent of the popular vote, the RRP became the main and single opposition party and gained 178 seats. Turkey began to be ruled by a single majority-party government with a very strong executive structure. After having had a series of extremely problematic coalition governments, the general public opinion before the election in Turkey was to point out the need to put an end to the existing ineffective and undemocratic governing structure that had been operating totally detached from society and societal needs. In this context, this new governing structure has been welcomed by the different segments of society in the name of political stability and effective governing as a solution to the severe economic problems of Turkish people.

The way in which the JDP gained an electoral victory sufficient enough to form a single-party majority government consisted of a three-dimensional electoral strategy. Through this strategy the JDP established a successful organic linkage with different segments of society. First, by understanding that the November 3rd national election was a society-centered election in which economy was the dominant issue, the JDP presented itself to society not as an Islamic party but as "a center-right party," claiming to have the strong will to govern society effectively on the basis of well-prepared and efficient policies to overcome the economic crisis. Second, the JDP has argued that in its attempt to create a new impetus for economic change by cleaning up the cronyism and corruption that have hobbled Turkey's banking and financial system for decades, it would also act in the service of society at large by listening caringly to the needs and demands of different segments of society, especially those groups that have directly faced the problems of unemployment, inequality, and poverty. Thus, as opposed to the RRP's economic program, prepared by Kemal Derviş in accordance with the unquestioned acceptance of the IMF structural-adjustment program, the JDP presented itself to society as a center-right party that would place the deep problem of "social and distributive injustice" at the center of its immediate economic program, even if it creates a conflictual relationship with the IMF. Third, in establishing its organic linkage with society at large, the JDP insistently and repeatedly argued that democracy constitutes the fundamental and effective basis for the long-term solution to Turkey's problems. This heavy and special emphasis placed on democracy has been maintained and voiced strongly in the JDP's discourse on the protection of individual rights and freedoms, as well as in its full support for Turkey's integration into the EU as a full member.

I would argue that it is through this three-dimensional electoral strategy that the JDP successfully established an organic linkage with society and won the election. This three-dimensional electoral strategy also enabled the JDP to present its identity to society not as Islamic but as a center-right party whose primary aim was both to overcome the problem of inequality/poverty and to work for the further democratization of state-society relations in Turkey. Thus the JDP created a suitable ground on which to differentiate itself from its main competitor by suggesting that the economic program it would initiate to overcome the crisis was more humanistic than the one proposed by the RRP and Kemal Derviş. The JDP's economic program was designed to pay more attention to the problem of social and distributive injustice, as well as to support the medium- and small-scale industrialists necessary to vitalize the production side of the Turkish economy.

It is through these points of differentiation that the JDP found social support, especially from the medium- and small-scale industrialists whose numbers and economic activities have been growing throughout society. It also established class alliances with the poor and disadvantaged groups and mobilized civil-society organizations voicing the needs of religious segments of society in terms of recognition. Since the attitude of the Turkish electorate in the election had given primacy to the immediate need to solve the problems of unemployment, inequality, poverty, and economic growth, the JDP became the choice of the majority, due precisely to its claim that its economic program was both different than other parties' and more adequate in finding effective solutions to severe economic problems (Öniş and Keyman 2003).

The JDP's economic program can be defined as a communitarian-liberal synthesis that operates on the basis of three basic principles:

1. An effective and postdevelopmental state that is democratic, transparent, and accountable in its interaction to society, but at the same time "caring" and assuming a supervisory role in relation to the economy. In this context, the JDP claims that in its governing it will create an effective postdevelopmental state that focuses on the needs and demands of society in a caring fashion.
2. A regulated free market that is not destructive and corrupt but enriching, contributing to economic development and social justice. The JDP argues that it promotes a free-market economy and sees it as the basis for growth, to the extent that it will contribute to the further industrialization of Turkey by creating both financial stability and a strong real economy.
3. Social justice, which is to be established both in terms of the distribution of wealth and welfare services and with respect to the domain of recognition in which social segments will not be discriminated against in terms of their cultural beliefs. In doing so, the JDP argued that a strong, stable, and trust-based economy cannot be established without solving the problem of social justice in distribution and recognition.

Working on the basis of these principles, the communitarian-liberal synthesis means at the very general level an articulation of the free market with communitarian values that promote religious beliefs, societal norms, and local characteristics. More concretely, the communitarian-liberal synthesis calls for a just society not organized on the basis of pure egotistical individualism, but as a democratic regulation of state-society relations in which free-market rationality is regulated by the effective and democratic state that takes into account the problem of inequality/poverty as a central issue of effective governance. The communitarian-liberal synthesis, put into practice by the JDP's strong single-party majority government, could be a chance for Turkey to create sustainable and stable economic growth as a way to solve its worsening problems of inequality/poverty.

It is most likely that the JDP's communitarian-liberal synthesis will be challenged by the IMF and its structural-adjustment program. As noted, as a country whose recent attempts to overcome its worst economic crisis are financed by the IMF, and whose "strong economy program" is dictated by the IMF's structural-adjustment policy, Turkey must live with the IMF. This means that any governing party in Turkey is always in the position of having to face the challenges and demands (even impositions) coming from the IMF. The JDP is no exception. If its government's economic policies contradict the structural-adjustment program, the JDP will definitely find itself challenged by the IMF. More concretely, as the JDP attempts to give primacy to the problem of social and distributive injustice, and approaches the problem of inequality/poverty as its central concern, it will create tension in its relations with the IMF. Similarly, if the JDP acts as a postdevelopmental state trying to create resources for medium- and small-scale industrialists without creating financial macroeconomic stability, it will again face challenges from the IMF. On the other hand, however, if the JDP does not attempt to pursue these developmental strategies and goes hand in hand with the IMF's structural-adjustment policy, it will face the danger of losing its societal support and interclass alliances.

Of course, the JDP will make its own choices. The choices made by coalition governments in the 1990s accepted the primacy of macroeconomic stability over the problem of inequality/poverty. These choices were made in the name of economic stability, but not only have all of them failed to achieve their goal, they have also created devastating and tragic results for ordinary people. Inequality and poverty have social, cultural, political, and ethical consequences, and are a great source of human misery today. Therefore, any political actor who wants to deal effectively with social-justice issues must employ a "direct approach" to the problem of inequality/poverty by recognizing its multidimensional constitution. Whether or not the JDP can show such political will still remains to be seen.

As I have pointed out, such political will is not utopian but rather a realistic response to the increasing problem of inequality/poverty in Turkey, in particular, and also in our post–Cold War world in general. Insofar as the problem of inequality/poverty has the potential to cause more human misery than terrorism and identity politics, democratic visions of the world in which we live today require taking the question of social justice seriously. In doing so, we should approach the problem of inequality/poverty as a central issue in human development and define it as a complex problem involving both distribution and recognition. This way, rather than glorifying or rejecting globalization, we accept that we live and will continue to live in a globalizing world. What is important in this context is to attempt to transform the existing predatory face of globalization into democratic global governance. It is here that the significance of having the political will to fight against inequality and poverty lies.

## Notes

1. Hereafter, I will use the term "the problem of inequality/poverty." Of course, inequality and poverty are interrelated but nevertheless separate problems. However, I put a "slash" between them to indicate that together they constitute a central problem in human development and for democratic governance.

2. This section of the chapter is based on research I have done on the question of "the impacts of globalization on Turkey" by focusing on powerful and effective economic actors and their discourses and strategies. The research was part of the "cultural globalization" project directed by Peter Berger of Boston University. For details, see Özbudun and Keyman (2002), Keyman and Içduygu (2003), and Öniş and Keyman (2003).

3. For a detailed analysis of the "Washington consensus," see Williamson (1993). For a philosophical discussion of the discourse of post–Washington consensus, see Beitz (2001) and Pogge (2001).

# 4

# South Korea: Globalization, Neoliberal Labor Reform, and the Trilemma of an Emerging Welfare State

*Jae-jin Yang and Chung-in Moon*

Constructing a viable welfare state to cope with income and power inequalities emanating from market forces has been at the center of intellectual debates on new social contracts in Western European countries since World War II (Esping-Andersen 1985; 1990). The postwar social contract was predicated on securing risk pooling, social equity, and redistribution through such welfare programs as pensions, unemployment benefits, and health care insurance. But it was not confined to the provision of the welfare state, but extended to the idea of labor market protection. The institutionalization of collective bargaining on wages and working conditions, as well as legislation protecting jobs and basic employees' rights, exemplify such trends (Regini 2000; Crouch 1993). Thus it can be said that the welfare state and labor market protection have grown in tandem.

Since the 1980s, however, profound changes have taken place. Waves of globalization have begun to threaten the foundation of the postwar social contract, calling for a renegotiation on conditions of the welfare state and labor market protection in the West (Mishra 1984; 1999). Welfare disease, social rigidity, and declining competitiveness have provided the pretext of the renegotiation. Globalization has been exerting the same pressures on the developing world by precipitating the race to the bottom (Rudra 2002; Kang and Ma 2001; Schmitz 2000). Global competition has not only seriously undermined efforts to move toward the welfare state, but also compelled governments to abandon labor market protection in the name of its flexibility.

The 1997 financial crisis and subsequent neoliberal economic reform in South Korea offer a classical example in this regard. The Kim Dae Jung government significantly deregulated the labor market to increase flexibility and thereby facilitate corporate restructuring. The Kim government, however, tried to compensate workers, one of its main political support bases, for their job insecurity by vigorously strengthening a wide range of

71

social-welfare programs in the name of "productive welfare" (Office of the President 2000).[1] Korea appears to be an anomaly in the global trend toward a retrenchment of the welfare state (Moon and Yang 2002a; Yang 2000; Shin 2000). Yet the neoliberal labor market reform turned out to be one of the biggest obstacles to the materialization of a mature Korean welfare state as statutory social insurance schemes failed to reach most of non-regular workers,[2] whose number increased rapidly after the labor market reform. What is worse, the long tradition of fiscal conservatism within the Korean state and neoliberal economic managerialism put a cap on the social spending necessary to induce low-income irregular workers to voluntarily join the social-insurance system. Therefore, despite its prowelfare stance, South Korea seems to follow liberal welfare states in dealing with the trilemma of postindustrial economies by prioritizing fiscal discipline and employment growth over income equality (Yang 2003; Iversen and Wren 1998).

Against the backdrop of the above observations, this chapter attempts to explore the impacts of globalization on social equality in South Korea by looking into dynamic correlates of globalization, neoliberal labor reform, and their welfare consequences. The first section offers an analytical overview on the relationships between globalization, labor market reforms, and the welfare state. The second discusses how South Korea's neoliberal labor reforms cope with the challenges of globalization and economic crisis. The third section elucidates the social-welfare consequences of neoliberal labor market reform, with particular attention paid to the casualization of labor, decreasing job security, deteriorating income distribution, and faltering social-insurance coverage expansion. The concluding section draws some comparative theoretical and policy implications from the South Korean case.

## Globalization, Labor Market Reforms, and Social Inequality: Some Analytical Considerations

### Globalization and Neoliberal Reform Mandates

Globalization can be defined as grand historical processes that transform the world into organic and functional networks of complex interdependence by tearing down artificial national boundaries. Economic globalization, which is predicated on the integration of national economies into the world economy through production, investment, market, and information networks, constitutes the crux of this process. Economic globalization is Janus-faced, however. On the one hand, it can be seen as a major vehicle for enhancing economic growth and expansion through a relatively easy access to capital, technology, and overseas markets (Ohmae 1990; Burtless et al. 1998). On the other hand, some scholars argue that economic global-ization is not necessarily gentle, beneficial, and welfare-maximizing. On the contrary, forces of spontaneous globalization can accompany new con-straints, challenges, and devastating trauma that can critically undermine such national values as democracy, economic security, social stability, and social welfare (Cox 1997; Mittelman 1996; Rodrik 1997).

Among others, the impacts of globalization on social welfare have been quite extensive. As national economies become more open and thus more subject to external economic influences and less amenable to national control, the autonomy of national governments to manage their economies for full employment and economic growth has been significantly curtailed. Globalization also has strengthened the bargaining power of international capital considerably against host governments and labor by providing for-eign capital with an "exit" option, whereas the end of full employment has weakened the leverage of organized labor. Moreover, given the openness of economies and the increasing importance of trade, international competi-tiveness is at a premium (Mishra 1999; 1984). It is in this context that retrenchment of the welfare state and "flexibility" of the labor market emerge as neoliberal managerial responses to the challenges of globaliza-tion.

These neoliberal managerial responses usually involve two compo-nents (Mishra 1999). One is macroeconomic stabilization measures com-posed of fiscal and monetary austerity, devaluation of exchange rates, and wage control, and the other is structural adjustment measures that include industrial restructuring, banking and financial reforms, liberalization of trade and investment, privatization, labor market reforms, and the adoption of market-conforming economic management policy, including a sound competition policy. Of these neoliberal responses, labor market reforms, primarily aimed at greater labor market flexibility, bear the most important welfare implications. The greater flexibility of the labor market consists of "less generous unemployment insurance provision in terms of benefit pay-ments, duration of benefits, and qualifications of benefits; wider earnings dispersions; lower levels of unionization and less centralized wage bargain-ing; less government intervention in the wage bargaining process; fewer restrictions on hiring and firing of employees; and lower social insurance charges and other non-wage labor costs, such as the amount of paid vaca-tion" (International Monetary Fund 1994: 36).

By taking advantage of globalization trends, international financial institutions and transnational capitalists have been exerting great pressure on host countries to adopt and implement neoliberal labor reforms. Such pressures have not been limited to developing countries plagued by eco-nomic crises and obligations of complying with IMF conditionalities, but also extended to advanced industrial countries such as those in Europe that have long suffered from the "Eurosclerosis" resulting from rigidity of labor markets and social-protection programs. From the standpoint of international competitiveness and economic growth, job protection and income maintenance emerge as major impediments to the swift and profitable deployment of labor and, therefore, to the enhancement of international competitiveness (Mishra 1999: 3–11).

### Three Ideal-Type Responses and Trilemma

Responses to the neoliberal labor reform mandate, however, have varied by country, depending on the governing structure of social welfare and labor (Esping-Andersen 1999; Esping-Andersen and Regini 2000; Huber and Stephens 2001) and more specifically on patterns of interaction between the labor market and the welfare state (Soskice 1999; Esping-Andersen and Regini 2000; Hall and Soskice 2001; Esping-Andersen 1999). At the risk of oversimplification, interactions between labor markets and welfare states can be categorized into three different types: (1) the liberal regimes of the United Kingdom and the United States; (2) the conservative regimes of the continental and southern European countries; and (3) the social-democratic regimes of the Scandinavian countries (Iversen and Wren 1998; Esping-Andersen 1999: chap. 5; Lodovici 2000: 32–35).

The liberal regime can be characterized by a limited role of the state, which intervenes in "bad risks" only—such as long-term unemployment, poverty, and social exclusion—while protection of other social risks tends to be left largely to the operation of the market and self-reliance. The liberal model prioritizes unregulated labor markets and employment protection is governed by common law, which relates only to the violation of individual rights such as unfair dismissal. Decentralized and uncoordinated industrial relations at the firm level govern wage determination.

Meanwhile, the conservative regime is predicated on the combination of high employment-protection regulation and compulsory social insurance, complemented with more or less ad hoc residual social-assistance schemes. Welfare schemes are usually fragmented according to occupational status. Income support during unemployment is guaranteed for core workers or male breadwinners, while the family provides care services and support for the secondary component of the labor force. The conservative model favors a passive approach to employment management. Active labor market policies (ALMP) tend to be marginal, and the management of unemployment is a question of family support or of induced labor supply reduction (discouraging married women's careers and favoring early retirement, for example).

Finally, the social democratic regime is based on the notion of a citizen's right to comprehensive risk coverage through the provision of universal and generous social-welfare schemes. Although employment protection is stronger than in the liberal regimes, the labor market is not so rigid, due to ALMP. Based on Nordic "productivism,"[3] ALMP offers various training, retraining, and employment promotion programs for the unemployed to facilitate labor mobility and industrial restructuring. Wage setting and regulation of working conditions are left to centralized collective bargaining between unions and employers' associations.

The impacts of globalization are most visible in countries that have adopted a liberal regime. Facing the challenges of globalization, they have consolidated a process of combining weak, decentralized industrial relations with weak employment protection, while emphasizing fiscal restraint at the expense of social-welfare schemes. Close to neoliberal managerial responses, the liberal regime has achieved relatively high private-sector employment, averting the high unemployment problem annoying many European countries. Nevertheless, deteriorating job protection and social-welfare systems have resulted in increasing income inequality.

On the other hand, social-democratic regimes have opted for a combination of high labor market flexibility, albeit lower than the liberal model, with strong social guarantees to the individual worker—partly in the form of very generous social protection, and partly in the form of ALMP (refer to Table 4.1). A striking feature of the social-democratic regime is that, unlike other regimes, social democracy sees the state as a necessary tool to achieve its traditional egalitarian and full-employment objectives, and this has involved a certain measure of deliberate sheltering from the inegalitarian effects of labor market flexibility through an expansion in public services and employment. Under the circumstances, budgetary restraint tends to be sacrificed and long term productivity growth and fiscal stability are often called into question.

The conservative regimes of continental Europe and the Mediterranean countries have maintained very strict levels of employment protection for those in employment and welfare-state arrangements, while stressing fiscal and monetary restraint. Employment protection and welfare-state measures help maintain earnings equality, but the priority on fiscal stability makes it hard for the state to absorb increasing labor market participants through expanding public provision of services, as in the social-democratic regimes.[4]

In a word, it can be said that advanced industrial countries are caught in what Iversen and Wren (1998) called a "trilemma" that allows the state to pursue simultaneously only two of the three core policy objectives—fiscal discipline, income equality, and expansion of employment—and forces it to abandon the other. The liberal-regime countries have followed the neoliberal reform mandates, deliberately abandoning income equality, one of the key components of postwar social contracts between the state and its

**Table 4.1    Labor Market Flexibility Ranking**

| Regime type | Countries | Unemployment benefit as a percentage of IAPW[a] | Minimum wage as a percentage of IAPW | Synthetic labor market flexibility ranking[b] |
|---|---|---|---|---|
| Liberal | Australia | 32 | — | 4 |
| Regimes | Canada | 32 | 35 | 3 |
| | New Zealand | 31 | 45 | 2 |
| | UK | 23 | 40 | 7 |
| | USA | 14 | 39 | 1 |
| Conservative | Austria | 43 | 62 | 15 |
| Regimes | Belgium | 57 | 60 | 16 |
| | France | 48 | 50 | 13 |
| | Germany | 43 | 55 | 14 |
| | Italy | 5 | 71 | 20 |
| | Netherlands | 58 | 55 | 8 |
| | Portugal | 42 | 45 | 18 |
| | Spain | 41 | 32 | 19 |
| Social | Denmark | 60 | 54 | 4 |
| Democratic | Finland | 45 | 52 | 9 |
| Regimes | Norway | 40 | 64 | 10 |
| | Sweden | 30 | 52 | 12 |

*Source:* Esping-Andersen (1999: 22). Table 2.2 is reformulated.

*Notes:* a. IAPW = income of average production worker. Unemployment benefits are net, after tax as a percentage of average production worker earnings.

b. This is based on an average index based on four different rankings of employment protection and refers to the situation in the late 1980s to the early 1990s.

citizens. The conservative-regime countries opted for job security and income equality, but this strategy has brought about ever-increasing high unemployment, another breach of the postwar social contract, full employment. The social-democratic countries also could not be free from making a choice under the mounting pressures of globalization. Their commitment to equality and full employment, not only through labor market flexibility buttressed by ALMP but also through public employment, seems to be a better choice for preserving postwar social contracts, but the costs have cast doubt over achieving fiscal discipline, calling into question their long-term economic stability and growth, the key element.

## The South Korean Case in Historical Perspective

South Korea did not belong to any of the three ideal types discussed above. Having been classified as a Confucian welfare state, the South Korean state played a very limited role in providing most social-welfare functions except education. It was by and large families that replaced the role of the state in satisfying welfare needs (Jones 1990; Palley 1992). Moreover, labor was victimized in the process of rapid industrialization. During the past authoritarian regimes where the ideology of the developmental state—"growth first, and distribution later"—prevailed, labor was placed under the tight corporatist control of the state, which was in turn responsible for facilitating a greater labor market flexibility through wage control and limits on workers' collective action (Deyo 1989).

Unlike Latin America's newly industrialized countries, where inward-looking, import-substituting industrialization provided a safe haven for profit making by local entrepreneurs, South Korea's outward-looking strategy was predicated on export price competitiveness in the world market. Thus, economic imperatives under the developmental state for export promotion were such that social spending should be kept minimal and institutional social-welfare programs be delayed as long as possible (Yang 2000: chap. 4).[5]

For the same reason, labor legislation reflected the economic rationale to ensure labor peace by minimizing the influence of trade unions, which slowly but steadily increased their membership as a result of industrialization. One of its features was the requirement for trade unions to affiliate themselves with industry-specific intermediate labor organizations under a single, government-sponsored peak organization, the Federation of Korean Trade Unions. This quasi-monopolistic trade union structure, characterized by a close connection among union leaders, large employers, and the government, was maintained until the late 1980s. At the enterprise level, authoritarian rule tended to strengthen management prerogatives, while collective bargaining was little developed (OECD 2000: 43–45; Koo 2001). In short, the Korean developmental state was a minimalist welfare state, with labor being tightly controlled.

However, we can detect some kind of "social contract" between the authoritarian developmental state and the Korean people. In return for restrictions on social spending, the government promised continuous economic growth and income rise through which individual social-welfare demands were to be satisfied (see Table 4.2).

Also, in exchange partly for its repressive industrial relations, the South Korean government adopted and strengthened protective labor regulations to stabilize employment and protect wages and working conditions (OECD 2000). The Labor Standards Act, for example, regulates the permissible types, durations, and conditions for termination of labor contracts rather than leave such contracts between employers and employees, as is seen in liberal-regime countries such as the United States. Under the act, individual and collective dismissals of regular employees are allowed only for "just cause." Although dismissal for the reasons of poor performance or lack of competence has always been possible in principle, it was rarely implemented in practice, precisely because the Labor Relations Commission (the initial appeals board in dismissal cases) has in the past applied high standards vis-à-vis the "just cause" provision (OECD 2000: 62). Thus,

**Table 4.2    Real Income Growth in Selected Middle-Income Countries (percentage per year)**

| Country | Period | GDP per capita | Manufacturing wage | Agricultural wage |
|---------|--------|----------------|--------------------|--------------------|
| Brazil | 1963–1991 | 3.19 | 1.64 | –0.73 |
| Chile | 1963–1992 | 1.17 | 2.10 | — |
| Indonesia | 1970–1991 | 4.21 | 5.52 | 3.74 |
| Korea | 1966–1991 | 7.44 | 9.09 | 7.06 |
| Mexico | 1970–1991 | 1.56 | –1.20 | 1.25 |
| Pakistan | 1963–1988 | 3.00 | 4.89 | 2.94 |
| Peru | 1963–1986 | 0.68 | –0.97 | –2.03 |
| Thailand | 1970–1990 | 4.89 | 3.00 | — |
| Turkey | 1960–1985 | 2.75 | 2.64 | — |

*Source:* World Bank (1995: 149).

OECD (1999) ranked Korea among the highest groups of OECD members in terms of the strictness of employment protection.[6] Furthermore, democratic opening and consolidation since 1987 have made this highly regulated labor market all the more rigid, as workers were able to exercise greater collective bargaining power over employers and the state.

In the wake of globalization and an economic crisis in 1997, however, the labor market regulations and social-welfare arrangements of the developmental state could no longer be sustained. Leaving the broken social contract behind, the South Korean government's new strategic response to overcoming the economic crisis was to combine neoliberal labor market reforms with strengthening the social-welfare system. In other words, the South Korean government tried to rescue its falling economy by undertaking neoliberal economic reforms, but to minimize the accompanying social costs by carrying out aggressive social-welfare programs in the name of the "productive welfare" initiative (Office of the President 2000). As will be discussed below, however, the new extensive social-welfare program has not been able to resolve the predicament of one of the major victims of the neoliberal labor reforms, namely irregular, temporal workers, whose numbers have since increased enormously.

## Globalization, Economic Crisis, and Labor Market and Welfare Reforms

### Globalization and Economic Crisis

Despite its outward-looking orientation, South Korea has remained a die-hard mercantile state. While it was trying to maximize its national wealth through its state-sponsored assertive export promotion strategy, it tightly protected domestic markets from external competition. However, as South Korea showed a remarkable performance in economic growth, industrialization, and balance of payments, it was under enormous outside pressures to terminate mercantile practices. Encountering bilateral pressures from the United States and other Organization for Economic Development and Cooperation (OECD) countries for market opening in the name of strategic reciprocity, multilateral pressures resulting from the Uruguay Round negotiations and the subsequent launch of the World Trade Organization in the early 1990s, and eroding international competitiveness of domestic firms compelled the Kim Young Sam government to undertake the *segyehwa* (globalization) campaign. The move reflected a major shift in economic management thinking from a defensive, mercantilist adaptation to external changes to a positive accommodation of outside stimuli. As part of the globalization campaign, South Korea not only ratified the Uruguay Round, but also applied for membership in the OECD, both of which were predicated on the liberalization of trade, investment, and foreign-exchange regimes as well as of the capital, financial, and banking sectors. Another related move was labor market deregulation (Sechuwi 1998; Samuel Kim 2000).

The Kim Young Sam government was burdened with two contradictory labor-reform objectives: the democratic mandate to compensate workers through equal burden sharing and distributive justice and the neoconservative globalization campaign to enhance international competitiveness through flexible labor market conditions. While the democratic mandate favored workers by pushing for labor reforms that included the lifting of the ban on multiple labor unionism,[7] third-party intervention during labor disputes, and unions' political activities, the *segyehwa* campaign to enhance international competitiveness drove the government to side with management by advocating reforms for labor market flexibility. The two conflicting objectives continued to dominate the discourse on labor reforms during the Kim Young Sam government. Although new labor reform bills were enacted in early 1997, a messy stalemate continued until the outbreak of the 1997 financial crisis in Asia (Moon and Kim 2000).

The Kim Young Sam government's push for globalization ended up with a major disaster. South Korea was severely hit by a major financial crisis in November 1997. Several factors were responsible for the crisis (Moon and Mo 2000). While low profitability and high debt levels in the corporate sector, moral hazard, the snow-balling size of nonperforming loans, the paralysis of the banking and financial sector, and government and political failures to monitor and regulate firms and banks proved to be the domestic sources of the crisis, hasty globalization, heavy reliance on short-term loans, contagion effects and panic behavior, and international financial instability served as external trigger variables. Although financial markets started to stabilize in early 1998 with the injection of IMF rescue financing, GDP dropped by 6.7 percent and the labor market was hit hard, in marked contrast with the near full-employment situation before the crisis. Many Koreans lost their jobs and unemployment rose to 7.0 percent in 1998 before peaking at 8.6 percent in February 1999. The real wage also fell dramatically by 9.3 percent from 1997 to 1998. Soaring unemployment and falling wages aggravated poverty and inequality. The Gini coefficient of urban households jumped from 0.25 in 1996 to 0.28 in 1997, and 0.31 in 1999 (Moon and Yang 2002a: 183–185; Sung 2002: 50).

## Neoliberal Labor Market Reform and Strengthening Social Safety Nets

The Kim Dae Jung government, which was inaugurated in the middle of economic hardship in February 1998, was burdened with complying with conditionalities imposed by the IMF in return for its rescue financing. They varied from macroeconomic stability to corporate, financial, and banking reforms, privatization of public enterprises, and transparency. One of the most pronounced conditionalities was neoliberal market reforms to allow flexible layoffs (see Table 4.3). The mandate of neoliberal labor reforms imposed by the IMF as part of its conditionalities put the Kim Dae Jung government in a very delicate position since it won the presidential election with strong labor support. It is in this context that the Kim Dae Jung government sought to combine labor market deregulation with strengthening social-safety nets. Although the Kim Dae Jung government pursued a market-based open economy and a more flexible labor market as seen in the liberal regimes, strengthening social-safety nets was considered essential in sustaining its political support base. The historic social compromise reached through the Tripartite Commission in February 1998, which was composed of labor, capital, and the government, offered a major turning point in this direction (Yang 2000).

As Table 4.3 illustrates, the 1998 tripartite agreement led to a radical revision to the Labor Standards Act by allowing redundancy dismissal and employment adjustment for "urgent managerial needs," which were further defined by a reference to "transfers, mergers and acquisitions." The 1998 Labor Standards Act provides minimum protective measures for workers, specifying that prior to layoffs, employers must make every effort to avoid dismissal; apply fair standards in selecting employees for dismissal; and consult with trade unions or other worker representatives on efforts to avoid dismissal and on fair and reasonable selection criteria. Moreover, worker representatives have to be informed sixty days prior to planned dismissals for managerial reasons. Thus the Korean labor market was still considered as highly regulated. Nonetheless, the new layoff provisions were clearly a step forward in the direction of increasing the freedom of firms to shed surplus employees (OECD 2000).

**Table 4.3    Key Contents of the Tripartite Commission's "Social Compromise to Overcome the Economic Crisis"**

| | |
|---|---|
| Management transparency and corporate restructuring | Improvement of the corporate financial structure<br>More responsible and more transparent corporate governance<br>Promotion of business competitiveness |
| Enhancing labor market flexibility | Permission for employers to dismiss workers in cases of managerial need<br>Permission for the establishment of temporary work agencies |
| Policies to promote employment stability and combat unemployment | Expansion and improvement of employment insurance<br>Livelihood support for the unemployed<br>Expansion and improvement of the public employment service<br>Expansion of vocational training<br>Job creation through public works and business start-up subsidies<br>Consultation and re-hiring requirements in case of redundancy dismissals |
| Enhancing labor rights | Permission for public servants to form workplace associations<br>Permission for teachers to join trade unions<br>Permission for trade unions to engage in political activities<br>Right of dismissed and unemployed workers to join trade unions |
| Extension and consolidation of the social security system | Integration of social partners in social security steering committees<br>Wage guarantee in bankruptcy cases<br>Extension of social insurance coverage to nonregular workers |

*Source:* Organization for Economic Cooperation and Development (2000: 49).

Employment flexibility has been further enhanced by the operation of temporary work agencies under the Dispatched Workers Act, starting from July 1998. Dispatching agencies were allowed to hire out workers to user firms for up to two years in twenty-six occupations that require special expertise and experience. In addition, an employee may be hired out in all industries and occupations in order to fill vacancies due to temporary absences of other employees. Since then, dispatch work has increased rapidly. At the end of 1998, only six months after the legislation, the Ministry of Labor estimated that the number of licensed agencies rose to about eight hundred and of hired-out personnel to 42,000. Other estimates give a much higher figure of dispatch workers, which include those hired by illegally run agencies operating even before the adoption of the 1998 legislation (OECD 2000: 63–64).

Not surprisingly, the share of nonregular workers (i.e., fixed-term, dispatched, temporary, and daily workers) increased further during and after the economic crisis, as seen in Table 4.4. Korean employers took full advantage of the opportunities provided by labor market flexibility meas-

**Table 4.4    Change in Employment Structure (in 1,000s of persons; in percentages)**

|  | Regular workers (A) | Nonregular workers | | Total (B) | Share of nonregular workers B/(A+B)*100 |
|---|---|---|---|---|---|
|  |  | Temporary workers | Daily workers |  |  |
| 1997 | 7,282 | 4,236 | 1,886 | 6,122 | 45.7 |
| 1998 | 6,534 | 4,042 | 1,720 | 5,762 | 46.9 |
| 1999 | 6,135 | 4,255 | 2,274 | 6,529 | 51.6 |
| 2000 | 6,395 | 4,608 | 2,357 | 6,965 | 52.1 |
| 2001 | 6,714 | 4,726 | 2,218 | 6,944 | 50.8 |
| 2002 | 6,862 | 4,886 | 2,433 | 7,319 | 51.6 |

*Source:* National Statistical Office (2002).

ures in avoiding permanent employment contracts. South Korean employers' behavior does not seem exceptional. In the United States, for instance, firms tend to externalize their employment in order to enhance numerical, scheduling, and wage flexibility as well as to undercut the organizational base of the regular workers (Pfeffer and Baron 1998). In view of this, the increasing share of nonregular employment can be attributed in part to employers' corporate strategy to circumvent the relatively high level of employment protection legislation and labor costs for permanent employees, including social-insurance contributions, severance pay requirements, and other corporate welfare provisions.

As noted before, South Korea has lagged behind other OECD members in securing social-safety nets. Keenly aware of the social and political backlash associated with structural reforms and unprecedented mass unemployment, however, the Kim Dae Jung government was swift in strengthening social-safety programs. In managing the backlash effects, the government first introduced extensive temporary measures such as public works,[8] while enacting a new social-assistance program as well as extending social-insurance programs to the hitherto excluded workers in the informal sector and the self-employed. At the same time, the coverage of the employment insurance system was radically expanded. It was initially limited to workers in companies with more than thirty employees. The scheme rapidly expanded in four steps: in January 1998, to firms with ten or more employees; in March 1998, to companies with more than five workers; in October 1998, to enterprises with fewer than five workers, that is to say, to all companies. Finally, in July 1999, temporary workers (employed at least one month per year), part-time workers (working more than eighteen hours a week), and day workers (who work less than 30.8 hours a week) were covered (Gazier and Herrera 2000: 344).

The state-administered national pension and work injury schemes also significantly expanded. The national pension expanded to include about 10 million self-employed persons and workers in companies with fewer than five employees (or half of the economically active population) from the previous 4.9 million company employees and 2.1 million farmers and fishermen. The industrial injury insurance plan, which had covered 7.5 million workers in industrial firms with five or more employees, was extended to include an additional 1.6 million workers in small businesses with four or less employees in July 2000. Employers in small businesses also became eligible for the work injury insurance scheme.

Since the medical insurance already began to cover the entire population in 1989, four major statutory social-insurance programs now cover all workers both in the formal and informal sectors.[9] This universal coverage is quite unique among the developing countries, and the speed at which the statutory social-insurance programs expanded is also extraordinary among countries with universal coverage (Y.-M. Kim 2000).[10]

## Social-Welfare Consequences of the Neoliberal Labor Market Reform[11]

### Casualization of Labor

In managing economic crisis, the Kim Dae Jung government adopted and implemented the neoliberal reform mandates in a methodical way. Yet, in or order to minimize negative social and political consequences resulting from the neoliberal reforms, it assertively pursued social-safety nets in the name of a productive welfare initiative. The South Korean experience reveals a paradoxical ensemble of neoliberal and social-welfare mandates. Nevertheless, the ensemble proved to be deceptive. The social-safety nets cast in the process of structural adjustment have not been able to counter the negative consequences of the neoliberal labor market reform due to a "casualization of labor," which has become widespread in every sector of the South Korean economy except mining, where employment itself has been shrinking (see Table 4.5). The casualization of labor is still continuing, with immense negative implications for social inequality.

*Widening income differential and poverty.*    The increase in the nonregular employment bears several negative consequences for social welfare. First, as shown in Table 4.6, there is a wide disparity in earnings between regular workers and nonregular (temporary and daily) workers.

The average hourly wage of regular workers was 8.2 thousand won in 2000, while that of temporary workers was 4.3 thousand won, about half of the hourly wage of permanent regular workers. What is worse is that daily workers get paid an average of 3.8 thousand won per hour, less than half of regular workers' earnings. As the share of nonregular workers rises, income

**Table 4.5    Change in Employment Structure by Industry (in percentages)**

|  | 1996 | | | 2000 | | |
|---|---|---|---|---|---|---|
|  | Regular (permanent) | Temp. | Daily-hire | Regular (permanent) | Temp. | Daily-hire |
| Total employment | 56.6 | 29.4 | 14.0 | 47.1 | 34.4 | 18.5 |
| Agriculture, forestry, fishing | 14.1 | 23.9 | 62.0 | 8.3 | 14.6 | 77.1 |
| Mining | 61.4 | 26.3 | 12.3 | 74.0 | 16.9 | 9.1 |
| Manufacturing | 66.2 | 24.9 | 8.9 | 57.7 | 29.8 | 12.6 |
| Utilities | 92.5 | 5.3 | 2.2 | 74.6 | 14.9 | 10.5 |
| Construction | 28.8 | 15.8 | 55.4 | 25.2 | 17.7 | 57.1 |
| Retail, wholesale, accommodations, food services | 35.6 | 54.4 | 9.9 | 23.7 | 56.3 | 20.0 |
| Transportation,storage, communications | 80.9 | 16.0 | 3.2 | 71.8 | 21.6 | 6.6 |
| Finance, insurance, real estate | 68.6 | 28.6 | 2.8 | 54.9 | 39.1 | 6.0 |
| Business, personal, public services | 68.3 | 25.6 | 6.1 | 57.0 | 29.4 | 13.5 |

*Source:* National Statistics Office (2000) in Ahn (2001: 22).

**Table 4.6    Hourly Wages by Employment Type, 2000 (in won/hour)**

| Duration of employment contract | Fixed-term contracts | | Contracts of an indefinite period | | |
|---|---|---|---|---|---|
|  | Less than one year | One year or longer | One year or longer | Less than one year | Average |
| Average | 3,894 | 7,632 | 6,364 | 3,520 | 6,061 |
| Regular | — | 7,632 | 8,284 | 3,840 | 8,225 |
| Temporary | 4,165 | — | 4,307 | 3,352 | 4,251 |
| Daily-hire | 3,766 | — | 3,941 | 3,586 | 3,811 |

*Source:* National Statistics Office (2000) in Ahn (2001: 38–39).

differentials among workers have become further widened, aggravating the already deteriorating disparity in income distribution.

Figure 4.1 shows the widening earnings gap among "employed" workers. As the South Korean economy has rebounded since the 1997 economic crisis, overall income distribution improved, although it could not recover the precrisis level. Economic growth and falling unemployment contributed to the improvement of overall income distribution. However, income inequality among employed workers continues to deteriorate regardless of

**Figure 4.1    Trend of GDP Growth, Unemployment, and Income Distribution**

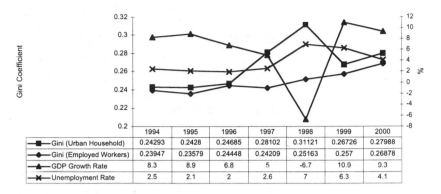

| | 1994 | 1995 | 1996 | 1997 | 1998 | 1999 | 2000 |
|---|---|---|---|---|---|---|---|
| —■—Gini (Urban Household) | 0.24293 | 0.2428 | 0.24685 | 0.28102 | 0.31121 | 0.26726 | 0.27988 |
| —◆—Gini (Employed Workers) | 0.23947 | 0.23579 | 0.24448 | 0.24209 | 0.25163 | 0.257 | 0.26878 |
| —▲—GDP Growth Rate | 8.3 | 8.9 | 6.8 | 5 | -6.7 | 10.9 | 9.3 |
| —✗—Unemployment Rate | 2.5 | 2.1 | 2 | 2.6 | 7 | 6.3 | 4.1 |

*Source:* Sung (2002: 50) and Ministry of Finance and Economy (2003).

the economic recovery, with the Gini coefficient reaching 0.269 in 2000 from 0.242 in 1997.

Therefore, it is not surprising to observe that poverty is more common in the households of the nonregular working group (see Table 4.7). The poverty rate of households with nonregular blue-collar workers as their head of family is six times higher than that of white-collar workers' households, almost twice the regular blue-collar workers' family, and even higher than the households of unemployed heads. The long-term poverty rate is also highest among the nonregular working people. Given that nonregular workers now account for more than half of the whole work force, a growing number of workers are suffering from low wages and poverty. In view

**Table 4.7    Household Poverty by Working Status of the Head of Family, 1998–2000 (in percentages)**

| Working type of house-head | Poverty rate | Long-term poverty rate[a] |
|---|---|---|
| White-collar | 5.4 | 3.2 |
| Regular blue-collar | 18.4 | 12.6 |
| Nonregular blue-collar | 33.5 | 23.4 |
| Employer | 7.1 | 4.6 |
| The self-employed | 15.9 | 10.2 |
| The unemployed | 26.6 | 21.8 |

*Source:* Lee and Chung (2001).
*Note:* a. Long-term poverty is defined as experiencing poverty for consecutive 12 quarters (i.e., 3 years).

of this, nonregular workers are the greatest victims of the economic crisis and the subsequent neoliberal labor market reforms.

### The Korean Welfare State Caught in Institutional Mismatch and Trilemma

As noted above, the Kim Dae Jung government has attempted to compensate workers by providing them with more extensive social-safety nets. Coverage of the four major statutory social-insurance schemes was extended to all workplaces, including small firms with less than five employees, and even to temporary and daily workers (in the case of unemployment insurance) and all residents (in the case of medical insurance and pensions). Therefore, the coverage should be universal. However, effective coverage rates have fallen well short of our expectations because of the problem of huge contribution evasion (see data in Table 4.8).

Contribution evasion is critical because South Korea's social-insurance schemes are basically funded by payroll contributions split between the employer and the employee (in the case of company workers) and solely by contributions of the self-employed. Without a contribution history, no one can claim benefits. As of 2001, effective coverage rates for industrial injury, unemployment, health, and pension schemes are estimated to be 59.4 percent, 46.9 percent, 54.3 percent, and 51.8 percent, respectively, indicating that half of the targeted insured do not pay contributions (H.-G. Lee 2001: 6; Y.-M. Kim 2000: 10–11).

It can be expected that the maturing of the newly expanded systems

Table 4.8    **Effective Coverage Rate of Social Insurances and Severance Pay (in percentages)**

|  |  | Pension | Health insurance | Unemployment insurance | Severance pay |
|---|---|---|---|---|---|
| Regular workers |  | 92.7 | 94.8 | 80.0 | 94.3 |
| Nonregular workers | Temporary | 16.6 | 19.4 | 18.3 | 10.6 |
|  | Part-time | 1.0 | 2.3 | 1.5 | 1.5 |
|  | On-call | 0.0 | 0.0 | 0.3 | 0.0 |
|  | Special employ. | 22.8 | 24.9 | 22.2 | 18.9 |
|  | Dispatch | 48.5 | 50.4 | 48.1 | 46.2 |
|  | Subcontract | 46.3 | 55.2 | 43.8 | 35.6 |
|  | Tele | 9.7 | 10.4 | 8.5 | 9.7 |
|  | Total | 19.3 | 22.2 | 20.7 | 13.6 |
|  | Total | 51.8 | 54.3 | 46.9 | 49.3 |

*Source:* National Statistics Office (2001) in H.-G. Lee (2001: 6).

would entail increased coverage rates. But given the institutional mismatch between the "casualized" labor market and social-insurance systems, which are predicated on stable employment and contributions of the insured, such expectations might be too optimistic. One of the structural difficulties in expanding social-insurance coverage is the significantly low coverage rate of nonregular workers, whose numbers have been increasing since the neoliberal labor market reform. In contrast with almost universal coverage of regular workers, the coverage rate for nonregular workers is only about 20 percent. A similar pattern can be noticed in the case of severance pay (refer to Table 4.8). It is natural for low-paid nonregular workers to heavily discount future benefits in preference for the consumption needs of today. They have every reason to avoid contributions. So do small-business owners in the low value-added marginal sector. Under severe price competition, they have little incentive to voluntarily enroll their workers and contribute. Without government financial inducements such as subsidized contributions or matching contributions, both small-business owners and nonregular workers remain reluctant to abide by social-insurance laws.

Unfortunately, the Korean state has been financially conservative, despite its strong commitment to the expansion of social-insurance schemes. The government can neither pay contributions nor provide institutional arrangements like basic benefits funded by a general tax for those uninsured. Budgetary restraints or fiscal conservatism, a key component of neoliberal economic management seems to have prevented the progressive Kim Dae Jung government from channeling more state funds into social-safety nets. Indeed, it is true that the Kim government's public spending and financial commitment to social security have grown since 1997. However, in recent years those figures began to decline again (see Table 4.9), making it impossible to overcome an already low level of total social spending by international standards (see Table 4.10). Therefore, for all the Kim government's prowelfare efforts, South Korea is still regarded as a variant of the liberal welfare regime in that it sacrifices income equality in pursuit of employment growth and conservative fiscal management under

**Table 4.9  Public Spending and Central Government's Commitment to Social Security (percentage of GDP)**

|  | 1997 | 1998 | 1999 | 2000 | 2001 | 2002 | 2003 |
|---|---|---|---|---|---|---|---|
| Public Spending (% of GDP) | 20.4 | 23.7 | 24.8 | 24.6 | 24.9 | 24.5 | 24.3 |
| Expenditure on Social Security (% of GDP) | 0.93 | 1.01 | 1.26 | 1.55 | 1.97 | 1.80 | 1.78 |

*Source:* Ministry of Health and Welfare (2003).

**Table 4.10    Comparison of Total Social Spending Among OECD Countries, 1999 (percentage of GDP)**

| OECD (Average) | Sweden | Norway | Germany | Netherlands | USA | UK | Greece | Spain | Poland | Turkey | Mexico | S.Korea |
|---|---|---|---|---|---|---|---|---|---|---|---|---|
| 22.37 a | 34.14 | 28.16 | 29.24 | 28.57 | 14.68 | 25.59 | 22.73 | 19.71 | 23.27 | 13.31 | 8.23 | 9.77 |

*Source:* Ministry of Health and Welfare (2003).
*Note:* a. Mean of 28 OECD member states excluding Korea and Hungary.

the conditions of the trilemma of the postindustrial economy (Yang 2003; Iversen and Wren 1998; Esping-Andersen 1999).

## Conclusion: Summary and Policy Implications

### Summary

As with other developing countries, South Korea fell prey to the dynamic process of globalization, resulting in an acute economic crisis in 1997. The South Korean government undertook sweeping structural reform measures in order to overcome the economic crisis. Implementation of the neoliberal labor reform, primarily aimed at enhancing labor market flexibility as well as international competitiveness, produced an increasing number of nonregular workers. Employers put the nonregular workers under less favorable working conditions, while having them perform the same tasks. Employers have used nonregular employment as an expedient to reduce costs and avoid the more protective labor regulations of regular employment. It is clear that South Korea now has a more flexible labor market and an improved employment record. But the overall social-welfare consequences of labor market reform have turned out to be negative.

The Kim Dae Jung government made unprecedented efforts to mitigate the negative backlash of the neoliberal reforms by compensating workers through the strengthening of social-safety nets. Despite mandates that urged the retrenchment of the welfare state, the South Korean government sought universal and comprehensive social-safety nets based on social-insurance schemes. It could be seen as a major anomaly. However, this delicate balance between the neoliberal labor market reforms and provision of extensive social safety did not last long.

The neoliberal reform and subsequent increase in nonregular employment have proved to be the greatest impediment to the government's effort to build a strong social-welfare system. Although the statutory social-insurance programs should be universal, their effective coverage rate remains low due to huge contribution evasions, leaving the large segment of low-income irregular workers uncovered. If the Kim Dae Jung government had provided financial inducement measures such as copayments and subsidized contributions or tax-based insurance schemes, coverage loopholes would have been minimized. However, having to stay within the parameters laid down by neoliberal economic mandates, the government could not opt for such measures without a steep rise in social expenditure. Given the lack of a strong leftist party and class-oriented labor movement, a new financial equilibrium, which would be reestablished by power politics, is hardly expected in Korea.

### Theoretical and Policy Implications

The South Korean case strongly suggests that welfare states in the developing world face harder times than in the preglobalization era. First, policy initiatives increasing flexibility in the labor market are bound to clash with efforts at building a mature welfare state, since social insurance, the backbone of the modern welfare state, is predicated on stable employment. Second, neoliberal financial and monetary management leaves little room for social spending, which is necessary to make up for the loopholes in the social-insurance system. Without strong prowelfare pressures from below, even a progressive government will have a hard time striking a new equilibrium between public spending and financial stability. But the problem is that labor market flexibility pursued by reformist governments erodes the power resources of prowelfare political forces.

What policy lessons can be drawn from the Korean case? First, the Korean case vividly demonstrates that strengthening formal social-safety nets alone is not enough to protect workers in developing countries faced with the challenges of globalization. There should be extraordinary efforts to protect nonregular workers. To this end, developing countries should refer to the Dutch "miracle" economy where "flexicurity" is practiced (Van Oorschot 2001; Visser and Hemerijck 1997). The Dutch Flexibility and Security Act of 1999 is regarded as a cornerstone of new labor law reconciling employment growth through flexibility and labor market protection by reflecting the rights and interests of all workers in various employment arrangements arising from changes in industrial structure (Ahn 2001; S.-Y. Kim 2001). Second, South Korea strongly suggests that it is necessary to exert more financial efforts to meet the new challenge of labor market dislocations. Although neoliberal reform mandates allow governments much less leeway, developing countries should manage to avoid the pitfalls of liberal welfare states in which income equality is sacrificed for fiscal health. As Iversen and Wren (1998: 515–516) note, it will be possible for governments to achieve strong employment growth without sacrificing financial health only if they pursue a "modest" success both in equality and financial stability, as seen in Netherlands.

The South Korean trilemma reminds us that improvement in working conditions and protections for irregular workers are not easy tasks. But without these benefits, materializing a mature welfare state in developing countries will remain just a dream.

## Notes

1. Given the relative low coverage of unemployment benefits and the weaknesses of the social-assistance system, international financial institutions including the World Bank and the IMF also endorsed the government's effort to weave stronger social-safety nets (Moon and Yang 2002a).

2. "Nonregular" employment refers to temporary work (fixed-term work and dispatch work) and daily work. Temporary workers are employed for a determined length of time, usually longer than a month and shorter than a year. Daily workers are employed on a daily basis. Part-time employment can be categorized into daily work.

3. Superficially, this seems like an echo of what Americans call "Workfare." But, Workfare in the United States implies that social benefits are conditional on accepting work, while Nordic productivism implies that the welfare state must guarantee that all people have the necessary resources and motivation to work (Esping-Andersen 1999: 80).

4. The responses of southern European countries are somewhat different from those of continental Europe. Their employment protection is exceptionally high for core workers, while external flexibility is obtained, partly through the use of short-time and early retirement schemes, usually financed by the state, and partly through expanding small firms and self-employment.

5. For example, in 1990 South Korea's total social expenditure was 4.1 percent of GDP while developing countries in Latin America such as Brazil and Argentina spent 10.8 percent and 9.8 percent respectively (International Labour Organization 2000: 312–314). Likewise, the timing of social-insurance introduction is far belated in South Korea in comparison with counterparts in Latin America. In Korea, unemployment insurance was introduced in 1995, pensions in 1988, health insurance in 1977, and the work injury program in 1963, while in Brazil, for instance, the unemployment benefit was introduced in 1965, pensions in 1923, health insurance in 1924, and a work injury program in 1916 (U.S. Social Security Administration 1999).

6. The OECD study placed Korea at second place next to Portugal in "overall strictness of protection against dismissals," at second place next to the Netherlands in "regular procedural inconveniences," among the medium group in "notice and severance pay for no-fault individual dismissals," and at fifth place in "difficulty of dismissal."

7. The Korean Confederation of Trade Unions, the peak labor organization of democratic unions, called for lifting the ban on multiple labor unionism because the ban prevented its legalization.

8. In 1998, a total of 10.7 trillion won was allocated for employment stabi-

lization and construction of a social-safety net. The creation of new jobs through public works and investments in small and medium-sized firms and venture companies was given top priority, receiving 5.2 trillion won, more than half of the entire budget. A social-safety net for the unemployed, including unemployment benefits, minimum cost-of-living support for the destitute, and scholarships for children of the unemployed, received the second largest share, 2.1 trillion won; 1.9 trillion was allocated for minimizing unemployment through financial support of small and medium-sized firms; and 896 billion won was allocated for occupational training and job conversion. The construction of a social-safety net through fiscal stimulus is one of the boldest Keynesian initiatives in South Korea's history. The Kim Dae Jung government allocated 9.2 trillion won in 1999 for the same purposes (Moon and Yang 2002b).

9. Besides, the Labor Standard Law has come into effect in small-sized workplaces with less than five employees from 1999. Therefore, hitherto excluded marginal workers are now protected by the government. The minimum-wage system, which took effect only in firms with ten workers or more, was also extended to cover workplaces with five workers and more in September 1999. Thus, about 85 percent of all workers are now protected by the minimum-wage system (Shin 2000).

10. In Korea, it took only twelve years from its introduction for the medical insurance plan to reach the whole nation in 1989; four years for the employment insurance in 1998; eleven years for the national pension in 1999; and thirty-seven years for the industrial injury insurance in 2000.

11. This section draws on Yang (2003).

# 5

## The Philippines: Poor and Unequal, but Free

### *Aprodicio A. Laquian*

Globalization may be defined operationally as a process that includes four key elements: (1) rapid dissemination and receiving of information worldwide, (2) unfettered trade and commerce across national boundaries, (3) easier movement of people internationally, and (4) immediate effects and impact of important global events on people's lives. In this chapter, I add five other elements that are closely related to the first four to the definition of globalization: (1) instantaneous transfer of financial resources all over the world, (2) increased activities and power of international financing institutions, (3) use of international legal regimes and standards, (4) expanded role of transnational corporations, and (5) rapid spread of sociocultural influences. As noted by the United Nations Center for Human Settlements in its *Global Report on Human Settlements 2001*, what distinguishes globalization from other international processes are: that it functions at much greater *speed,* it operates on a much larger *scale,* the *scope* of connections it generates is multidimensional, and the interactions it creates are more *complex.* In this sense, globalization is a relatively recent phenomenon made possible by computers, the Internet, fiber optics, communication satellites, cell phones, pocket organizers, ATMs, and jet planes.

Based on the above definition, the Philippines may not rank as high as Singapore or other Asian tigers on the globalization index (Kearney 2002: 1–8) but most Filipinos will argue that their country is significantly "globalized." Filipinos have good access to information through 11.5 million radios. They can get CNN, MTV, and other global programs on 3.7 million television sets hooked to thirty-one TV broadcast stations. Many Filipinos are computer-savvy—in 2002 the Philippines had more than a million Internet users served by thirty-three service providers. Filipinos can easily call overseas on 3.8 million telephones linked to foreign networks through nine international gateways, satellites, and earth stations. The Philippines is now a regional hub in e-business (America Online maintains a facility in the former Clark U.S. Air Force Base where Filipino technicians trained to speak unaccented English respond to global queries about computer problems). Filipinos are so adept at using e-mail, cell phones, and "texting" that during the 20 January 2001 "people power" demonstrations in Metro Manila, close to a million people were mobilized in a matter of hours to oust former president Joseph Estrada from office (Laquian and Laquian 2002: 33).

The Philippines is an active participant in international trade. In 1994, Philippine external trade accounted for 54.3 percent of gross domestic product (GDP). Foreign direct investments jumped from $1.3 billion in 1992 to $5.1 billion in 1994. In that same year, foreign equity market capitalization made up 86.9 percent of GDP. To facilitate foreign trade, the Philippines passed Executive Order No. 264 in 1995 that would adjust tariff rates until they reach a uniform rate of 5 percent by 2004 as required by the Philippine commitment to the Common Effective Preferential Tariff agreement it signed with other countries in the Free Trade Area (FTA) of the Association of South East Asian Nations (ASEAN).

It is estimated that from 7 to 8 million Filipinos are currently working in 140 countries, including more than 4.8 million overseas Filipino workers (OFWs). In recent years, 500,000 to 700,000 OFWs have departed the country, bound for the Middle East, Japan, Hong Kong, Singapore, Italy, Canada, the United States, and other countries. More may leave if given the chance—a public opinion poll conducted in January 2003 revealed that about 19 percent of Filipinos interviewed said they believed conditions in the country were so hopeless that they were planning to emigrate.

In 1998, OFWs remitted about US$7 billion back home, funds that accounted for about 19 percent of export earnings and 2.5 percent of gross national product (GNP) (Brillantes 1998: 137–155).[1] In March-April 2002, the unstable situation in the Middle East and the economic slowdown caused by the 9/11 terrorist attacks in New York and Washington, D.C., resulted in a decline of dollar remittances to less than $6 billion because about 100,000 Filipino overseas contract workers lost their jobs. In February 2003, uncertainties created by a possible war in Iraq, coupled with the launching of a "second front" in Mindanao in the global war on terrorism, reduced remittances. War jitters also caused the Philippine peso to plummet to a record low of Php 54.60 to US$1.00.

Since the late 1980s, the Philippine government has pursued policies that have integrated its economy more closely with that of Asia and the world. It was one of the founders of Asia Pacific Economic Cooperation (APEC) in 1989 and joined the AFTA in 1992. In 1994, the Philippine Senate ratified accession to the Uruguay Round of the General Agreement on Tariffs and Trade, making the Philippines one of the founding members of the World Trade Organization. In February 2003, the Philippine legislature approved a money-laundering law to comply with procedures and standards demanded by the Financial Action Task Force.

With 94 percent of Filipinos functionally literate and many of them able to understand and speak English, they are keenly attuned to foreign cultural influences. First-run Hollywood movies are shown in theaters and are widely available on video. McDonald's golden arches and Kentucky Fried Chicken outlets dot rest areas along superhighways and adorn plazas in prosperous towns. Middle-class Filipino parents worry that their children are aping U.S. teenagers too much (Rap, hip-hop, spiked hair, tattoos, body piercing). Like their U.S. counterparts, they are concerned about pornography, sexually-transmitted diseases, HIV/AIDS, and drugs. Most recently, their apprehensions and fears have been focused on the effects and impact of the war in Iraq and terrorist acts in malls and other public places.

By all accounts, therefore, the Philippines is very much a part of the global community. In this chapter, I explore what influences globalization has had on the country's economic development, income inequality, and practice of liberal democracy.

## Effects and Impact of Globalization

Conventional theories of globalization propose that higher levels of global integration are directly correlated with: (1) higher levels of economic development, (2) reduced income inequality, and (3) greater political freedom and liberal democracy. It is my contention that the Philippines does not conform to the first and second parts of these suggested relationships. However, because of historical and cultural factors related to globalization, the Philippines has been able to achieve a relatively high level of liberal democracy.

### Globalization and Economic Development

Supporters of globalization hypothesize that there is a positive correlation between globalization and economic development. They suggest that trade liberalization opens up competitive markets, creates greater demand for goods and services, and encourages higher productivity. They contend that the rapid spread of technological innovations, made possible by great improvements in communication, spurs development. International legal regimes that ensure the predictability of economic conditions enhance foreign investments that, in turn, create employment and new products. The free movement of capital, material resources, people, ideas, and goods and services (factors closely associated with globalization) are the foundations for high and sustainable levels of socioeconomic development.

The Philippine situation, however, shows a weak correlation between globalization and economic development. While the country has become more globalized during the last two or three decades, annual rates of GDP growth since the 1970s have barely exceeded 3 percent on average, which is only slightly above the population growth rate of 2.7 percent. The annual Philippine GNP per capita of US$3,670 compares poorly with $6,490 for Thailand, $7,730 for Malaysia, $24,350 for Korea, and $29,230 for Singapore. In 1999, per capita GDP plummeted as the Philippines was wracked by scandals during the waning days of the Estrada administration. GDP rose by 3.3 percent during the second quarter of 2001 under President Gloria Macapagal-Arroyo, but this lagged behind Asian regional growth rates exemplified by China's 7.8 percent. In 2002, the Philippine government projected annual growth rates of 4.0–4.5 percent despite the adverse economic effects of the 9/11 terrorist attacks on the United States and the expansion of its global war on terrorism to Mindanao. These targets are considered overoptimistic by many as the country continues to be plagued by basic problems arising from both domestic and global factors.

The weak performance of the Philippine economy is reflected in agriculture, where productivity has not been enhanced by global developments. The contribution of agriculture to GNP at present is a low 15.1 percent despite the fact that 37.4 percent of the employed labor force works in the sector. Agricultural productivity had declined from an annual rate of 6.5 percent in 1970–1975 to a low of 0.3 percent in 1980–1983 (Balisacan 1994: 39). This had risen to 3.9 percent in 2001–2002 but this was mainly due to the fortuitous blessings of good weather and the absence of typhoons. Filipino farmers, whose cost of production is about twice as high per ton of rice compared to their Thai and Vietnamese counterparts, find it hard to compete in the international market (the Philippines imported 500,000 metric tons of rice in 2003). Widespread smuggling of fresh vegetables and frozen chicken from Taiwan and China as well as rice, yellow corn, sugar, and other products from Thailand, Vietnam, and India has worsened the plight of Filipino agricultural producers and traders.

The scientific discovery of high-yielding rice and corn varieties has not significantly increased yields on Philippine farms. In the meantime, Filipino officials and environmental activists wrangle over the benefits or dangers of genetically modified foods. While the global demand for cash crops for export such as bananas, mangoes, and citrus fruits has dramatically increased, producing these locally has been hampered by debates on domestic issues such as land reform that favors allocation of small plots to subsistence farmers. Some entrepreneurs have advocated large "corporate farms" to produce cash crops, but their proposal has been seen as merely an effort to evade land reform and has not received much support. It is feared that the benefits of corporate farming will mainly go to transnational corporations and their rich Philippine partners, not to small farmers.

Like many developing countries, the Philippines joined the global boom in electronic manufacturing in the 1990s. During the administration of former president Fidel Ramos (1992–1998), the country aggressively pursued export promotion policies that accelerated the country's links to the outside world. The export of manufactured goods grew from 54.8 percent in 1985 to 78 percent in 1995, largely because of the production of "electrical equipment, parts, and telecommunication components" that made up 41 percent of the total value of manufactured exports.

The problem with the Philippine reliance on electronic exports, however, was the fact that in reality, many of the so-called Philippine electronic firms were little more than "soldering gun and screwdriver" enterprises producing switching blocks, motherboards, and electronic components. They relied mainly on the nimble fingers of thousands of Filipino women working long hours on repetitive tasks in long assembly lines. Electronics hardly used local materials as input; about 47 percent of Philippine imports mainly consisted of "semi-processed raw materials" (electronic components) that were merely assembled by local companies. The electronic firms were located in gated special economic zones (SEZs) linked primarily to export markets that did not do much to enhance developments in their surrounding areas. With the recent collapse of e-business worldwide, electronic component inventories in Philippine firms have piled up and there have been massive layoffs in local electronics plants. Linking up to global markets, therefore, exposed Philippine industry and labor to the vagaries of the international market. Unfortunately, with schemes like unemployment insurance, social benefits, and "safety net" provisions still largely underdeveloped in the Philippines, these economic dislocations placed workers and laborers at a great disadvantage.

A major element in Philippine participation in globalization has been the "labor export policy" that has resulted in the sending of 7 to 8 million overseas Filipino OFWs all over the world. On the surface, this policy seemed to have been beneficial to the Philippines because of the US$7–8 billion in remittances that have come to the country each year. Supporters of the policy have also pointed out that OFWs learned new skills and technical know-how that they brought back to the country. Some of the remittances had supported the education and training of family dependents, enhancing the development of social capital. Returning OFWs have also gone into entrepreneurial ventures that have increased income and generated employment. While most of these economic and social benefits are real enough, the labor export policy has also created critical shortages in certain skills and trades (carpentry, masonry, nursing, medical technology). Family separations have created a lot of social problems (child neglect, juvenile delinquency, infidelity, etc.) that have strained the social-service system. Some critics have even blamed the policy for the delayed emergence of a

Filipino middle class because the country's best and brightest have left or continue to leave the country.

Global investments are mainly determined by the decision of foreign entrepreneurs whether to locate in a country or not. This makes the "competitiveness" of the Philippines extremely important because foreign investors do have a wide field of choice in Asia. Here, the Philippines is at a tremendous disadvantage compared to its Asian neighbors. The World Competitiveness Report in 1992 ranked the Philippines overall as thirty-third among forty-one countries, the lowest in Southeast Asia. The country's worst ranking was in infrastructure, where it was in thirty-ninth place (only the Czech Republic, Hungary, and Poland ranked lower, but these countries have vastly improved since then while conditions in the Philippines have stagnated) (Fabella 1996: 423–484).

A similar survey carried out by the Japan External Trade Organization (JETRO) in 1995 highlighted the poor condition of infrastructure in the Philippines. With the exception of Japan, the Philippines had the highest electricity cost in Asia (11 cents per kilowatt hour). It had the second highest truck freight rates ($75 as against Japan's $100) and the second highest rate in marine freight ($103 per twenty-foot equivalent). Interestingly, the JETRO survey also indicated that the Philippines had the lowest customs clearance fees in Asia ($14) but it did not mention that the informal, illegal "grease money" involved in customs transactions was extremely high.

Recognizing that international trade is one of the hallmarks of globalization, the Philippine government has made many attempts to liberalize foreign trade. The 1981–1985 tariff reform program under President Ferdinand Marcos narrowed down tariff rates from 0–100 to 10–50 percent. In 1986, during the Corazon Aquino administration, the tariff rate on crude oil was reduced from 20 percent to 10 percent. For the period 1991–1995, Philippine tariff guidelines were set at a minimum of 10 percent and a maximum of 30 percent. The liberalization process, at the same time, was accompanied by stronger safeguards against unfair trade practices such as the passage of the antidumping law and the setting up of a comprehensive import surveillance system under an agreement with the Societe Generale de Surveillance that took over supervision in the Customs Bureau. Penalties for smuggled goods were also considerably increased.

The Ramos administration is credited with having unilaterally put in place tariff reduction and import liberalization programs that have profoundly changed the pattern of Philippine foreign trade. It passed laws that gradually adjusted tariff rates to conform to AFTA standards. Although the Philippines has tried to follow international tariff agreements, however, other countries with much greater economic clout have continued to impose tariff and nontariff barriers. Australia, for example, has imposed restrictions

on Philippine imports. The United States has also adopted a number of protectionist policies. With the relatively weaker Philippine economy forced to
operate in a nonlevel international playing field, it has been significantly
disadvantaged.

Side by side with trade liberalization, the Philippines has relaxed foreign investment rules as part of its globalization strategy. In 1991, the passage of the Foreign Investments Act allowed foreign equity in Filipino
enterprises to exceed 40 percent provided the firm did not ask for incentives. Foreign banks were allowed to own up to 60 percent of voting stocks
of local banks. The Philippine stock exchange was opened to foreign
investors. Foreign exchange regulations were relaxed to allow the peso to
float in relation to other currencies. Exporters were allowed to retain their
foreign exchange earnings in full and banks were permitted to create loan
assets against their foreign currency deposit liabilities. As in the case of tariffs, the benefits expected from foreign investments did not really fully
materialize. Despite the incentives and concessions offered by the
Philippines, not that many investors became interested. The investors who
were attracted tended to be high-risk money managers and speculators who
were quick to pull out their money at the first sign of trouble. Other people
attracted were shady characters mainly interested in laundering dirty
money.

The Philippines had traditionally enjoyed positive balance-of-trade
relationships with the United States. During the 1990s, however, its foreign
trade shifted away from the United States toward Japan, Korea, and, more
recently, Hong Kong, Singapore, Taiwan, and other Asian countries.
Exports to the United States declined from 38 percent in 1990 to 34.5 in
1995. Exports to Japan also declined to about 16 percent, but those to the
Asian newly-industrialized countries (NICs) such as Hong Kong,
Singapore, and Taiwan increased significantly.

The same pattern of reduced trade with the United States and increased
trade with Asian countries was shown in Philippine imports, where the
share of the United States declined from 25 percent to 17 during the same
period. The shift in trade toward Asia has increased the Philippine trade
deficit. The trade deficit with Japan, which supplies capital goods and venture capital funds to the Philippines, has increased dramatically, accounting
for 50 percent of the total Philippine trade deficit.

To summarize, globalization has not significantly contributed to
Philippine economic development. Low agricultural productivity continues
to plague Filipino farmers, and with much higher costs of production compared to their Asian counterparts, they are unable to effectively compete in
global markets. The lifting of trade barriers under international agreements
has negatively affected local producers and traders that have grown weak
under decades of protectionist policies. The country's poor infrastructure

serves as a hindrance to foreign investments but financial terms for joint ventures tend to be too onerous for local partners and international loans for infrastructure development are hard to get because the country is already saddled with huge international debts. Without an adequate indigenous supply of energy, the Philippines is vulnerable to severe fluctuations in international oil prices.

Although the Philippines has abandoned an import-substitution strategy in manufacturing and industry, the country's foreign trade is skewed toward the export of electronic products that are subject to wide international fluctuations. The possibility of using tourism as a source of valuable foreign exchange is hampered by local conditions of insecurity, rapid deterioration of tourism facilities, and poor international marketing. A labor export policy that has sent 7 to 8 million Filipino workers to 140 countries has benefited the country with remittances but it has also created labor and skill shortages in key economic areas. All in all, structural weaknesses in the Philippine economy and adverse terms of trade that have hindered economic development in the country seem to have been exacerbated by globalization.

## Globalization and Inequality

Conventional globalization theory proposes that free trade and commerce, the spread of technological innovations and ideas, international migration, and the unfettered movement of capital, goods, and services worldwide will increase productivity. A larger economic pie means larger slices for each citizen. As more wealth is created it will tend to be distributed more equitably among members of society.

The A. T. Kearney/*Foreign Policy* magazine study of globalization has concluded, however, that "the level of income disparity in an economy might have more to do with history, economic growth, price and wage controls, welfare programs and education policies than with globalization or trade liberalization" (Kearney 2002: 7). This conclusion certainly has strong applicability to the Philippines where, historically, economic and social inequalities have been severe. Furthermore, although some economic benefits of recent globalization processes have "trickled down" to the poor, these benefits have not equitably gone to marginalized socioeconomic groups and geographical areas. In other words, globalization has made inequality in Philippine society a lot worse and the income gap between rich and poor will probably continue to widen in the future.

The profound inequality in Philippine society is captured in the statistic that at present, the top 20 percent of Filipinos own about 52.3 percent of the country's wealth. Seen in another way, the bottom 10 percent of Filipinos consume only 1.5 percent of resources while the top 10 percent consume 39.3 percent. It has been said that the Philippines is actually run by no more than sixty elite families (Karnow 1989: 22).[2] In 1987, a revised Philippine constitution banned family dynasties from dominating politics but the legislature never approved statutes to implement the provision. This was not surprising because a 1994 study found that of the 199 members of the 9th House of Representatives, 145 (72.9 percent) came from political families. The proportion of representatives from political families in the 8th Congress was even higher (82.5 percent) (Gutierrez 1994).

About 34.2 percent of Filipinos live below the poverty line, defined as making do on less than US$1.00 a day (Balisacan 1994: 39). In 2001, the government claimed that only 25.4 percent of people were below the poverty line, but this was based on a per capita income of Php 38.12 per day (roughly 69 U.S. cents) that had been criticized as unrealistically low. Poverty in the Philippines, as well, is unevenly distributed geographically—while about 30 percent of Metro Manila residents live below the poverty line, more than 45 percent of people in Mindanao barely survive below that line (Muslim 1994: 32).

The situation in Mindanao shows the immediate impact of global forces that cause gross inequality. A local secessionist struggle on the island has been thrust into the world's headlines by the kidnapping and beheading of foreign tourists and the fielding of three thousand U.S. soldiers in Basilan and Sulu. The intense media coverage, however, completely glosses over the historical struggle of Muslim Filipinos to preserve their cultural identity. It ignores the suffering of refugees (70,000 in Cotabato alone) and the economic losses from the abandonment of farms and plantations. It fails to indicate that with the unleashing of U.S. and local soldiers in a tiny part of the Philippines, the global war is helping to impoverish Mindanao and is rapidly widening the income gap between its citizens and those in other parts of the country.

The global information revolution has opened up the world to most Filipinos as the transistor radio, television, cell phones, and videos have reached even the most remote rural areas. The most important impact of this global exposure has been massive rural-urban migration, which, in the minds of many Filipinos, is only the first step to international migration. Very large cities such as Metro Manila, Davao, Cebu, and others have grown very rapidly. Unfortunately for many migrants, moving to the city has only meant trading rural poverty for urban misery. Rapid urbanization has made social class polarization even more visible. In very large cities, the rich live in gated communities protected by armed guards, high walls, and razor wire while the vast numbers of the poor are packed in slum and squatter communities with practically no access to basic services.

At present, an estimated 25 million people all over the Philippines are living in slums and squatter areas and more than a third of Metro Manila residents are living in informal settlements. It is significant that about 82 percent of households financed the construction of their homes with their own resources, 12 percent were financed by the private business sector, and only 6 percent by the government. The massive investments of the poor in their own dwellings have been estimated by the Peruvian economist Hernando de Soto to amount to US$133 billion. However, since these investments are considered "dead capital" because they are in the informal sector and have not entered the capital market, they have not played a significant role in the country's development (de Soto 1989; 2000).

The Hernando de Soto mission to the Philippines in 2000 provides an example of how fashionable international ideas can influence developments in a country. Building on the research findings of the de Soto mission, the Macapagal-Arroyo government launched an "assets formation campaign," designed to "monetize" the hidden assets of the poor. President Macapagal-Arroyo established a task force assigned to preparing recommendations on how the "informal tenure" of squatters and slum dwellers can be "formalized and regularized" through such mechanisms as actual sale of land and issuance of land titles; awarding of long-term land leases; accurate definition of alienable land parcels through better mapping, cadastral, and aerial survey techniques; simplification of the administrative process for land registration; and computerization of land records and registers and their linkage to real estate tax rolls. By accelerating the formalization of land and housing ownership, the task force hopes that the assets of the poor will be "securitized," thereby transforming "dead capital" into active assets.

As the task force pursues its work, however, it is becoming quite clear that the proponents of the assets-formation campaign have grossly underestimated the difficulties and costs of surveying, titling, and registering land. They also seem to have neglected to consider the considerable effects of corruption in the legalization of land ownership. Unfortunately for the urban poor, the extensive research and policy studies carried out by the task force in the pursuit of an exciting international idea seem to be taking the place of actual poverty-alleviation programs. The output of the campaign will most likely be a well-written report that, by itself, will not solve the problem of inequality.[3]

Another element of globalization, the Filipino diaspora, has also not contributed significantly to greater equality in Philippine society. It is true that the millions of dollars remitted by Filipinos living abroad have increased family incomes even in rural areas. Surveys of communities where the emigrants and OFWs have come from have shown that larger and more houses have been built, families own more physical assets like TV sets, refrigerators, and even private vehicles, and the children of workers left behind have been able to pursue higher education. However, the drain on the Philippine economy and society of the departure of millions of

Filipinos has been considerable. The resulting lack of a middle class (as potential members of that class elect to live in other countries) has served to widen the gap between a small agglutinated elite and the poor rural and urban masses. The sense of hopelessness among the poor, therefore, does not make it surprising that almost a fifth of Filipinos want to leave the country for a better life abroad.

Since the end of World War II, the Philippines has received many loans and grants from the IMF, the World Bank, the Asian Development Bank, and other agencies both multilateral and bilateral. In some ways, pursuance of ideas embodied in the so-called Washington consensus that favors the role of the market in economic development and the importance of unrestricted international trade have had some inimical effects. For example, housing projects financed through international loans abhor subsidies because it is alleged that they make projects nonreplicable and not sustainable. As a result, so-called bankable housing projects usually take the form of housing that is beyond the poor's capacity to pay. Some international loans for projects such as rapid transit in Metro Manila, mass rapid transit to the provinces, or the cleaning up of the Pasig River have involved the razing down of slum and squatter shanties and the relocation of the urban poor to far-flung resettlement sites. Expressways and superhighways have benefited car-riding elites rather than the "jeepney"-riding masses. The emphasis on market-oriented approaches persists despite ample evidence showing that the government should intervene and help with programs that really benefit the poor. Innovative approaches, such as the Community Mortgage Program, whereby nongovernmental organizations (NGOs) have organized urban poor communities and encouraged them to purchase the lots they have been occupying, have tended to be shelved and have been defunded.

To sum up, globalization does not seem to have helped in reducing income inequality in the Philippines. In some ways, this may be related to the fact that globalization has not significantly enhanced economic development in the country. With a smaller pie to share, it seems only natural that a small and powerful elite would keep as much of the pie as possible. The integration of Philippine society into the outside world arising from the explosion of information technology has mainly benefited urban residents and has neglected rural areas. Free trade has also been monopolized by traditional elites, who have used their control over politics, government, and trade and commerce to pursue their particularistic interests. Some Filipino families have prospered somewhat by the departure of some of their members for work abroad. However, the social cost of the Filipino diaspora in terms of personal and family difficulties has been very high.

The Philippines, as a nation, has pursued a vision of an economically robust, socially equal, and democratically liberal society. As I have indicated, I believe that it has failed to achieve the first two elements in this vision and that globalization has not helped Filipinos achieve those goals. In the following section, I try to analyze why, despite the failure to achieve economic development and equality, the Philippines has been able to actively practice a unique but workable form of liberal democracy.

### Globalization and Liberal Democracy

Most Filipinos are committed to a system of liberal democracy and they strongly adhere to the principle that sovereignty resides in the people. They define liberal democracy, in its ideal form, as a regime where leaders propose visions and policies on how to achieve the public good and the people elect the leaders they feel most capable of achieving it. Under this notion of liberal democracy, public and private decisions are governed by a set of formal and predictable laws. Citizens actively participate in public affairs from vision setting, policy formulation, policy implementation, and monitoring and evaluation to ensure that the public good will be attained. The actions of public officials are transparent and accountable. When public officials do not perform their tasks according to people's expectations, they are booted out of office in a legitimate process that is carried out smoothly, harmoniously, and without resorting to violence.

The type of liberal democracy currently enjoyed by Filipinos falls short of the ideal mentioned above, but most people accept it and enjoy its uniquely colorful and at times turbulent processes. Filipinos are particularly proud of the two "people power" revolutions that ousted two presidents accused of corruption from office. They feel that civil-society groups in the Philippines have shown that greater citizen participation in politics and governance can bring about positive results in such fields as electoral reform, poverty alleviation, social justice, and human rights. The Philippine press and the mass media, despite acknowledged cases of corruption and blind partisanship, serve an important informational and fiscalizing role. Political parties function as opportunistic alliances of political leaders and followers but they do work as mobilizing devices during elections and sometimes raise valid issues in the legislature. There is still a tendency on the part of the masses to vote for movie actors, TV anchors, star athletes, and other popular personalities, but some people with excellent educational and professional qualifications are starting to enter the political arena. There is a general feeling that "there is too much politics" in the Philippines, but it may precisely be this deep involvement in politics and overwhelming fascination with political processes that are making this "Filipino-style" variant of liberal democracy so vibrantly workable in the country.

Globalization exerts strong influences in the practice of liberal democracy in the Philippines. With their excellent access to the mass media,

Filipinos are informed about both domestic and international issues. Armed with timely and accurate information, they can make rational decisions. It is a rare Filipino who does not have relatives or friends living abroad and the information and ideas mediated through these contacts give many Filipinos a global perspective. It is worth noting that the Philippines has just passed legislation giving Filipino citizens temporarily living abroad the right to vote in national elections. Proponents of the law are hoping that the direct participation of overseas Filipinos in the political process will help elect better officials because the estimated 3.5 million absentee voters may not be as easily influenced to vote on the basis of purely partisan considerations.

A very important element in the practice of liberal democracy in the Philippines is the growing importance of civil society in public affairs and governance. Many Filipinos, in fact, believe that they have played a very important role in the global civil-society movement because of the two "people power" revolutions they waged in 1986 (against Marcos) and 2001 (against Estrada). In the Philippines, civil society is defined as "the realm of collective public action that lies between the private sphere and the state" (Silliman and Noble 1998: 13). Civil society is the "politically active popular sector" that seeks the institution of democratic rule and the "pursuance of a range of social and economic reforms to uplift the conditions of the poor" (Lane 1990: 1).

To achieve democratic goals, civil society in the Philippines has mobilized NGOs, people's organizations, community-based organizations, and cause-oriented groups. These organizations are deeply concerned about specific issues such as poverty alleviation, civil liberties, human rights, housing rights, gender and development, labor unionism, the welfare of indigenous peoples, and environmental protection. To achieve their goals, civil-society activists carry out advocacy campaigns, comanagement of programs and projects, cofunding of developmental activities, policy-oriented research, education and training, monitoring and evaluation, capacity enhancement, and institution building.

At present, there are more than 58,000 civil-society organizations in the Philippines officially registered with the Securities and Exchange Commission. There are probably thousands more that are active at the local community level that have not taken the trouble of registering with the government. Many of these civil-society groups are directly linked with international organizations and donors. For example, more than half of the Canadian financial and technical assistance to the Philippines is channeled through civil-society groups. Development assistance from United Nations agencies as well as bilateral assistance from the United States, Germany, France, and Japan is also targeted to assist many civil-society groups.

To sum up, widespread access to information, international migration, and the spread of ideas related to civil society seem to have contributed to the practice of liberal democracy in the Philippines. However, other elements of globalization (international trade and commerce, activities of transnational corporations, global legal regimes and standards, international financial institutions) have had only marginal effects on liberal democracy as practiced in the country. With many elements of globalization proving to be inadequate explanatory variables for the high level of liberal democracy in the Philippines, I believe it is necessary to look at the historical roots of globalization in the country to more fully understand the relationships between globalization, economic development, income inequality, and liberal democracy.

## Historical Roots of Globalization in the Philippines

To facilitate our discussions on the relationships between globalization on the one hand and economic development, income inequality, and liberal democracy on the other, I make a distinction between recent globalization processes and the long history of foreign influences in the Philippines. As pointed out by Amartya Sen, "globalization is neither new nor necessarily Western . . . over thousands of years, globalization has contributed to the progress of the world through travel, trade, migration, spread of cultural influences, and dissemination of knowledge and understanding" (2002: A2–A5). The Philippines has been open to foreign influences as a Spanish colony from 1571 to 1898 and a U.S. colony from 1900 to 1946. The basic features of the Philippine economy, polity, and society, therefore, were formed during these colonial periods.

### Economic Development

The reasons for the low level of economic development in the Philippines are rooted in a long history of international influences that have existed long before the advent of globalization. Basically, lack of economic development may be explained by considering four domestic factors: (1) agriculture, (2) manufacturing and industry, (3) energy supply, and (4) infrastructure.

*Agriculture.* A major problem in Philippine agriculture is the fact that almost all the arable land has already been cultivated. The logging industry, responding to the demand for timber in Japan, Korea, and other countries, has practically cut down all the country's forests. Logging, in turn, has opened the way to "slash and burn" agriculture. The application of traditional farming techniques to marginal land has not significantly increased crop yields, but it has caused tremendous damage to the environment (e.g., soil erosion, flash floods, siltation of rivers and streams). In recent years, global demand for Philippine resources has shifted from traditional exports such as Philippine mahogany, Manila hemp, copra, and sugar to food items such as bananas, mangoes, canned tuna, prawns, and seaweed. Filipino producers, however, have found it difficult to maintain the quality of exports and lack facilities for storage, shipping, and marketing. Production of marine food items has been hampered by widespread environmental pollution and harmful practices (e.g., dynamite fishing, destruction of mangrove forests and coral reefs). Beset with these problems, Filipino producers have lost out to more technologically savvy entrepreneurs in Thailand, Taiwan, China, and Vietnam.

A persistent issue in Philippine agriculture is protectionism that has been heavily influenced by historical events. The establishment of special "reciprocal trade relationships" between the Philippines and the United States during the first half of the twentieth century encouraged production of cash crops such as sugar and coconut. The preferential price paid by the United States for these products greatly benefited landed elites. Protected prices did not encourage Philippine planters to improve crop yields or modernize their processing plants because the U.S. quotas guaranteed purchase of all their exports at higher than prevailing global prices. Instead of introducing mechanization in their farms, the hacienda owners relied on the cheap labor of migratory seasonal workers (*sacadas*), who were abused and exploited. In recent years, the U.S. demand for Philippine sugar has declined and the local sugar industry has become moribund. The political clout of the "sugar block," however, continues to be strong and the industry enjoys its protected status.

Another cause of low agricultural productivity in the Philippines that is deeply rooted in the country's colonial past is the skewed pattern of land ownership. Despite the government's official commitment to land reform, Philippine agriculture is still dominated by very large land holdings. The hacienda system constitutes a legacy of the Spanish colonial system whereby the king of Spain awarded "land grants" to favored officials, including Church authorities. To this day, tenancy continues to be a big issue. In the coconut industry, the continued dominance of big landlords is revealed in the failure of the government to allocate the earnings from the controversial coconut levy fund to poor farmers. This levy, which has now grown to an estimated Php 700 billion, was imposed by the defunct Marcos administration on small farmers, but big coconut planters now want to control the funds.

An important issue in Philippine agriculture is the government's monopoly over rice trading. Since 1983, the National Food Authority has been importing rice—in 2002, rice imports to make up for domestic shortages were estimated at 350,000 metric tons. The Asian Development Bank

(ADB), in pursuance of its trade liberalization policy, approved a loan of $175 million in 2000 to encourage the Philippines to live up to its free-trade commitments. However, politicians know that people will not vote for an official responsible for an increase in the price of rice. In April 2002, the ADB called on the Philippines to deregulate the rice trade, but fear of shortages due to the El Niño phenomenon (and the fact that the presidential election in 2004, won by Gloria Macapagal-Arroyo, worked against any major changes in policies), have prompted the Philippine government to postpone liberalization of the rice trade.

It is clear from this analysis of Philippine agriculture that the country's low level of productivity and the failure of agriculture to contribute to economic development are rooted in historical factors related to colonial patterns of land ownership, types of products raised, protectionist economic policies, outmoded technological approaches, and poor agricultural management. At the same time, recent globalization realities such as the strong competition from neighboring Asian countries, overdependence on a changing U.S. market, uncontrolled smuggling of food items, and governmental policies to import rice and corn rather than accelerating production are all contributing to underdevelopment of the agricultural sector. Recent globalization processes have not contributed to Philippine economic development. However, this has been mainly because of the persistent influence of historical factors that have shaped the nature of Philippine agricultural development.

*Manufacturing and industry.* During the colonial period in the Philippines, Spanish and U.S. colonizers mainly encouraged extractive industries such as mining and logging. Predictably, the contributions of these two sectors to Philippine development have drastically declined. Aside from near exhaustion of mineral and forest resources, a strong concern for environmental protection has made resource exploitation more difficult. Local activists, supported by global environmental and human rights groups, have successfully blocked mining exploration ventures. The newly approved Philippine Mining Act has also empowered indigenous people living in targeted areas to aggressively protect their ancestral lands.

Many of the problems currently facing manufacturing and industry in the Philippines can be traced to the government's adoption of import-substitution strategies after World War II. The strategies protected "infant and necessary industries" by imposing tariff and nontariff barriers on imported items. Many of these protected industries, however, turned out to be "assemble and package" enterprises that did not create much added value. For example, canned-milk factories basically imported powdered milk, tin cans, and printed foreign labels and added local water. So-called automobile production plants did nothing but assemble components from abroad. Textile and garment factories relied on imported materials right down to the buttons and threads, took advantage of cheap Filipino labor, and then claimed the garments as valuable exports.

Implementing the import-substitution strategies, of course, generated considerable corruption. Import control permits were bought and sold, and trade in these items became more profitable than actual manufacturing. U.S. dollars from Central Bank allocations for importation of specific items were traded in the black market. Rationing of imported goods encouraged smuggling. After a couple of decades, Philippine officials realized that import-substitution strategies did not work. However, grave harm had already been done to the economy before these programs were abandoned.

Some of the rapid growth in Philippine manufacturing has been attributed to the concentration of investments in special economic zones, industrial parks, high-tech enclaves, and export-processing zones. The former U.S. military bases of Clark and Subic Bay were transformed into SEZs where large firms such as Federal Express, Acer Computers, Enron, and Reeboks were located. While this approach dramatically increased Philippine manufacturing output and exports, it has not created significant multiplier effects in the economy. For example, the SEZs did not generate economic development in their surrounding areas because they were linked more to global activities. In the case of Clark and Subic Bay, the SEZs even had negative externalities by attracting gambling, prostitution, drugs, and other unsavory developments in nearby Olongapo City and Angeles City.

*Energy.* A major bottleneck in Philippine economic development is the high price of energy. Here again, global forces have created domestic difficulties. During the Marcos administration, a contract was signed between the Philippine government and Westinghouse for the installation of a Php 1 billion nuclear power-generating plant in Bataan. It was exposed, later, that the deal involved massive kickbacks to the Marcos family. Furthermore, the plant was located on a dangerous seismic zone along the Central Luzon fault line. After many years of litigation, the nuclear power plant contract was canceled. By that time, however, it had practically exhausted most of the country's budget for power generation. The sorry state of the power industry came to haunt the Aquino administration when Metro Manila and the Luzon grid suffered from frequent brownouts. Former president Ramos "solved" the power crisis by fast-tracking the installation of power-generating plants dependent on fossil fuels and entering into lopsided power purchase agreements that have made energy costs in the Philippines the second-highest in Asia (next to Japan).

Since the Philippines has no oil resources, it has initially relied on coal as an energy source. Later, geothermal energy was tapped and now supplies about a quarter of electricity in the country. International investors have expressed a great deal of interest in the development of natural gas, and vast quantities have been identified in Malampaya Sound. Gas pipelines from the offshore fields are now being constructed to supply the energy needs of Metro Manila and surrounding regions. There are also plans to tap wind power in two areas of Luzon. However, at present, the major potential source of energy in the country is natural gas.

*Infrastructure.*   The sorry state of infrastructure has been identified as a major cause of underdevelopment because it discourages international and domestic entrepreneurs from investing in the country. Traffic congestion in Metro Manila is so bad that during rush hours, the average speed of vehicles is less than twelve kilometers per hour on Edsa, the city's main thoroughfare. The expansion of the light-rail transit system promises to ease traffic, but its operation has been marked by labor problems and even terrorist attacks. Meanwhile, the city relies on eight thousand diesel buses, many imported secondhand, and on the ubiquitous "jeepneys," converted World War II Jeeps that serve as the cheapest transport mode for the poor. Traffic in Metro Manila has caused such critical levels of air pollution that the World Health Organization has issued warnings on its effects on mental retardation among children.

Metro Manila's residents produce 5,400 metric tons of garbage per day and more than 10 percent of that ends up in canals and rivers because of poor collection. The metropolitan area has run out of garbage dumps and neighboring municipalities have refused to be the sites of proposed sanitary landfills. In 1996, competitive bidding was conducted for establishing an incinerator and energy-generating plant for Metro Manila. The bid was won by Jancom Environment Corporation, an Australia-based company teamed up with Philippine partners. A build-operate-transfer contract for $350 million over twenty-five years was signed in 1997, but the losing bidders filed a case against Jancom, alleging that corruption was involved in the deal. The following year, the Philippine legislature passed a law banning incineration, so Jancom revised the contract to set up a sanitary landfill, revising its tipping fee for garbage from $59 to $32 per metric ton. Because of the litigation, the contract was not signed by former presidents Ramos and Estrada. In April 2002, the supreme court of the Philippines ruled that the Jancom contract was valid but that, in order for it to be implemented, it had to be signed by President Macapagal-Arroyo. The incumbent president refused to sign the contract and called it "flawed," so the issue remains unresolved.

The Jancom case highlights the problems faced by international investors in the Philippines who find that large infrastructure projects invariably become very political and the object of corruption. Investors complain that when the legal system itself becomes politicized and corrupted, outcomes cannot be predictable and investments become too risky.

Thus, some U.S. entrepreneurs have complained to President Macapagal-Arroyo that even when contracts have been won by legitimate bidding, losing companies often bribe judges to issue temporary restraining orders that delay project execution. They have argued that unless the legal system could make contracts and agreements binding and government decisions could be made more predictable, it would be extremely difficult to conduct global business in the Philippines.

## Inequality

The historical roots of inequality in the Philippines are usually traced to the country's colonial background, but even in precolonial times Philippine society had already been divided into three social classes: the rulers, with their rank indicated by titles of *sultan, rajah, or datu;* regular citizens who owned lands and property and supported the rulers in local wars; and slaves and serfs, usually made up of individuals captured in war or children indentured to pay their parents' debts. In colonial times, the social class structure was perpetuated by the intermarriage of indigenous royals with the Spanish colonizers. Social inequality was also enhanced by awarding land grants only to families of loyal subjects and confining participation in the lucrative Manila-Acapulco galleon trade to powerful and influential elite families.

U.S. colonialism tried to make Philippine society more egalitarian by introducing compulsory public education and teaching occupational skills to poor people. However, the economic reforms were short-lived and were interrupted by World War II. Although political independence after 1946 created economic opportunities that allowed many Filipinos to achieve upward mobility, the hold of elite families on economic development, social affairs, and politics has continued. This is highly visible in the near monopoly of power by a few families in the closely intertwined fields of private business, government, and politics.

Like many developing countries, the Philippines, in the past, has relied heavily on government to provide infrastructure and services. In recent years, however, the Philippines has encouraged large-scale privatization of government functions in the hope that the efficiency of private enterprise could be introduced into public affairs.

A good example of privatization efforts is the awarding of the development and management of Metro Manila's water and sewerage system to two concessionaires partnered with international companies. This privatization scheme has not been too successful. In April 2002, the two concessionaires sought permission to raise their water rates by 16 percent. Because water service had not improved since the system was privatized, consumers objected to the higher rates. It turned out that the higher water rates were the direct result of the global economic downturn caused by the 9/11 terror-ist attacks in the United States. The two water companies admitted that only 51 percent of the new rates were due to the actual costs of water pro-duction—a full 49 percent took the form of "foreign currency differential adjustments" and "currency exchange adjustments," which were the direct result of foreign borrowings. Not surprisingly, customers vigorously object-ed to these costs being passed on to them and there were cries for boy-cotting the private firms. In January 2003, one of the water concessionaires affiliated with a French company withdrew from its contract, alleging that the government had not allowed it to raise water rates to cover its losses.

The problems faced by the Metro Manila privatization scheme serves as a good case study of social inequality and the power of elite families. One of the concessionaires in the water project was the Lopez family, whose business concerns also include the company that supplies electricity to Metro Manila. The Lopezes have holdings in sugar, publishing, TV net-works, and real estate. They own the largest television network in the coun-try, ABS-CBN, where a number of broadcasters, anchors, and media stars who have been elected to the Philippine Senate and other top positions have come from. Their family members have included a former vice-president of the country. The Lopez family is so powerful that many observers see it as a virtual political party. The other water concessionaire was the Ayala fami-ly, who owns most of Makati City and is big in real estate, insurance, hous-ing development, and resort development. While Ayala family members have not directly ventured into politics, they have openly supported key individuals who have in turn favored their business ventures upon being elected to office.

The economic hold of elite families that is strengthened by linkages with transnational corporations extends to other fields. For example, it is known that the Philippine cement industry is a local cartel controlled by Lafarge (a French company), Cemex of Mexico, and Holcim of Switzerland. In April 2002, contractors charged that the three international companies, which reportedly controlled the Philippine Cement Manufacturer's Corporation, tried to block importation of cement into the country by imposing high tariff rates. The higher price of cement that immediately occurred placed President Macapagal-Arroyo and the Department of Trade and Industry in an awkward position, especially in the light of outcries in the Philippine press about the alleged operations of the cement cartel and its local partners.

Inequality in the Philippines does not only exist in socioeconomic class distinctions. It is also most marked in geographic distribution of the bene-fits of development. Metropolitan Manila, for example, accounts for about 40 percent of the Philippine GDP. About ninety of the country's hundred largest corporations and 60 percent of manufacturing firms are located in the metropolis. The Metro Manila city-region employs 45 percent of the country's nonagricultural labor force.

On the other hand, the island of Mindanao has been lagging behind the rest of the country in economic and social development. About 45 percent of Mindanao's population lives below the poverty line, compared to 34.2 percent for the whole country. Infant mortality in the island is 93.3 per 1,000 live births compared to the national average of 54.1. Life expectancy in Mindanao is 55.3 years, compared to 63.7 years for the whole country and 64 years in Metro Manila. The historical forces that have caused under-development in Mindanao are depicted in the section below.

### Globalization and Inequality in Mindanao

The so-called Mindanao problem has its origins in age-old global conflicts that may be linked to what has been called the "war of civilizations." Muslim Filipinos (Moros) were never conquered by Spanish and U.S. colonizers. What could not be won by war, however, was achieved by internal colonization after the Philippines became independent. Land laws patterned after the homesteading act in the United States encouraged many Christian Filipinos to go to Mindanao. The influx of Christian Filipinos immediately created violent ethnic conflicts.

Globalization reached Mindanao through transnational corporations. By 1994, about 5.3 million hectares of land, more than half of the total land area of the island, were occupied by agribusiness plantations, logging concessions, industrial tree plantations, and mining concessions. That same year, 3.1 million hectares of land, representing 30.2 percent of Mindanao, were owned by 145 big corporations, 54 of which were foreign-owned or controlled (Muslim 1994: 34). Government positions were also largely held by Christians.

It is not surprising that poverty and inequality have triggered a secessionist movement in Mindanao. The Moro National Liberation Front (MNLF) launched a rebellion in the 1960s aimed at establishing an autonomous Islamic state over twenty-three provinces. However, the region claimed by the MNLF was only 22 percent Muslim, and only five of the provinces had Muslim majorities. Interestingly, when the issue was raised with the Islamic Foreign Ministers Conference (IFMC), the IFMC did not support the MNLF's secessionist aims. Reasons advanced for this included the fear of other Asian countries with restive Muslim populations of setting a bad example for secession, and a tacit agreement among Southeast Asian governments not to interfere in each other's internal affairs.

In 1977, the MNLF abandoned its secessionist objectives and settled for the creation of the Autonomous Region of Muslim Mindanao. However, another group, the Moro Islamic Liberation Front split from the MNLF and pursued a secessionist line. A much smaller group of Muslims, the Abu Sayyaf, engaged in kidnapping and other violent activities. The killing of two U.S. citizens by the Abu Sayyaf led to its branding as a terrorist group linked to Al-Qaida by the United States. In February 2003, the United States sent more than 1,700 soldiers to Mindanao as "advisers" to Philippine troops. The Tausug ethnic group, the main residents in Sulu island, promised the U.S. troops a "hot reception," recalling events in 1913 when more than 2,000 of their ancestors were killed by U.S. soldiers under the command of General John J. "Blackjack" Pershing. Thus, a local Philippine problem, with roots in a violent past, has become a major global concern with potential repercussions for other peoples all over the world.

## Liberal Democracy

With its tradition of "people power," a thriving civil society, a rambunctious free press, decentralized local governance, and a history of free and open elections as an institutionalized way of transferring formal government authority, the Philippines can be regarded as one of the more robust liberal democracies in the world. Historically, Filipinos have been voting for public officials since 1903. Political parties have been active since that time. The country achieved political independence in 1946. Authoritarian rule was imposed for twenty-one years by the Marcos dictatorship, but a popular revolution restored democracy in 1986. Another similar revolution also ousted former president Joseph Estrada from power in 2001. At present, Filipinos are talking of setting up a constitutional convention or a constituent assembly to revise the 1987 Philippine constitution, and there are open debates on the merits and disadvantages of a presidential versus a parliamentary form of government. Newly elected President Macapagal-Arroyo has indicated strong support for a parliamentary system, but her opponents cynically interpret this as an effort on her part to remain in power even after her constitutionally mandated six-year term limit is over.

There are many socioeconomic variables that may explain the relatively high level of liberal democracy in the Philippines. Most of these are rooted in historic events and others are traceable to more recent globalization processes. The most important of these variables are: (1) U.S. colonial influence, (2) compulsory public education, (3) community-based cooperative action, (4) the rapid growth of civil society, and (5) a freewheeling mass media.

### U.S. Colonial Influence

Filipinos of a certain age fondly remember "Peace Time"—the U.S. colonial regime between 1900 and 1941 when food was plentiful and cheap, buses and trains ran on time, jobs were available, civil servants were honest, and politicians were responsive, honorable, and not corrupt. Taking their pledge to prepare the Filipinos for independence seriously, U.S. colonial administrators introduced municipal elections for selecting local leaders as early as 1903. They encouraged the formation of political parties—the Federalistas who advocated joining the United States, the Nacionalistas, who clamored for immediate independence, and the Liberals, who stood for economic nationalism. Young bright Filipino scholars (*pensionados*) were sent to the United States to prepare them for leadership roles. A professional civil service was established where advancement was based on merit, entry was attained through competitive examinations, and promotion depended on performance. Political mechanisms for referendum and plebiscite, citizen reviews and recall, and impeachment of erring officials were adopted and used.

In politics, the colonists upheld the principle of "one person, one vote," although in the 1903 election they had to agree to limit voting to the *principalia* (elite community leaders), who insisted that only persons who owned property, paid taxes, and could read and write should be allowed to vote. This exclusivist principle raised so much protest among the great majority of Filipinos, however, that universal suffrage was introduced soon after that. At a more basic level, the U.S. colonial administrators popularized the holding of citizen assemblies (patterned after the New England town meeting) to resolve local issues.

Under U.S. colonial rule, the Filipinos developed a rather idealized concept of liberal democracy. For most of the colonial period, liberal democracy seemed to have worked quite well. The Filipinos had national leaders such as Manuel Luis Quezon, Sergio Osmeña, Claro M. Recto, and Manuel A. Roxas who were charismatic, eloquent, and upright citizens. The *pensionados* sent to the United States returned to the country and assumed top leadership positions. The Filipino clamor for national independence unified them.

The fight for independence, however, could not paper over the fact that there were aspects of indigenous Philippine culture that predisposed Filipinos toward "hard-boiled" pragmatic politics characterized by bargaining and accommodation among elite groups to achieve particularistic goals rather than the general welfare. Filipino politicians engaged in wild and woolly unrestricted contests in order to achieve partisan interests. In this Manichean world, the group with the most money, cunning, and the wickedest means for inflicting violence became the winners.

Even with these politically aberrant patterns of behavior, however, U.S. colonial influence succeeded in introducing basic elements of liberal democracy in the Philippines. The rule of law, spearheaded by an independent supreme court coequal with the legislative and executive branches of government, has been generally respected. A constitution-based Commission on Elections attempts to make suffrage open and free. The foundations for a professional civil service have been set up. A free press and a vigilant civil society consistently clamor for economic and political reforms. Some critics may say that the United States' experiment with liberal democracy in the Philippines has been a disaster, but it cannot be denied that despite their economic and social problems, Filipinos remain one of the most freely democratic peoples in Asia, if not the whole world.

## Compulsory Public Education

Another lasting influence of U.S. colonization that has significantly contributed to the practice of liberal democracy in the Philippines is compulsory public education. At present, almost all Filipino children of school age are in school and 77 percent of male and 78 percent of female students aged twelve and above reach high school. Only 6 percent of people aged twelve and above cannot read or write. Most Filipinos view education as the primary means for achieving economic and social mobility.

When the United States took the Philippines as a colony, they made public education compulsory. In 1901, 1,074 U.S. teachers came to the Philippines to teach the Filipinos (since 509 of these teachers came on board the U.S. transport *Thomas,* they became known as the Thomasites). Faced with no less than seventy-six languages and dialects spoken by Filipinos, the U.S. teachers made English the medium of instruction. More important, however, the Thomasites "saw themselves as bringing more than just the basic literacy and numbers skills. They were charged with inculcating democratic values and ideals into young Filipino minds, with a view to making the country a model of American-style democracy in the Far East" (Racelis and Ick 2001: 4).

To a great extent, compulsory public education has brought about a revolutionary change in Philippine society. The elitism of the old Spanish-dominated society was eroded. Gender inequality was dramatically changed as girls did much better in school and enrolled in the sciences, medicine, engineering, and other fields formerly considered male preserves. The curriculum used in schools emphasized love of country, good moral character, civic conscience, and vocational proficiency. It stressed the importance of civic duty and the need for people to get actively involved in public affairs. Education opened the eyes of students to the outside world, especially to political practices in liberal democratic countries such as the United States and Europe. Education also made it possible for many Filipinos to move to foreign countries.

Not surprisingly, a major effect of general education in the Philippines is the high rate of participation of Filipinos in governmental affairs. In public meetings, elections, campaigns, and demonstrations, people tend to be directly involved. Voting turnout in local and national elections rarely goes below 85 percent. High literacy rates enhance access to information, which helps to guide rational choice.

Unfortunately, in recent years, the quality of education in the Philippines has gone down dramatically, especially in public schools where low teacher salaries and political interference in administrative decisions have negatively affected teacher morale. A shift toward a more vocational orientation has taken place whereby instead of students going into traditional fields such as law and medicine, they are taking up nursing, medical technology, computer programming, or enrolling in trade schools to become plumbers, auto mechanics, electricians, or radio operators. The most noticeable aspect of these choices is the fact that they are the ones required of individuals who would like to go abroad as contractual workers or immigrants. Families and clans even pool their resources together to select the brightest children, finance their education and training, send these individuals abroad to work, and then benefit from the remittances they send home. Once Filipinos gain a foothold in a foreign country, other members of the family or clan join them as sponsored family members. Education, therefore, has served as the passport of many Filipinos to a globalized way of life.

### Community-Based Cooperation

The seeming natural affinity of Filipinos to democratic decisionmaking is culturally based on traditions of community cooperation rooted in an agricultural way of life. To the average rural *tao* (common folk), the practice of *bayanihan* (voluntary assistance) is the key to survival and a productive and harmonious life. The time for field preparation, planting, and harvesting is short and one needs the voluntary and reciprocal help of neighbors to do the job properly. Building a house, constructing and maintaining irrigation systems, surviving floods and other calamities, and dealing with officious and corrupt officials all require community solidarity and common action. Transferring the practices and rituals from rural agriculture to politics, the average Filipino becomes a functioning democrat.

An interesting effect of community-based cooperation on politics is the creation of political machines designed to organize and mobilize people for political action, especially during elections. Usually, influential individuals in a community become political *liders* (leaders) who report to party "bosses" in the provincial capital, who, in turn, are loyal to national politicians and their clans. To be a *lider* is to be an organizer and facilitator—helping constituents find jobs, accompanying individuals to health clinics and other government offices to ensure immediate attention, telling the boss which individuals in the community need help, attending birthdays, baptisms and wakes, etc. All these "services" of the *liders* are done in the name of the boss or top official. Thus, when election time comes, these IOUs are cashed in by the *liders* in favor of their candidates.

The transition from traditional community mutual-aid patterns to political party formation is an important step in political socialization. To most Filipinos, local issues are occasions for direct involvement in civic affairs. This is one of the main reasons why there has been such a strong movement for decentralization and local autonomy in the Philippines. The Local Government Code of 1991 has devolved key functions of government to provinces, cities, municipalities, and villages. Using their traditional patterns of mutual aid, cooperation, coordination, and political accommodation, Filipinos are able to make liberal democracy function at the local and national levels.

### Civil-Society Activism

One of the most significant developments in Philippine political culture has been the emergence of civil-society groups. These groups have become the main instruments for effecting community cooperation in Philippine localities. Many civil-society leaders come from the educated middle class. They champion universalistic causes such as housing for the poor, health services for women and children, environmental protection, and drives against drug addiction, gambling, prostitution, graft, and corruption. They have also started strong alliances with church leaders, business entrepreneurs, and professionals to fight corruption and abuses by top officials. Civil-society groups were prominently involved in the ouster of Marcos and Estrada from power.

The rising importance of civil society in Philippine politics raises the issue of what it means in terms of the creation of the middle class. The usual relationship between globalization and political democracy proposes that as a country becomes more globalized and gains better information about the outside world, a growing middle class becomes dissatisfied with authoritarianism and demands greater participation in public decisionmaking. Carolina Hernandez points to South Korea and Taiwan as good case studies of this pattern. She describes what happened in these countries as follows: "No longer content with being participants in the economy and the society as a consequence of increased mobility, education, and information, [the middle class] sought political liberalization and eventually, democratization of the polity" (Hernandez 1996: 121).

A real Filipino middle class, however, has been very slow in evolving. Many of the upwardly mobile educated Filipinos mainly work as poorly paid civil servants or employees in private firms. They are so preoccupied with the daily struggle just to survive that they are not able to pay a lot of attention to political and civil-society matters, except, perhaps, during times of crises. Fed up with the lack of development in the country, millions of middle-class Filipinos have left the country to seek a better life in North America, Australia, and Europe. Others have gone abroad as contractual workers but, after a number of trips abroad, they have ended up as permanent residents and immigrants. For some time, therefore, Philippine politics is likely to continue to be dominated by economic and social elites. Civil-society activists, mainly drawn from the middle class, might be able to bring about social changes such as the ouster of Joseph Estrada, but if genuine economic and social reforms do not take place after such upheavals, the prospects for true liberal democracy in the Philippines will still be far into the future.

### Mass Media and a Free Press

Filipinos are proud of the fact that they have a freewheeling press and media sectors that serve as critics, evaluators, monitors, and watchdogs of public and private actions. Government officials, business leaders, church functionaries, or military officers—no one is exempt from the prying eyes of the press. As such, the Philippine media plays an effective fiscalizing role and contributes immensely to achieving liberal democracy.

One of the key factors in winning an election in the Philippines is popularity and name recognition. Prominent media personalities have tended to go into politics—with rather mixed results. Former president Estrada, a former action movie star who styled himself the hope of the Filipino masses, is the best example of how "stardom" can lead to the highest political office in the land. With his impeachment and incarceration, some social analysts have hoped that Filipino voters would become less prone to elect individuals purely on the basis of their popularity. However, in the 2000 elections, a television broadcaster named Noli de Castro topped the senatorial winners and quite a number of media stars also got elected. Among the current members of the Philippine Senate are three popular television anchors, a former movie actor, an actress, and a former basketball star. Potential presidential candidates in the 2004 elections included Loren Legarda and Noli de Castro, both popular television "stars" who continue to run their TV programs even though they have been elected to the Philippine Senate.

The important role of mass media in political life has led some dominant politicians to buy and own newspapers, radio stations, and television stations that they use for propaganda and "spin doctoring" purposes. As one newspaperman once observed, some politicians see a newspaper as a "gun in the holster" that can be used both for attacking opponents and praising partisans. What is probably saving the Philippine situation is the fact that there are so many media groups that they pretty much counterbalance each other's influence. People find out the particular bias of individual newspaper or media channels rather quickly and learn to take what they read or hear from those groups with tons and tons of salt.

The Philippine media are notorious for their cavalier attitude toward the truth and for widespread corruption. The country's rather lax libel laws allow media practitioners to print and broadcast even rumors, gossip, and lies. Many reporters, columnists, and editors are reputed to be engaged in "AC-DC journalism" (Attack and Collect–Defend and Collect). During press conferences of key officials and politicians, sealed envelopes with money are customarily distributed, giving rise to the term "envelopmental journalism." Although salaries of press and media people are very low, many of them live an opulent lifestyle that can only be possible with "sideline occupations" and corrupt practices. Some journalists are known to be on the payroll of politicians, political parties, or government offices where they are known as "15/30" employees because they only come to collect their pay envelopes on the 15th and 30th day of each month.

International observers of the Philippine situation are often amazed at the seeming openness of the press and mass media. The fact that most of the newspapers are in English adds to this semblance of openness. However, because of the partisanship, corruption, and free-for-all nature of the Philippine press, finding out what is true and what is spin requires very careful reading. One has to know, for example, who owns the newspaper, the political friends of certain editors and columnists, what schools they graduated from, what families and clans they belonged to, etc. Since these alliances and networking activities are in constant flux, it is an extremely difficult task to interpret what one reads, sees, or hears in the media.

Despite the existence of corruption and partisanship, however, the Philippine press and the mass media still manage to have a rather positive role in political development. For one thing, it is virtually impossible to bribe all media practitioners, so there is always somebody who can criticize a public official's actions. Increasingly, also, there are some dedicated journalists who take their fiscalizing role seriously and refuse to be bribed, coerced, or intimidated. Staff members of the Philippine Center for Investigative Journalism (PCIJ), for example, have steadfastly and courageously upheld the freedom of the press. They were mainly responsible for the investigative reports that exposed the corruption during the Estrada administration and provided the evidence that helped to have him impeached. It has not been easy for PCIJ, however, to take on this crusading role. Happily, it has been encouraged to carry out its investigative work by the support of civil-society groups and some assistance from international donors committed to truth in journalism.

## Conclusion

In this chapter, I have proposed that globalization has not significantly con-tributed to economic development in the Philippines. Globalization has also not helped to reduce social and economic inequality in Philippine society. At the same time, however, despite low rates of economic growth and per-sistent inequality, Filipinos have been able to achieve a high level of liberal democracy. In trying to explain these developmental relationships, I have looked at the effects and impact of recent globalization in the Philippines and have analyzed those linkages in the context of centuries-long historical processes and cultural factors that have influenced that country's economy and society.

Students of Asian development suggest that countries in the region can choose between the so-called East Asian model, where economic growth was pursued with the use of strong state powers, or a liberal democratic model, where democratization preceded a drive toward economic develop-ment. Some Filipinos believe that poor economic performance has been the price their country has had to pay for its commitment to liberal democracy. They note that a number of neighboring countries such as Taiwan, Korea, and Singapore were able to achieve high levels of economic growth by ini-tially adopting "strong state" regimes. The Philippines, on the other hand, has opted for the messier and less "efficient" democratic path. Unlike China and Vietnam, it did not go through communist rule to correct social cleavage—it persisted in relying on democratic ways even as it remained relatively poor and unequal. The primary challenge to the Philippines then, according to one political observer, is how to successfully face the power-ful combination of increasing globalization and deepening problems of inequality while maintaining its commitment to democracy (Almonte 1996: 12–22).

Many Philippine social scientists take great pride in the Filipino's strong commitment to liberal democracy and believe that this will be attained despite inequality and a slow pace of economic development. Carolina Hernandez, for example, cites the overthrow of the Marcos dicta-torship as proof of the people's love of freedom. She believes that the polit-ical culture of Filipinos is historically marked more by dissent than blind obedience to higher authority. Thus, she argues that the authoritarian path to economic development taken by Taiwan, Korea, Singapore, Vietnam, and China is not acceptable to most Filipinos. She suggests that even if the Marcos dictatorship had been able to achieve high levels of economic development, the freedom-loving Filipinos would have thrown him out just the same. After all, Hernandez argues, the Filipinos fought against Spanish colonization, Japanese occupation, and even "benevolent assimilation" by the United States throughout their history. They also used "people power" to evict former presidents Marcos and Estrada from the presidential palace (Hernandez 1996: 122).

Since it attained political independence in 1946, the Philippines has been committed to achieving *both* economic development and liberal democracy. Interestingly enough, despite low levels of economic growth and worsening income inequality, the Philippines is achieving a higher state of liberal democracy. Much of this achievement is traceable to historic factors such as U.S. colonization, compulsory public education, democratic elections, and encouragement of community-based participation and civil-society activism. There are some problems facing liberal democracy in the Philippines, such as a cultural yearning for authoritarian leaders, poorly managed elections, and widespread graft and corruption. However, as a general tendency, recent globalization processes such as increased access to international information through the Internet, an ability to network globally with civil-society groups, and the possibility of introducing electronic technology to improve election management in the Philippines may tend to enhance liberal democracy.

This chapter proposes a number of structural and institutional factors that need to be overcome if the Philippines is to achieve higher rates of economic growth, greater equality, and more liberal democracy in the context of future globalization. The Philippines has to increase agricultural productivity by introducing modern technology in rice and corn production, reinvigorating the land reform program, encouraging research and development, and expanding agricultural inputs such as irrigation, small-scale credit, and agricultural extension. Government policies and programs rooted in nationalistic protectionism have to be changed because they have traditionally benefited only the economic and political elites. If the Philippines wants to be a key player in regional organizations such as AFTA, ASEAN, and APEC, it needs to commit itself to the rules of the global game and not base its decisions on purely local political interests.

Also, while free trade and the unhindered flow of capital, goods, and services between the Philippines and other countries are important for economic development, the government has to ensure that selective interventions to correct market imperfections are instituted. Protection of the environment, certainly, needs to be ensured. The basic rights of individual workers, especially of women and children, have to be respected. The welfare and rights of indigenous populations living in areas targeted for resource-extraction activities such as mining and logging need protection. In general, improving the quality of life of the poor and underprivileged beyond the random benefits of "trickle down" processes or the offering of "safety nets" is absolutely necessary if the government is to achieve peace and security as well as liberal democracy.

Happily, the Philippines to date, has been able to achieve a workable level of political development despite slow and erratic rates of economic growth and continuing income inequality. The transfer of political power has been achieved through periodic elections that, while marred by cases of violence, vote manipulation, and cheating in some areas, still manage to place into position leaders who are the true choices of the people. There is freedom of assembly, of movement, and of the press. People actively participate in public decisionmaking either through political parties or civil-society groups.

A key challenge to Philippine development that is closely related to globalization, inequality, and political democracy is corruption. At present, the Philippines is ranked the third most corrupt country in Asia (behind Indonesia and India). Not surprisingly, this notoriety has discouraged foreign investments in the country. At the same time, however, corruption in the Philippines has attracted "hot money" from the drug trade and other illegal sources. The Philippines has been prominently listed among countries where the banking system is used for laundering illicit funds. The Philippine stock exchange has unearthed scandals involving insider trading and stock manipulation. Favored traders with global connections have been allowed to use government service insurance resources and social security funds for stock investments. Gambling lords from Macao, Hong Kong, and other countries have found the Philippines a haven for their investments. The legitimization of gambling has brought corruption to the highest levels.

There are some people who fervently hope that globalization will help to limit corruption in the Philippines because increased access to information, the demand for greater transparency in public transactions, and the need to adhere to international standards and "codes of conduct" in business operations will help curtail corrupt practices. For example, the recent passage of a law adding the Philippines to the list of twenty-nine countries subscribing to the Financial Action Task Force that are committed to preventing money laundering is a move in the right direction. The installation of a computerized system of evaluating bids for procurement and execution of infrastructure projects in the Philippine government is another good move. Anticorruption measures now required by the World Bank, Asian Development Bank, and other international agencies in the execution of projects in the Philippines also promise to curtail graft and corruption.

Because of the importance of elections in selecting able leaders, some people have expressed the hope that globalization may help to bring electoral reform to the Philippines. They look to better international communication, combined with local media dynamism and the watchful eyes of international election observers, to improve electoral management. They view computerization of the electoral process and the use of sophisticated vote-counting machines as excellent methods for preventing cheating. Some people are even suggesting that a parliamentary form of government should replace the presidential form so that expensive local and national elections currently conducted every two years can be avoided. There are also hopes that allowing Filipino citizens temporarily living aboard to vote in national elections would help improve the quality of leaders in the country.

At present, Filipinos accept that they are poor and their society is marked by serious social inequalities. However, they glory in the fact that politically they enjoy a great deal of freedom. They readily admit that Philippine politics has many shortcomings. It is primarily transactional and public decisions tend to be based on bargaining and accommodation among elite groups. Often, the general welfare is not given enough consideration in governmental deliberations. Political actions depend more on personalities rather than on principled stands focused on important public issues. Political parties are merely opportunistic coalitions of individuals and factions and lack coherent platforms. Graft and corruption remain uncontrolled. Despite all these shortcomings, however, most Filipinos are proud of their democratic way of life. As a people, they are optimistic and often proclaim that they are as pliant as the bamboo in the face of economic difficulties and social adversities. If, in the not too distant future, globalization processes will help them achieve higher levels of economic development and reduce social inequalities, they are hopeful that their already high level of liberal democracy will become even better.

## Notes

1. See also Constable (1997).
2. Karnow was quoting Fr. John Doherty, a U.S. Jesuit Scholar at Ateneo de Manila University.
3. For a critique of de Soto's ideas, see Gilbert (2002: 1–17).

# 6

# Brazil: Globalization, Poverty, and Social Inequity

## Simon Schwartzman

Brazil is a country with reasonable levels of economic development, but serious shortcomings in the social sphere. The *Human Development Report,* published in 2002 by the United Nations Development Program (UNDP), puts Brazil in the seventy-third place in the overall ranking of social development. With US$7,600 per capita, it ranked fifty-ninth on income, but lagged behind in indicators such as infant mortality and literacy. Brazil is also supposed to have one of the worst income distributions in the world (United Nations Development Program 2002; Urani 2002). In this chapter, I will discuss to what extent this situation is due to external factors affecting Brazilian society, or internal ones. I will also provide some information on the nature and scope of these social shortcomings and on the possibilities for dealing with them.[1]

## The Impact of Globalization

In the second semester of 2002, as the presidential campaign intensified and the likelihood of a victory for the leftist opposition candidate increased, Brazil experienced the full impact of globalization. For several months, the country had been resisting contamination from the Argentine debacle, which plunged that country into a terrible financial crisis. The Argentine problem had very concrete effects for Brazil, on trade and all other economic transactions between the two main partners of Mercosur, effects that were amplified by the perception, in international financial markets, of the growing risk of "Latin" debt, in spite of the large differences in the conditions and economic policies of the two countries. However, the impact of Argentina on the Brazilian economy was much smaller than the effects that public opinion polls showing the growing support to the candidate of the Laborers' Party (PT) had on the assessments of a few rating companies, which caused the "Brazil risk" to soar and the country's currency to lose about 50 percent of its value in a few months (see Figure 6.1).

The rush of foreign investors to get out of Brazil at any price was labeled by the Brazilian financial authorities of the time as an "irrational" behavior of a nervous market, unrelated to Brazil's economic reality. There was a clear risk, however, of a self-fulfilling prophecy. As the *real* fell, interest rates soared; long-term debt papers were replaced by short-term ones, often indexed to the dollar; and the likelihood of a debt default increased. This was a typical "globalization" event—the fate of countries does not seem to depend any longer on the hard realities of their economies, but on the fleeting waves of good and bad feelings and expectations that washed anonymous markets in New York or London.

This situation led to joint action between government and the opposition, through which the government negotiated a $30 billion loan with the International Monetary Fund (IMF), and the main opposition candidate made a public commitment to honor it. Once in power, President Luis Inácio Lula da Silva kept his word, in a clear turnabout regarding the views expressed by the party and its allies until then. Before, it was common to hear proposals to stimulate the economy with the expansion of public expenditures and drastic reductions of interest rates, and to postpone, renegotiate, or cancel the payment of the international debt.[2] Once in power, the

**Figure 6.1    Election Polls and Exchange Rates**

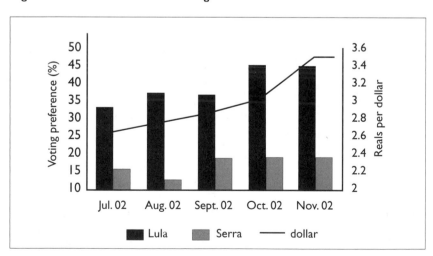

*Source:* Election polls data taken from the DataFolha surveys published in the daily press. Exchange rates are mean values, as posted by the Brazilian Central Bank.

new stand was that the government would not "reinvent the wheel" in economics, would not overspend, would not tinker with inflation and the interest rates, and, to make sure that it was committed to this policy, a former top executive of Bank Boston was invited to head the country's Central Bank.

Economic conservatism was justified in terms of realism, to be compensated by strong and immediate actions in the social sphere, dealing at once with the problems of hunger, illiteracy, housing, health care, and poverty. In the long run, the economic model inherited from the Cardoso government, which placed integration with the international economy ahead of the social needs of the people, would be replaced by a different economic policy, still to be described in detail.

In this chapter, I argue that the notion that there is an option to be made between a policy of international integration, leading to poverty and social inequity, and a policy of national self-sufficiency, leading to economic development and social equity, is a false dilemma. The debates in Brazil have always evolved around two juxtaposed issues, the internal versus external dimensions, and the relative weight of state versus market, or society, in the economy and in the implementation of social policies. There is a tendency to identify "state" with "national," and "market" or society with "international" or global. However, this is in large part an ideological argument, or a rhetorical device.

From this perspective, I will examine some of the key social issues facing Brazilian society, trying to ascertain to what extent they have been shaped and influenced by external or internal forces. My conclusion is a simple one. Global trends have their impact, as they always have, on the internal life of countries, with the peculiarities of place and time. The main novelty of recent years is perhaps the speed and depth of short-term fluctuations in international perceptions and, consequently, in international capital flows, as well as the sheer scale and availability of these resources. It is necessary, however, to distinguish these abrupt fluctuations from the long-term effects of the country's insertion in the international economy. It is also necessary to distinguish between the economic and the broader social implications of external conditions. The economy places a strong limit on what can be done in the social realm, but it does not determine all the choices; it is always possible to do better, or differently, with the existing resources.

## Concepts: From Dependency to Globalization

Global integration is nothing new to Brazil, nor its links with poverty and social inequity. The country started in 1500 as a colonial enterprise of the Portuguese Empire, and expanded using slave labor for the production of sugar, gold, and coffee for international markets. Administrative cities, trade, and military outposts were established along the coast to handle the colonial interests, and a population of mixed-blood, impoverished freemen grew in the shadows of the export economy. Political independence in the early eighteenth century was a direct consequence of the Napoleonic wars. The new country relied on England for international recognition and on the Rothschild bankers to finance its imperial government, which fell at the end of the century when Britain decided to stop the international slave trade. In the early days of the republic, coffee production depended on millions of immigrants arriving from Europe and Japan. Brazil suffered the impact of the 1929 crisis, its economy was reorganized to participate in the military efforts of World War II, and, since then, benefited or suffered the impacts of the expansion of international trade, the Cold War, and the industrial and technological revolutions of the late twentieth century.[3]

In the 1960s, as a political exile in Santiago de Chile, the Brazilian sociologist Fernando Henrique Cardoso wrote a book in partnership with Enzo Faletto arguing that the political, economic, and social conditions of underdevelopment in Latin America could only be interpreted in terms of the countries' international dependency. Poverty was a central concern, as the most obvious face of social and economic underdevelopment.[4] The notion was that, to overcome it, the countries should create a modern industry that would generate a modern and strong proletariat, which would in turn strive for a social-democratic or socialist regime. The local oligarchies, in partnership with foreign interests, kept the economy tied with the production of primary goods, and did not allow for modern industry to grow. The struggle for economic development and against poverty should be a struggle against the alliance of local oligarchies and foreign interests. Hopefully, national bourgeoisies could emerge and join arms with peasants and workers in this fight against local oligarchies, international interests, poverty, and dependency. If not, the national state should fulfill this role.[5] In the 1950s and 1960s, it was inevitable that these views would have strong international consequences, with countries and political movements aligning themselves with the Soviet block, or trying to create a third path between the two conflicting camps in the Cold War. With some variations, these notions were already present in the economic papers of Raul Prebisch and the early works of the United Nations Economic Commission for Latin America, and in a growing literature on colonialism and underdevelopment in Asia, Africa, and Latin America; but Cardoso and Faletto dressed it in Marxist terms, and the authors came to be known as the founders of a new school of thought in the social sciences.[6]

The dependency theories did not resist the emergence of the so-called Asian tigers and the end of the Cold War. How could it be that Korea and Taiwan, poorer than Brazil in the 1950s, became rich in the 1980s, while Brazil and other Latin American countries lingered through the "lost decades"?[7] Why, in Latin America, did some countries, such as Mexico,

Costa Rica, and Chile, seem to move forward, while others, such as Honduras, Peru, and Bolivia, stagnate? During the Cold War, it was still possible to try to explain these differences by each country's peculiar place in the international arena: Korea and Taiwan were supposed to be pawns in the Cold War, and to have benefited from this special condition. Soon, however, it became obvious that the achievements of these countries in education, technology, and industrial development required deeper interpretations, having to do with their values, attitudes, and past policies in human resources and social organization.

Two streams of thought followed from this new context. In the first, globalization was perceived as bringing a new era of prosperity, through the free flows of capital and knowledge. An initial, but shortsighted explanation for the achievements of the "Asian tigers" was purely external: these countries were successful because they had kept their economies open to the international markets, while countries such as India, Brazil, and others did not. However, this explanation was not sufficient. It was necessary to go back to the countries and to try to understand, beyond the circumstances of the Cold War and short-term economic orientations, why some were able to carry internal and external policies that allowed them to reap the benefits of the international economy, making their societies richer and more egalitarian, while others did not. This included some old questions, like their climate and natural resources (Landes 1999), and others not so old, like the way their governments were organized, the extent and quality of public education, the space allowed for free enterprise, how they dealt with science and technology, and the legal, institutional, and cultural conditions for the operation of efficient public administration and modern business enterprises. The World Bank, a central institution in the new global world, has had an important role in fostering this line of inquiry, trying to influence countries to reform their institutions and harvest the benefits that were supposed to flow from the new international scenario.[8]

The second approach was to put the emphasis not on the countries, but on the new international context, described now by the term "globalization," as something different and more overwhelming than the old "internationalization." There is no consensus on what this new globalization actually means; but the starting point is the intense penetration of national societies by all kinds of international networks, associations, institutions, and cultures—financial markets, large multinational companies, nongovernmental organizations, the international media, academic circuits, religious movements, and new international and multilateral institutions, from NATO and the European Union to the Arab League. Globalization is seen as a multidimensional trend, with economic, military, cultural, technological, political, and environmental aspects and consequences, each requiring special attention.[9] A common feature of this second approach is a rebirth, in new clothes, of the old dependency theory: the notion that the global constraints placed on individual countries are too strong to be countered by local policies, and a renewed concern with the need to reform the international order. Instead of the old imperialism and neocolonialism, the culprit is now globalization, with similar consequences and implications.

## History: From Isolation to Global Integration

In spite of the long history of being linked and shaped by international trends and conditions, Brazilians like to think of their country as a relatively isolated entity, and this is more than a simple image or false perception. Two possible explanations are the early decadence of Portugal as a world colonial power, and the country's sheer size. Countries that emerged under the influence of England or France have kept stronger ties with the language, culture, institutions, and business interests of their old metropolis, whether in harmony or in conflict. In Spanish Latin America, Spain remains an important cultural and institutional reference, even if its economic significance is often not very large. For Brazil, however, Portugal is little more than a sentimental memory. The intellectual and cultural contacts Brazilians have had with France, as well as their business links with England, have remained limited to the elites, out of the eyes and perceptions of most of the population.

Size contributed to this relative isolation. Since the sixteenth century, Brazil went through several economic cycles—sugar in the northeast, gold in Minas Gerais, coffee in Minas Gerais and São Paulo—all related to the external markets. As the business cycles evolved and moved from one region to the other, however, expanding the frontier, they left a growing population scattered in a large territory, living mostly in poverty, producing for subsistence and impoverished local markets (Furtado 1963; Prado Júnior 1967; Katzman 1977). Slavery, prevalent until late in the nineteenth century, was replaced by international migration at the turn of the century, which also fueled the expansion of cities such as Rio de Janeiro, São Paulo, and Porto Alegre. Gradually, the internal economy expanded, with the production of food for the internal market, and the beginnings of industrial and services activities around the main urban centers. Early in the twentieth century, when Brazil was the world's leading supplier of coffee and the country was mostly rural, the external sector accounted for almost 35 percent of the country's economic activity. After World War II, however, as the economy grew, the relative size of the external sector shrank, going down to 15 percent or less, with a small rebound in the last years of the Cardoso government (see Figure 6.2).

This relative isolation was reinforced by the social and economic policies that prevailed since the 1930s, which can be broadly described in terms

**Figure 6.2   The Closure of the Brazilian Economy, 1901–2001**

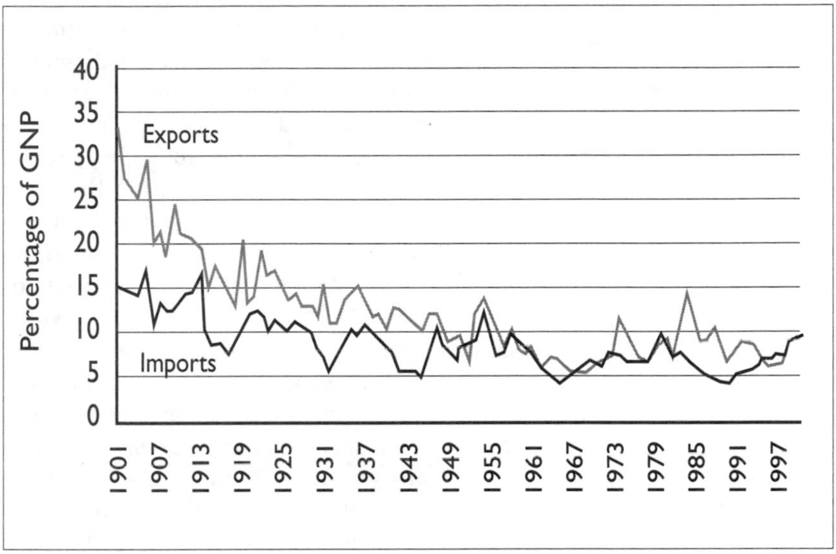

*Source:* I am grateful to Eustáquio Reis for providing the data for this chart.

of conservative modernization and import substitution.[10] Both policies depended on the generation and maintenance of significant revenues from the export of agricultural commodities, providing the government with enough taxes to transfer benefits and subsidize specific sectors and groups. When these resources became insufficient, they were replaced or compensated by inflation or debt.

Conservative modernization meant that industrialization, economic growth, and the advantages of a modern welfare state, which started to gather strength in the 1930s by copying the features of the industrialized and welfare states of Western Europe and the United States, benefited only the more organized sections of urban society in a few regions, leaving aside both the rural population and a growing number of urban settlers without qualifications and stable employment. This political alliance between the modernizing elites in the cities and the traditional oligarchies in the countryside was at the roots of political authoritarianism in so many countries, and Brazil was no exception (Moore 1966).

Import substitution meant that the government, making use of trade barriers, subsidies, and fiscal incentives, favored and supported the development of local industries producing for the internal market, without much need to compete for efficiency or cost. It is true that the most important industrial sector in the country, the automobile industry, has always been owned by some of the world's largest companies—GM, Fiat, Volkswagen, Ford, and Chrysler. Foreign companies were also strong in energy, chemicals, pharmaceuticals, and many other sectors. IBM was always the major supplier of information technology, even in the years of "market reserve" for personal computers. However, these multinational companies had to coexist with a select group of state-owned corporations in oil, electricity, telecommunications, mining, steel production, and others; the Brazilian financial system was dominated by state-owned banks, and closed to foreign firms; high tariff and nontariff barriers protected both the Brazilian and the local branches of multinational companies; and the relative size of external transactions in the economy remained relatively small.

The consequence was that accentuated levels of social and economic inequality came to characterize Brazil. In the main cities in the southeast, a modern society developed, with complex industries, well-financed universities and research centers, well-paid civil servants, and an organized working class enjoying the benefits of job stability, assured retirement, and health care. In the countryside and in small towns, there was little or no social protection, no public services, and no employment except for hard work and little income in extended export plantations, or precarious agricultural production for self-consumption or impoverished local markets. This huge imbalance led to heavy migration from the country to the cities and from the northeast to the south between the 1950s and 1980s, leading to the development of gigantic urban concentrations surrounded by large poverty belts, not only in São Paulo and Rio de Janeiro, but also in Belo Horizonte, Porto Alegre, Curitiba, Salvador, and Recife.

For many years, this combination of political centralization and market protection allowed for economic growth based on cheap labor, the exploitation of natural resources, and growing inflation. In the early 1970s, a period of military rule, Brazil went through a brief period of very rapid economic expansion, providing support to the ambitious project of Ernesto Geisel's government to turn the country into a mid-sized world power in a few years. In the early 1980s, however, the economy stagnated, the ambitious project was shelved, and the military returned power to the civilians.[11] At the end of the decade, the country was approaching hyperinflation, the economy was completely disorganized, and the government, paralyzed. It was time to try different roads.

## Brazil Reenters the Global World:
## Seeking Stability, Trust, and Transparency

Brazil's reentrance into the global world, after so many years of import substitution and relative isolation, is attributed to the first year of Fernando

Collor's presidency, and his description of the cars produced by the Brazilian automobile industry as *carroças*, old mule-driven farm carts. Collor was the first president to be elected in Brazil by popular vote since 1960, bringing an image of youth, renovation, anticorruption, and an attitude that is still very popular in the country, of being "against everything that is there" ("contra tudo o que está aí"). His policies, which ended up in disaster two years later, were to stabilize the currency at any price by freezing the bank assets of the population; to lower tariff and nontariff protection to local industries; and to dismantle the public administration through across-the-board dismissals and budget cuts. Underlying all this, there were elaborate procedures to generate kickback profits for himself and his cronies from all kinds of public contracts and dealings.

The opening of the Brazilian economy to international competition had important impacts in giving the population better access to consumer goods (including food, better cars, personal computers, and household appliances). Economic stabilization, however, required long-term policies that Collor did not have the inclination or competence to implement, and the exposure of his corrupt practices led to his impeachment in 1992, the first time a Brazilian president was deposed under popular pressure, and by legal means.

Collor's impeachment was the first and more dramatic episode in a long sequence of actions and decisions aimed to reduce the high levels of corruption in the Brazilian public sector, a direct consequence of an open press and the strengthening of the judiciary system. Other episodes included the dismantling, in 1993, of the gang of politicians that controlled the budgetary process in the Congress (the so-called "dwarfs of the budget"); the impeachment and arrest of judges and politicians involved in authorizing resources for public works that ended up as deposits in their accounts in Switzerland or the Cayman Islands; the impeachment of the president of the Brazilian Senate; and the closure of agencies such as the Superintendency for the Development of the Amazon Region (SUDAM) and the Superintendency for the Development of the Northeast (SUDENE), well-known sources of political patronage and corruption.

Corrupt behavior among politicians and civil servants is just one aspect of a broader pattern of financial disorganization and inflationary practices that prevailed in Brazil until recently and still remain in many sectors. With public accounts and expenditures out of control, the distinctions between corruption, patronage, and sheer inefficiency are academic at best. From this point of view, the control of extreme forms of public corruption that started with the impeachment of Collor in 1992 can be seen as part of an effort to bring balance, control, and transparency in the use of public resources, which was, arguably, the most important achievement of Fernando Henrique Cardoso's eight years of governance, 1995–2002.

The Cardoso period started, in practice, in 1994, the year before his investiture, with the success of the "Real" plan of economic stabilization, when he was the minister of the economy. Less visible, but probably more important, were the efforts to turn off the valves of irresponsible spending that fueled not only inflation, but the whole workings of Brazil's political system. Achievements in this area include the closure of the state banks, the renegotiation and control of the public debt of states and municipalities, the privatization of large, inefficient, and wasteful public companies, and the new law of fiscal responsibility for governments at all levels. Important administrative and management reforms were required and implemented, starting with the strengthening of the Central Bank, and the production of reliable and transparent public statistics and indicators on the revenues and expenditures of the public sector.[12]

These efforts to reduce irresponsible spending and corruption were an internal response to the unbearable situation that prevailed during the 1980s, leading the country to hyperinflation and the dismantling of the public sector. Many segments in society contributed to this change, including the judiciary, the press, and an active political opposition, but the merits of the financial authorities during the Cardoso period, at the Central Bank and the ministries of economics and planning, cannot be diminished.

These policies of economic equilibrium, transparency, and corruption control had a clear international dimension, since, to increase its presence in the international scene and attract foreign capital, Brazil had to present itself as an honest and clean player. Some of the policies implemented in those years were part of the standard recipes prevailing in international agencies such as the IMF and the World Bank, including the privatization of publicly owned companies, and the efforts to keep the public finances in equilibrium, policies which, in hindsight, are coming under severe criticism.[13] It is a mistake, however, to interpret the effort to organize the economy and make the public sector more efficient and transparent as a simple response to external influences, since they responded to unavoidable internal needs.

## Globalization and the Social Question

How did the policies of the 1990s affect the social conditions of the population? A simplified view of the period was that, as the economy opened up, the waves of globalization destroyed the country's industry, while the shrinking of the public sector led to a fall in the provision of public services, increasing poverty, social inequity, and misery. According to this view, globalization was the main culprit. This, however, is incorrect. It ignores the long years of inflation and institutional disorganization of the previous decade, to which the policies of economic stabilization, the control of public spending, and the opening of the economy tried to respond. It ignores also the substantial gains in several indicators of social well-being that took place in the 1990s (see Table 6.1). The stabilization of the currency in 1994, by itself, meant a very significant increase in the standards of living of the poorest segments, and a reduction of income inequality. As the economy stagnated in subsequent years, some of those gains eroded, but, even so, all the main social indicators improved throughout the decade.

The improvements in these indicators do not necessarily reflect the effects of recent policies, since some of them, such as the increase in life expectancy and the decrease of infant mortality, are continuations of long-term trends. But they disconfirm the notion that the policies of recent years have aggravated the social conditions of the population.

Positive as some of these improvements may be, they are not large enough, and the old problems are being compounded by a new generation of social issues related to urban violence, drug consumption, environmental decay, and the health and social security needs of an aging population. Some of these issues may be related to globalization—the spread of drug consumption, or the global changes in the technologies for services and industry—and there is also a clear global effect in the establishment of priorities as responses to whatever attracts more attention to the world media. There is a clear perception, however, that there is important homework to be done to improve the country's social conditions, which cannot continue to be blamed on the external factors and influences alone. The first step in this homework is to look at the facts, and, from there, to consider the policies that are being implemented or proposed.

**Table 6.1   Brazil: Main Social Indicators, 1991–2001**

|  |  | 1992 | 1995 | 1999 | 2001 |
|---|---|---|---|---|---|
| **People** |  |  |  |  |  |
| Life expectancy at birth | Men | 62.4 |  | 64.6 | 65.1 |
|  | Women | 70.1 |  | 72.3 | 72.9 |
| Infant mortality | per thousand | 43.0 |  | 34.6 |  |
| Cannot read or write | 15 years old or more | 17.2% | 15.6% | 12.9% | 12.4% |
| **Households** | Water from public supply | 68.1% | 71.1% | 76.0% | 77.6% |
|  | Public sewage system | 46.1% | 48.1% | 52.8% | 59.2% |
|  | Color TV | 46.7% | 60.9% | 79.7% | 83.0% |
|  | Refrigerator | 71.3% | 74.8% | 82.8% | 85.1% |
|  | Freezer | 12.2% | 15.4% | 19.6% | 18.2% |
|  | Washing machine | 24.0% | 26.6% | 32.8% | 33.7% |
|  | Fixed telephone | 18.9% | 22.3% | 37.5% | 51.0% |
|  | Cell phone |  |  |  | 31.0% |

*Source:* Instituto Brasileiro de Geografia e Estadística (2002).

*Poverty and Equity*

How many paupers are there in Brazil, how many are suffering from hunger, discrimination, and destitution? What is the situation regarding income inequality?

Brazil does not have an official poverty line, and the different estimates on the number of "indigents" and "paupers" in the country vary anywhere from 10 to 45 million people. There is no problem of widespread hunger in the traditional sense, as when food cannot be obtained and the population starves. On the contrary, Brazil is one of the world's largest producers of agricultural products, and very few persons are cut off from the internal markets. There are, however, millions with very little or no monetary income, the assumption being that they cannot afford to buy the minimum levels of food in the quantity and quality needed for their survival. In periods of drought, serious situations of deprivation can affect the peasant population in the Brazilian northeast, requiring prompt relief.

The main picture can be seen in Figure 6.3, based on the National Household Survey of 2001.[14] Ten percent of the families report a per capita income of around 40 to 50 cents per person per day, well below the World Bank poverty line of one dollar per person per day. Another 10 percent has about 90 cents. In the rural areas, 27 percent of the population is in the

**Figure 6.3    Household Income per Capita, in U.S. Dollars (by income deciles)**

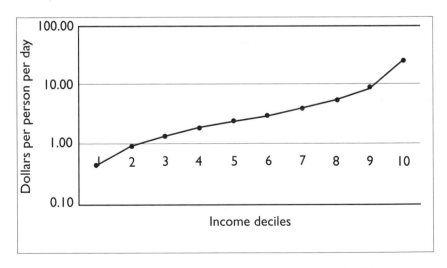

*Source:* Instituto Brasileiro de Geografia e Estadística (1992, 1995, 1999, 2001).

lower income bracket, and another 14 percent in the second lowest (see Figure 6.4). Since there is no systematic information on the nutrition conditions of the population, complex calculations are sometimes made to estimate the links between specific income levels and food consumption; but they are all subject to too many assumptions and interpretations to be taken literally (Rocha 2000).

A usual indication of income inequality is the Gini index, which varies from zero (everybody has the same income) to one hundred (one person has the whole income of a country or region). According to this index, Brazil had a Gini index of 59.1 in 1997, close to the level of Nicaragua (60.3), South Africa (59.3), and Honduras (59.0), and well above those of Japan (24.9), Italy (27.3), Mexico (51.9), and Chile (57.5) (U.S. Government 2002).These indexes are not the result of short-term policies, but the consequence of long-term conditions and trends. Figure 6.5 gives a more intuitive indication of the way income distribution has evolved in recent years. Historically, the added income of the richest 1 percent of the population has been higher than the added income of the 50 percent poorest. Data from the 1990s show a gradual improvement in this situation. It is important to note that these figures refer to income from work, and do not include differences in assets and wealth, on one hand, or on entitlements of different kinds, on

**Figure 6.4     Distribution of the Population by Income Deciles (by area of residence)**

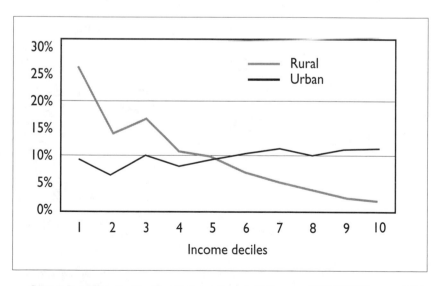

*Source:* Data from the Brazilian National Household Surveys (PNAD/IBGE, prepared by DIEESE (Departamento Intersindical de Estatística e Estudos Sócio-Econômicos). DIEESE (2002).

the other. They result from the high differences in economic development among Brazilian regions, and urban and rural settlers, and, mostly, from the large differences in revenues for people with different levels of formal education.

In the past, poverty and income inequality were seen as consequences of economic underdevelopment, bound to disappear as the economy improved. Now, it is clear that widely different levels of poverty and inequity are compatible with the same levels of economic development and require prompt actions. These actions, in turn, can be of three kinds. One is to redirect the existing social spending so that it benefits those with more needs. The second is to provide direct resources and support to the poorest, whether through cash, food baskets, food stamps, or other means. The third is to try to deal with the variables that are most likely to have a direct effect on the living conditions and earnings of the population—education, employment, credit, and access to land and property.

**Figure 6.5    Distribution of Income from Personal Work, 1988–1999**

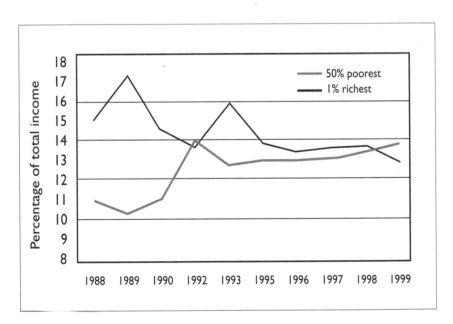

*Source:* Data from the Brazilian National Household Surveys (PNAD/IBGE, prepared by DIEESE (Departamento Intersindical de Estatística e Estudos Sócio-Econômicos). DIEESE (2002).

## Redistributive, Compensatory, and Remedial Policies

Ideally, the conditions of the poor should be improved without affecting the usually meager benefits already enjoyed by many segments of the middle classes. The fact, however, is that it has been impossible to increase social spending further without jeopardizing the need to keep the public sector in equilibrium. Social spending in Brazil is already high by international standards—about 20 percent of GNP, much higher than Chile (13.4 percent) and Mexico (13.1 percent)—and remained so during the 1990s (Fernandes, Rocha et al. 1998; Fernandes, Oliveira et al. 1998). Most of this spending is on retirement benefits, and is highly regressive. Estimations based on the Brazilian Institute for Geography and Statistics (IBGE) Living Standards Survey of 1996–1997 show that only about 13 percent of the social spending goes to the lower-income segments (Amsberg, Lanjuow, and Nead 2000). A program-by-program analysis made by Ricardo Paes e Barros and colleagues found that public expenditures in preschool and primary education are well focused on the poor; but pensions, unemployment insurance, and maternal, secondary, and higher education are strongly regressive (Barros and Foguel 2000). Public health expenditures are also very regressive: most public health care is delivered by private providers, but paid by the government. Since most of the private resources and equipment are in the richest regions and cities, their citizens get much better health care than those living in poorer areas. For private expenditures, a comparison between data from 1987 and 1996 showed that, in spite of the good purposes of the universalization and decentralization of public health promoted by the Brazilian Constitution of 1988, they are more regressive today than they were ten years ago (Médici 2002).

The need to reduce expenditures benefiting civil servants and other middle sectors is not just a question of social justice, but a crucial part of the effort to bring the public budget under control. Changes in expenditure levels or in the focalization of these programs, however, would affect the interests of highly organized and vocal groups. They could also lead to confrontations or be blocked by the judiciary, given the Brazilian tradition to consider "acquired rights" as not amenable to change. The Cardoso government was able to pass legislation reducing some outlandish benefits for civil servants, without, however, bringing the system under control or making it less regressive. The Lula government made a strong commitment to redress the inequities in the social-security system, going beyond what his predecessor was able to achieve.

While social spending is not increased or redirected, governments have started with policies and programs to deliver some resources to needy (or not so needy) segments of the population. Examples are the *bolsa-escola,* a program to provide cash to families with young children on the condition that they send them to school, adopted by the federal government and several municipalities and state administrations; *bolsa-alimentação,* a subsidy given to poor pregnant and nursing mothers; a subsidy for the acquisition of cooking gas; a program for the eradication of child labor; and several others. Many states and municipalities have followed suit, with, for instance, the *renda cidadã* in São Paulo and the *cheque cidadão* in Rio de Janeiro, a program to handle cash subsidies to families through evangelical churches. Several million people receive these benefits each month but, since these programs are not coordinated, there is no information on possible overlaps, proper coverage, etc.[15]

Another initiative was to try to stimulate welfare initiatives of the population, through donations and the mobilization of voluntary organizations and religious groups. The Cardoso government, with the leadership of the first lady, created a program of community work and solidarity *(comunidade solidária)* to bring together government and civil society, with activities targeted to the poorest segments in the countryside and in the periphery of the large cities. In the absence of assessments, it is difficult to know the real impact of these programs, but it is unlikely that, by themselves, they could have changed the general conditions of poverty and social inequity in a significant way.

The government of Luis Inácio Lula da Silva started with a high-profile "program against hunger," to make sure that all Brazilians could be assured of having at least three healthy meals a day. This program is supposed to dramatize his government's commitment to deal with the problems of poverty and inequity, and to compensate for its conservative economic policies. As of this writing, the details of this program are still being worked out, but some of the key components can be identified. They include the distribution of money to the poor to acquire food (either through food coupons or magnetic cards), education programs to teach the population about nutrition needs, incentives for the production of foodstuffs, and the mobilization of society to control the implementation of the program and the proper use of these resources. From the beginning, this program has been mired in controversy and criticized for its lack of focus and overlap with other social programs. There are several proposals to unify and simplify the current dispersion and overlap of social programs into one integrated program of minimum income, or negative income tax, and, for some of its critics, the "program against hunger" seems to be a step backward from this point of view.[16]

## Employment

The opening of the economy was feared to have a serious impact on the job market, by shrinking the industrial sector and increasing the number of people working in informal, short-term occupations. Some of these effects did occur, but not on the scale that is often proclaimed. During the 1990s, about 13 million persons were added to the labor force, mostly to the services sector. Industrial employment did not increase, and agricultural employment fell sharply (see Figure 6.6). Already in 1992, more than half of the workers, 56 percent, did not contribute to social security, meaning that they did not have regular job contracts, and were not entitled to benefits such as unemployment insurance, regular vacations, paid retirement, etc. (see Figure 6.7). There was a slight improvement in this situation to 54 percent by 2001. Open unemployment, the percentage of active workers temporarily out of work, grew by about 3 percent in the period, from 6.5 to 9.4 percent.[17]

There is a clear association between the stagnation of industrial employment and the opening of the economy, which led to intense capitalization and higher productivity in the industrial sector (Rossi Júnior and Ferreira 1999). One of the standard assumptions regarding globalization is that we are now in a new "knowledge economy," heavily dependent on

**Figure 6.6    Distribution of Economic Activities in Brazil, 1992–2001**

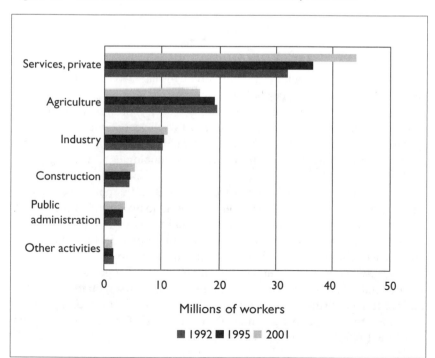

**Figure 6.7    Occupation of the Brazilian Population, 1992–2001**

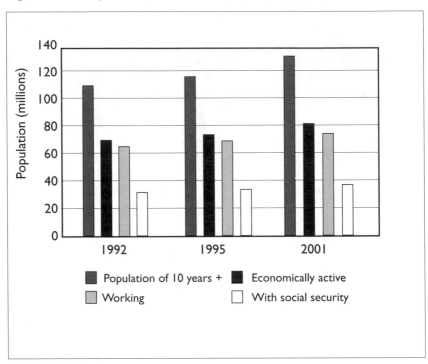

qualified manpower, making obsolete other forms of industrial production and the provision of services based on routine and unskilled work. It is true that, in recent years, the labor markets have been more favorable to those with more educational credentials, but most of the economic activities and employment opportunities that exist in Brazil and other Latin American countries are still based on more traditional technologies and arrangements (Schwartzman 2002).

The large number of informal workers in Brazil is not a consequence of the growth of the knowledge economy and globalization, but the persistence of an old condition related to the combination of low education and the high overhead costs and bureaucratic complications for establishing formal working contracts, which small firms try to avoid. Most self-employed workers, and about half the employers, do not pay social security of any kind. Making labor contracts more amenable to negotiation, and less subject to administrative oversight and legal disputes, could bring welfare protection to more people and increase the tax basis for the welfare system (Pastore 1998; Camargo and Urani 1996; Amadeo, Gill, and Neri 2000).

The Cardoso government tried to introduce some timid changes in the labor legislation, but they were strongly resisted by the unions and the opposition parties. The Lula government has promised to move forward with these reforms.

A special chapter in the area of employment is agrarian reform, an issue with a very high profile, thanks to the mobilization skills of the leaders of the Movement of the Landless Workers (Movimento dos Trabalhadores Rurais Sem Terra) and their supporters. The problem seems to be straightforward: there are many people without land, and too much land in a few hands. If land were distributed to the landless, family agriculture would develop, urban overcrowding would recede, and poverty would be reduced. In fact, most Brazilians already live in urban areas and, barring Cambodia, there are no examples of massive returns of populations from urban to rural areas. Familiar agriculture still exists, but tends to be unproductive and bound to shrink still further due to competition from agribusiness and the lures of urban life. The Fernando Henrique government is supposed to have settled about half a million peasants, at an estimated cost of 40,000 reais, or about US$12,000 per settlement; and there is strong evidence that most of these settlements are unable to sustain themselves. Given the high subsidies implied in this policy, there are reasons to wonder whether these resources could have been put to better use (Graziano 2003a).

## Education

If the economy does not create enough jobs, and the rigidity of the labor market cannot be changed, is it possible to improve employment through better education of the labor force? In the long range, probably yes. On short notice, however, it is not very likely. There is in Brazil a large fund named Fundo de Amparo ao Trabalhador (FAT), based on taxes levied on the country's firms, that can reach several billion dollars a year. Part of this fund is used by the National Development Bank to finance its operations; part is used for the payment of unemployment benefits; and part for an ambitious program to retrain the work force. FAT is administered by the Ministry of Labor and a council of participating business and trade union organizations, with decisions taken by consensus. Endowed with generous resources that are transferred to labor unions, universities, nongovernmental organizations, and other institutions, the program became an obvious instrument for political mobilization and patronage; but its impact and efficiency in reducing unemployment and improving the quality of the country's work force is still to be demonstrated.[18]

In formal education, illiteracy seems to be a serious problem, and has been given top priority by the Luis Inácio Lula da Silva government.

However, depending on how illiteracy is defined, it might not be so. The simplest information on illiteracy in Brazil is the answer, in the household surveys, of whether the person "can read and write." Most illiterates in Brazil, according to this definition, are older persons living in the poorest regions, and not many of them are likely to benefit from literacy campaigns and incorporate reading and writing habits into their daily lives. The other large group is the children that have still not learned at seven or eight. By the age of fourteen, illiteracy is limited to 2.5 percent of the population (see Figure 6.8).

Functional illiteracy, however, is another matter. There are strong indications that many students remain for many years in school without acquiring the basic literacy and numeracy skills. The key education problems in Brazil are the quality of public education, for the children who are already there, and the provision of basic education to adolescents and young adults who have dropped out of school.

The most important achievements in education of recent years were probably at the basic and secondary levels. The Brazilian constitution determines that the federal government should spend 18 percent of its resources on education, and state and local governments, 25 percent. A National Fund for Basic Education (FUNDEF) was established to make

**Figure 6.8     Illiteracy, by Age**

sure that this money is actually spent on education and to establish a floor, through compensations, for public expenditures per student and per teacher for the whole country. One of the effects of FUNDEF was to stimulate the involvement of local municipalities with basic education, reducing the size and bureaucracy of state education administrations. A traditional research institution within the Ministry of Education, the National Institute for Education Research, was reinvigorated and became responsible for the reorganization of Brazil's education statistics and the implementation of three large systems of education assessment—the Assessment System for Basic Education (SAEB), the National Examination for Secondary Education, and the national examinations for undergraduate course programs, known as Provão. Other policies included the development of new contents of basic and secondary education, and the improvement of several programs to transfer resources directly from the central government to the schools—schoolbooks, lunch, and cash.[19]

These actions, combined with programs implemented by the state secretaries of education in many regions, led to an increase in enrollments in preschool, fundamental, and secondary education, and to reductions in stu-

**Figure 6.9    School Enrollment by Age and Gender, 2001**

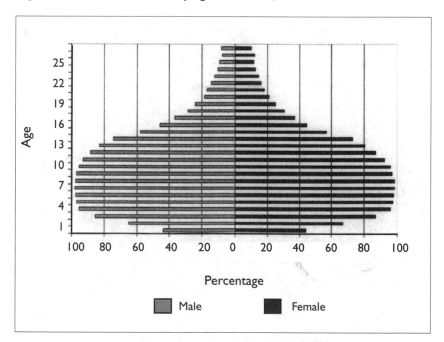

*Source:* Instituto Brasileiro de Geografia e Estatística (1992, 1995, 1999, 2001).

dent retention, more resources for teacher training and salaries, and more equipment and resources for schools. Today, practically all students aged seven to ten attend some kind of school (see Figure 6.9).

As seen in Figure 6.10, most youngsters between ages fifteen and seventeen are still not in secondary education. Because of retention, there are about 7 million students in basic education that are older than the reference group, and should not be there (giving a gross enrollment rate of 121 percent) (Figure 6.11). One consequence of this is that there is at least a 21 percent waste in the expenditures for basic education, which could otherwise be used to make the system better. In secondary education, about half the students are eighteen years or older, and should have already graduated. In higher education, which still matriculates only 9 percent of the age cohort, about half of the students are of age twenty-five or older. These distortions are related to a tradition of bad quality that limits the students' ability to learn, as revealed by SAEB and other assessments (Crespo, Soares, and Mello e Souza 2000), and generates high dropout rates as the young get into adolescence.

**Figure 6.10    School Enrollment of the Brazilian Population, by Age Groups**

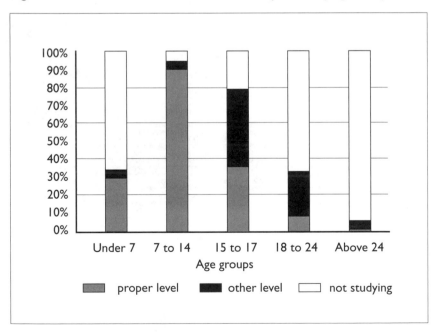

*Source:* Instituto Brasileiro de Geografia e Estatística (1992, 1995, 1999, 2001).

**Figure 6.11    Education Coverage in Brazil, 2001 (by education levels)**

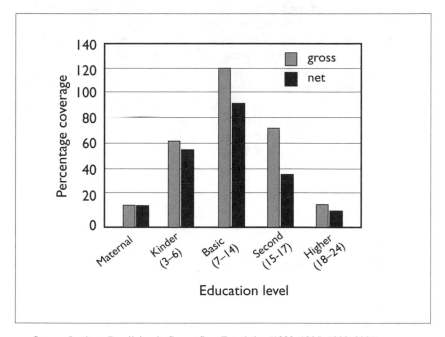

*Source:* Instituto Brasileiro de Geografia e Estatística (1992, 1995, 1999, 2001).

Achievements in higher education were less significant. Brazil has good graduate education and many well-recognized universities and professional schools, but the whole system is highly regressive, and unable to cope with the growing demand. The Brazilian federal government is responsible for an expensive network of public universities, which enrolls, however, only about 20 percent of the student body. Some other states, notably São Paulo, have their own universities, and there is a large private sector catering mostly to lower-income and working students through evening courses, and attending to about 70 percent of the student body. The high costs of public institutions are caused mostly by the salaries and retirement benefits of their academic and administrative staff, all civil servants endowed with job stability and early, fully paid retirement,[20] and by the maintenance of their teaching hospitals, which fill in, in practice, for the absence of adequate public hospitals in many places. These institutions are not free to establish their own salary scales, are not free to hire or dismiss staff, cannot charge tuition, have difficulty selling other kinds of services (like consulting, extension work, and technical assistance), and are not able or required to care for the efficient use of their resources. It may seem obvious that universities should not be organized as branches of the civil service, but as autonomous organizations entitled to manage their human and financial assets with flexibility; that governments should finance public higher education according to clear standards of efficiency and social needs; and that the private beneficiaries of higher education should also contribute to their costs. All these issues, however, are very contentious and political, and the Cardoso government was unable to introduce significant changes in this sector. The relationships between the teachers' and civil servants' unions and the Laborers' Party have been much more friendly, and there is hope that the current government will be able to face the problems of higher education without so much opposition.

## Deprived Sectors

The Cardoso government was also open to the demands and pressures coming from all kinds of nongovernmental and international organizations and movements, in Brazil and abroad—against racial discrimination, child labor, and police violence; for the protection of the Amazon rain forest; in favor of the Indian population, in support for women's rights, on behalf of gays and lesbians, and others. The Lula government is at least as open, if not more so. Each of these issues is important, and it is to the merit of these organizations and movements to have brought them to the foreground. At the same time, in a global world, they have the tendency to become national and international media events, with two consequences: they become simplified, in yes-or-no terms, and they may be given a priority that is not always justified. Two examples, race and child labor, can be mentioned to illustrate this problem.

The Brazilian statistical office collects information on the population "color," as a proxy for race: "white," "yellow" (now divided into native Brazilians and Orientals), "blacks," and "*pardos*" (mulattos).[21] On average, these last two segments, 44.6 percent of the population, come out as worse off than the white 53.7 percent in all indicators of income, welfare, and social opportunity. Racial discrimination may play a part in these differences, but it is not likely to be the most important factor, given the absence of a history of racial segregation, on one hand, and, on the other, the strong correlations between skin color and less access to good education, among other indicators of social deprivation. It would seem that policies aiming at improving the living conditions and opportunities of the poor would be the best approach to deal with racial inequality, without having to discriminate and stratify society according to racial lines, which, differently from the United States, are blurred and indistinct (Schwartzman 1999). The globalization of the race issue, stimulated by institutions such as the Ford Foundation, may have had the positive effect of bringing the question to the spotlight, but may have displaced the attention to secondary questions such as the introduction of racial quotas in higher education, favored by both the last and the current governments, without much consideration for their true need, as well as for the effectiveness and negative implications of such policies.

Regarding child labor, household surveys and censuses show the existence of several million children in Brazil doing some kind of work, most of them as part of their families' activities in rural areas. Usually, they work part time, and, statistically, working or not working has only a marginal effect on school attendance (Schwartzman 2001). Policies are clearly needed to take homeless children out of the streets, to prevent the abusive and exploitative types of child labor, and to provide better school opportunities and financial incentives to stimulate families to bring them to school. However, the dominant image of millions of children selling caramels or begging in the city streets, or working ten hours a day in sweatshops, or harvesting sugar cane, is distorted. This global image, enforced by the powerful pictures of Sebastião Salgado and institutions such as UNICEF and the International Labor Organization, has led to legislation forbidding child work in any circumstances, which is clearly unenforceable and counterproductive in many cases,[22] without addressing the real needs of important segments of the population. The largest child labor problem in Brazil, which does not gather headlines, are the millions of girls working as maids in private homes without any kind of protection or policies to relieve them from this condition.

These are very sensitive issues, emotionally charged and always controversial. When they appear as media events, the usual response from governments, from a public relations point of view, is to create other media events—to establish a working group, to create an agency, to sign a decree, to send a law to Congress, to start a legal procedure against someone. These responses, however, seldom lead to meaningful results.

## Social Policies for the New Millennium: An Emerging Consensus?

On balance, it is misleading to say, with Stiglitz, that because of globalization, "little if any progress has been made in reducing inequality [in Latin America], already the highest of any region of the world, and the percentages, let alone numbers, in poverty actually increased. Unemployment, already high, has increased by three percentage points" (Stiglitz 2002b). In the case of Brazil, at least, the picture is not as bleak, and the explanation has less to do with globalization than with the government's inability to redirect social spending and to implement better social policies. If the international scenario had been more favorable, the economy would be in better shape, and the government would have had more leeway to introduce social reforms without affecting so many interests. As it happened, the international context was not favorable, the government did not implement the reforms, and the country became much more vulnerable to the kind of crisis of confidence that took place in 2002. After the bad experiences of the 1990s, there is hope that the workings of global markets and global institutions will improve. However, they will not preclude active and well-conceived domestic policies to deal with problems of poverty and social equity.

A significant consensus is being built among Brazilian analysts about the causes and policies needed to confront the country's problems of poverty and inequity. It is clear that poverty is associated with the low quality and instability of the jobs available for the poorest and less educated segments of the population; that poverty and inequity would not disappear just through economic growth, requiring specific and well-focused policies; that social spending in Brazil is regressive and inefficient; and that it should be possible to do much better with the existing resources. The reduction of poverty and inequity is no longer seen as a weight or cost placing limits on economic growth, but, on the contrary, as an important instrument in bringing the Brazilian economy to new levels of economic performance. It is also part of this consensus that those in extreme conditions of poverty and need should not wait for the economy to grow or the social policies to improve, but rather require prompt assistance and support.[23]

There were, however, some important differences in perception and propositions along two interrelated main dimensions, one having to do with resources, the other related to social participation and mobilization. Regarding the first, there are those who hold that, instead of cutting expenses or redirecting social spending, it would be possible to increase public expenditures by raising the minimum wage, extending social-security benefits, investing more on public services, developing industrial policies for the production of goods for the popular markets, providing cheap loans for housing construction, and so forth (Medeiros 2002). These proposals have an unmistakable Keynesian flavor in assuming that the increase in the flow and distribution of resources would generate new demands for goods and services, thus stimulating economic growth. They have the additional advantage of not threatening the vested interests of unions and civil servants. Holders of the other view are skeptical about the possibility of raising public expenditures without fueling inflation, but more optimistic about the possibility of improving the quality and efficiency of social spending and of stimulating the economy through administrative and legal reforms, to allow for a more efficient and healthy market environment. For them, the new policies for economic growth and social equity should be geared to stimulate private initiative, to continuous efforts in the improvement of education, and an upgrade in the government's ability to use existing resources. This would entail the completion of the "first generation" of social reforms—social security, the labor market, and the tax system (Werneck 2002)—and a series of "second generation" reforms, including the streamlining of the judiciary, changes in the capital market and in property laws, better access to credit, better regulation and decentralization in the management of public services, and so forth (Instituto de Estudos do Trabalho e Sociedade and Urani 2002; Lisboa 2002).

The second dimension opposes two visions about the way society should be organized—one more individualistic, the other more collectivist. In the first vision, society should be formed by free and independent citizens, and it is the role of government to provide equal opportunities for each to exert her or his personal freedom and individual choices. The other vision wants to have society as a strong and integrated body of committed citizens, conscious of their collective responsibilities and duties, and working in tandem for the common good. Collective action takes precedence over administrative rationality, and political commitment prevails over technical competence.[24] For the holders of the first vision, social policies should be simple and automatic, with the minimum possible intervention of public bureaucracies, political parties, and social organizations and movements. Part of this view voices the concern with improving the efficiency of state bureaucracy, and the reliance on expert knowledge to identify problems, set priorities, and assess the outcomes. For the holders of the second view, who approach the social question from a strong moral and often religious perspective, political mobilization and communal solidarity are essential, not only to release the power and energy of social participation, but also to restrain and limit the bad effects of individualism and egotism.

It is not difficult to identify these beliefs in the attitudes and behavior of specific intellectuals, political parties, and social movements, but it would be incorrect to map the members and supporters of the previous government entirely on one side, and the members and supporters of the current government entirely on the other. The interplay and disputes between these two views on how society should be led and organized will continue for the years to come within all social and political segments. The country's ability to deal properly with its problems of poverty and inequity hinges largely on the way these philosophical orientations will play out. The international context of globalization will always set limits and affect what the country can do, but ultimately it is on the domestic front that the battle for economic progress and social equity will be won or lost.

## Notes

This text was originally prepared for the project "Getting Globalization Right: The Dilemma of Inequality," coordinated by the Woodrow Wilson International Center for Scholars. I am grateful to Bolivar Lamounier, Gary Bland, and Joseph Tulchin for comments and suggestions on an earlier draft of this chapter.

1. For an earlier overview, see Schwartzman (2000).

2. For instance, several institutions associated with the PT, including the Central Labor Union (CUT) and religious groups, supported a national plebiscite, carried on through a signatures campaign, on whether Brazil should or not pay its external debt. Not surprisingly, 90 percent of those consulted (about 5 million persons, or 5 percent of the electorate) agreed that the debt should not be paid without being submitted to a process of "public auditing." For the stand of CUT on the matter, see http://www.cut-sc.org.br/tp1_plebis.htm; for the results, see http://www.jubileu2000.hpg.ig.com.br/resultado/Tabperg2.doc.

3. For a bibliographical essay on the economic, social, and political conditions of Brazilian independence, see Bethell and Carvalho (1984). For the special role of England in the period, see Manchester (1964). For the slave trade, see Bethell (1970) and Klein (1999). For the freemen in the cities and the countryside, see Mattoso (1988) and Franco (1969).

4. This was the period when social scientists in Latin America were doing research and writing about "marginality," a concern coming both from the political left and from the "progressive" sectors of the Catholic Church. See, among others, Vekemans, Silva Fuenzalida, and Giusti B (1970) and Germani (1972).

5. A very influential author in the nationalist vein was Hélio Jaguaribe. See, among others, Jaguaribe (1966).

6. See Cardoso and Faletto (1969). In a highly critical overview of the *dependencia* movement, Robert Packenham argued that the original thesis had been the work of Andrew Gunder Frank; but Frank also drew on existing sources (Packenham 1992). Previous works on dependency include Pinto (1960); Fanon (1961); Lambert (1963); Frank (1967). For a personal testimony on Prebisch and the earlier work of the Economic Commission of Latin America, see "A dinâmica do sistema centro-periferia" in Furtado (1985).

7. Since the 1970s, a growing body of literature comparing Brazil and Korea emerged. See, among others, Looney (1975); Frieden (1981); Dahlman and Sercovich (1984).

8. This is evident from the subjects of most of the Bank's "World Development Reports" since the 1990s: poverty (1990), health (1993), infrastructure (1994), employment (1995), planning and markets (1996), the state (1997), knowledge (1998/1999).

9. A quick survey on the Library of Congress catalog found 1,177 books with "globalization" in their titles. For a good summary of the globalization issues in all these dimensions, as applied to environmental issues, see Viola (1996).

10. For detailed history of economic policies in Brazil in the twentieth century, with special emphasis on the links between internal and external conditions, see the several articles in Abreu (1990). On conservative modernization, see Schwartzman (1988) and Reis (1990); on import substitution, see Tavares (1972); on the origins of Brazil's welfare state, see Dean (1969) and Gomes and Araújo (1989).

11. See, for a summary and interpretation of the economic developments in this period, Fishlow (2000).

12. However, due perhaps to the constraints of the 1988 Constitution, the Cardoso government did not advance much in the reorganization of the public sector, compared with the achievements of Minister Hélio Beltrão during the military regime (Brasil Ministério do Planejamento 2002; Oliveira 1984).

13. Joseph Stiglitz: "The first true test of these policies [of the Washington Consensus], when the countries were freed from the shackles of overhanging debt, helps explain the sense of disillusionment. Growth during that decade was just over half of what it was during the pre-reform and pre-crisis decades of the 1950s, 1960s, and 1970s. Even in those countries which have seen significant growth, a disproportionate share of the gains have gone to the better off, the upper 30%, or even the upper 10%, with many of the poor actually becoming worse off." (Stiglitz 2002b). See also, for a premonition of the problems to come, Dornbusch and Cardoso (1988).

14. These are monetary earnings from work of all family members in the household, divided by the number of family members irrespective of age, as reported to the National Household Survey. It does not include transfers and nonmonetary gains, common in the rural areas. The exchange rate of 2.3 reais per dollar, current at the time of the survey, was adopted. This survey does not include the population living the rural areas of the Northern region. Households that reported no income whatsoever (estimated at 820,000) were excluded from the calculations.

15. See, for an overview and a careful evaluation of a small *bolsa-escola* program in the city of Recife, Lavinas, Barbosa, and Tourinho (2001). The assessment finds, among other things, that thanks to the careful targeting and the links established by the program between the grantees and the local schools, it was possible to increase attendance of students who would otherwise have dropped out.

16. The most well-known but by no means only promoter of a minimum-income program has been the Laborers' Party senator Eduardo Matarazzo Suplicy. See Suplicy (2002) and Carmargo and Ferreira (2001).

17. These rates are from the yearly household surveys—PNAD—and are known to be systematically higher than the figures produced by IBGE's monthly employment surveys—PME—adopted until recently. Both, in turn, are about half the figures produced according to the methodology adopted by São Paulo's SEADE Foundation, which works with a broader definition of unemployment.

18. For attempts to evaluate FAT, see Brasil Ministério do Trabalho (1998). The main achievements described in this document are institutional and ideological, not educational or professional. See also Rios-Neto and Oliveira (2000) and Barros, Andrade, and Perrelli (2000).

19. See, for official overview, Brasil Ministério da Educação and Secretaria de Educação Fundamental (2002).

20. Because of uniform, nationwide careers and salary scales, the costs for the government are high, but salaries paid to the more qualified staff are well below expectations, generating frustration and dissatisfaction on both sides.

21. The figures for the 2000 census were: white, 53.74 percent; black, 6.21 percent; Orientals, 0.45 percent; *pardos*, 38.45 percent; indigenous population, 0.43 percent; and without information, 0.71 percent.

22. For instance, for the young person who leaves basic school at fourteen, but is forbidden to do any kind of work until he is sixteen, a proper combination of work and study can make more sense than the blank prohibition to work.

23. An important contribution for this consensus was the work of economists, demographers, statisticians, and sociologists at IPEA, the Brazilian Institute for Geography and Statistics, the University of Campinas, Fundação SEADE, Getúlio

Vargas Foundation, the Catholic University in Rio de Janeiro, and other institutions. For a collection of papers, see Henriques (2000).

24. Aaron Wildavsky, following the work of Mary Douglas, has described these two orientations as contrasting cultures, or "ways of life," generated by different combinations of group cohesion and social hierarchy (Thompson, Ellis, and Wildavsky 1990). See also Schwartzman (1997: chap. 4).

# 7

# Mexico: Globalization and Democracy

## *Ilán Bizberg*

Although globalization is often spoken of as a homogeneous process that produces similar effects everywhere, this is obviously not the case. Each country has a particular economic structure that modifies the manner in which globalization affects it. The impacts of globalization on a country pass through economic, social, and political mediations; it does not simply impose itself on countries. One crucial mediation is that of government elites. According to Bruno Theret, globalization is not a phenomenon merely endured by the state, but is instrumentalized in terms of a strategy of government elites. In most countries in the developed world, but also in countries such as Mexico, governmental elites had seen their capacity for action strictly curtailed through the engagements implied by the welfare state, giving governments a low margin for financial maneuvering: most resources and the capacity for decisionmaking were established in advance by engagements in terms of education, social security, pensions, etc., directed toward different sectors of society. The political elites that, in the 1970s, took power almost everywhere in the world were imbued with the current neoliberal ideology, and modified it into a discourse on the ineluctability of globalization. The neoliberal project of reducing the weight of the state, which meant getting rid of its constraints, found an ally in the forces of globalization to weaken opposition to the transformation of the welfare state. In this sense, globalization substituted neoliberalism as an ideology to become a strategy of the new political elites (Theret 2001). This means that politics is crucial to understanding the way in which globalization translates through politics into economic constraints in each particular country, depending on the manner in which it is supported or resisted by the national elites and other social forces.

Most of the literature that deals with the influence of politics on the economic transition examines how the new economic model is either sustained by a new coalition of social forces or blocked by political interest groups that were formed in the old economic system (Nelson 1993; Kingston 1999; Eliot Armijo 1999; Starr 1999). By merely asking about the obstacles to the implementation of the new economic model, this literature leaves unquestioned the characteristics of the neoliberal reforms, which are not applied in the same manner everywhere. It does not draw all the possible implications of politics on economy. Politics is not only about the government's capacity, or lack thereof, to implement a preestablished economic model, but it is even more important as a factor that determines the characteristics of the economic model itself. This is because an economic model is not construed in advance: it does not exist in "pure" form, it has no inbred coherence, but like any social construct it is constituted by the action of society upon the economic structure. Politics is fundamental for determining the possibility of establishing a consensus about the new economic model, for assuring its coherence. Coherence of the model does not mean the "pureness" in which it is applied, as most governmental elites would insist, but rather the capacity of a society to negotiate the new economic model in terms that are both socially acceptable and economically viable. Any economic model has social impacts, both in terms of costs and gains, of winners and losers. Politics and its effects on the economy are thus also related to the capacity of the different social sectors to organize and represent their interests. These are the types of questions that are central for the "institutional school" and for the French "regulationist school."

In his well-known study, J. M. Maravall asks a fundamental question relating to politics and economics. He asks whether authoritarian regimes are more efficient economically, as is often thought, in that such regimes have a greater capacity to impose a definite economic policy. The opposite idea is that democratic governments are more inefficient reforming economies. It is true that where "the State dominates civil society and restricts rights and liberties, governments have a greater capacity to carry out their decisions" (Maravall 1997: 19). Nevertheless, he continues to say that although this dominance assures that a government is capable of applying a certain economic policy, this does not ensure that it is the most appropriate policy; in fact, on the contrary, a more predatory policy is probable. "Dictatorships possess greater independence from organized interests, but the power they exercise is also more arbitrary and discretional" (p. 19). They are thus more prone to predation and less capable of reacting to signs that tell them their policies are wrong. This idea thus comes from a very crude conception not only of politics, but also of what is economically efficient. Citing Douglass North, Maravall proposes that "democratic institutions are those best able to restrict the state's predatory instincts in the name of general interest . . . due to the incentives resulting from political competition, they also transmit the most efficient preferences and decisions better than authoritarian institutions do" (North 1990, in Maravall 1997: 30).

What the institutionalist school tells us is what Maravall speaks about when he cites Gourevitch in that "policies need politics" (North 1990, in Maravall 1997: 37). In an article comparing the economic performance of North America with that of Latin America, North, Summerhill, and Weingast draw the relationship between politics and economics. The reason why the United States became the richest economy of the world is closely related to the fact that it created a stable political democracy. The institutional foundations defined by the U.S. Constitution and a stable and well-specified system of economic and political rights allowed for a credible social contract, a necessary prerequisite for efficient economic markets (North, Summerhill, and Weingast 2002: 9–59). Although political order can be based on both coercion and consensus, social cooperation producing consensus, according to these authors, produces the most efficient societies in economic terms. The consensual order is founded on four principles. First, there must exist a sufficient agreement among the citizenry of a country that their political institutions are desirable; the disposition of citizens to live by the decisions taken by those institutions and their predisposition to defend these institutions against their abuse by political positions implies the creation of a system of shared beliefs (pp. 48 and 18). Second, successful societies are those that are able to establish institutions that limit the scope of political decisions, something that is achieved through a constitution that limits the influence of politics. This is so because the greater the extent of aspects that are subject to political decisions, the more relevant the decisions become. This in turn implies that those in power have less of a disposition to abandon it because they have too much to lose. On the other hand, those who are outside of power have a greater tendency to use extraconstitutional means to reach power or resist any onerous politics imposed by those who hold it (pp. 48 and 20). Third, the higher the instability of the rights of citizens as a consequence of a lack of a general social agreement, and the higher the stakes behind political decisions, the greater the social resources destined to compete for them. This situation generates a rent-seeking attitude that means that social resources are used to seek rents rather than to produce, which in turn diminishes wealth. At the limit of such a situation, everything is in question. In a society that lacks a basic agreement on the rights and rules that govern the political and economic elections, the greater part of their resources are spent in fighting against each other; society is characterized by clashes, crisis, political disorder, and economic contraction (pp. 49 and 20). This final proposition means that in order to warrant political order, the state has to engage in a credible manner in the establishment and maintainence of a variety of citizens' rights, assuring that they possess a sufficient degree of security from political opportunism and expropriation. Unless citizens have such an assurance, they do not sufficiently invest in economic activities. This is also crucial in order to maintain political and democratic rights, in that credible compromises require the creation of political institutions that have incentive to maintain the rights of their citizenry (pp. 49 and 21).

These general propositions of the "institutional school" regarding the relationship between political consensus, democracy, and economic development are posited in a different manner by Rueschemeyer, wherein he finds a link between capitalist development and the existence of a strongly organized labor class (Rueschemeyer, Stephens, and Stephens 1992). These propositions are further specified by the French "regulationist school." The regulationist school has developed a very profound analysis of capitalism. Its main proposition is that "capitalism is a force of change that does not have in itself a regulatory principle; this principle is to be found in the coherence of the social mediations that orient the accumulation of capital in the direction of progress" (Aglietta 1997: 437). By itself, this tremendous force of change does not generate the conditions of social well-being; on the contrary, it tends to incite conflicts and dysfunctions that can become obstacles to its own development. "Capitalism has the capacity to mobilize human energies in order to transform them into growth. It does not have the capacity to construct a global coherence from the choc of individual interests" (p. 420). In order to convert capitalism into an ordered productive force, "in order to make it capable to preserve the power of work that it needs, capitalism must be included in structures that constrain it. These structures are not the result of the reasoning of capitalists, nor of the spontaneous result of competition. These structures result from the creation of social institutions, legitimated by collective values that give society their cohesion" (p. 420). This latter is what is defined as a mode of regulation, "an ensemble of mediations that maintain the distortions that are produced by capital with limits that are compatible with the social cohesion within nations" (p. 412). In order to assure this cohesion it is necessary for capitalist growth to better the living conditions of the workers and to develop a wage society. This is what capitalism succeeded in doing throughout the thirty or more years that followed World War II, first through the fact that salaries increased regularly in that they were indexed to the growth of labor productivity (p. 431). Simultaneously, the creation of a system of a welfare state that assured workers their jobs, health service, and pensions generated what the regulation school calls the "fordist model." The state played a crucial role in it, giving the different social mediations their coherence and thus assuring its permanence for a certain period of time as the mode of regulation.

Wolfgang Streeck is in perfect accord with these ideas, and helps us to particularize some of their elements. He writes that "economists have succeeded in persuading most people that the performance of an economy improves as social constraints on self-interested rational action are removed [. . .] to the contrary, socially institutionalized constraints on the rational voluntarism of interest-maximizing behavior may be economically beneficial" (Streeck 1997: 197). As in the thought of the regulationists, an autonomous state is crucial because public policies emerge from the conflict and negotiation dynamics of social organizations, and are then applied by an autonomous state apparatus. This is the manner in which "the surrounding society, retaining and exercising a right for itself to interfere with the choice and pursuit of individual preferences," governs its economy (p. 198). But not only the state needs to be autonomous; the autonomous capacity of action of society is also necessary: "an economy can perform well only to the extent that it is embedded in a well-integrated society and that a society exists only to the extent that it is capable of imposing normative constraints, or social obligations, on the pursuit of individual interests" (p. 199). An important step in this direction has been the democratic transition, the demise of the hegemonic party, and the appearance of authentic political forces. But because beneficial constraints imply the existence of social organizations, democratization has to advance in the direction of civil society. Finally, political and social constraints on pure economic behavior are necessary if we take into consideration that

> improved economic performance requires a restructuring of identity [that] will not normally be sought for economic reasons and voluntarily. This is because rational choice cannot in principle adjudicate between alternative identities, but makes sense only under established second-order preferences (Hirschman 1992). Changes in the latter, in the kind of actor one wants to be, are accomplished through socialization and resocialization, i.e., through collective normative pressure rather than individual interest maximization . . . To stimulate strategic creativity beyond present interests and structures, having fewer options and less choice may be better for rational actors than having more, if foreclosed options are short-term remedies under unreformed second-order preferences. Constraining, choice limiting social obligations, like a high floor of general labor standards, may be economically beneficial because they may protect rational actors from spending time and resources on exploring sub-optimal options, and force them to concentrate their efforts on making successful use of potentially more productive alternatives. (Streeck 1997: 204)

It is perfectly clear that since the mid-1970s the fordist model of regulation produces crisis, due to changes in the way in which capitalism is working. In the developed countries with very extensive welfare states, or in others with job security assured by their collective enterprises, such as Japan, the institutional mediations (the constraints on capitalism) are under strong pressure to be transformed. Nevertheless, in countries such as Mexico, these mediations are being dismantled. This is possible because most of them were much less extensive and were originally created by the state. The state in Mexico did not merely act as the agent that gave coherence to different institutional mediations, but it created them. Their dependence on the state therefore made it possible to dismantle most of them. This in turn has had consequences on the effects of globalization on the Mexican economy and the type of model applied there. Authors such as Oxhorn and Ducatenzeiller who write from a Latin American perspective define what this means in socioeconomic terms: "Where civil society is strong, economic liberalism is likely to be inclusionary and lay the foundations for viable democratic regimes," but "where civil society is weak [. . .] economic liberalism is likely to be exclusionary. The same factors that inhibit the growth of civil society are likely to reproduce themselves in highly segmented social structures" (Oxhorn and Ducatenzeiller 1999: 37).

## The Politics of the New Economic Model

In contrast to most countries that underwent both an economic and a political transition after World War II, such as most of Latin America (excepting Chile) and especially central and Eastern Europe, political transition preceded the economic one. In the case of Mexico, the authoritarian regime was able to survive the 1982 crisis and was successful in implementing the new economic model that inserted the country into the global economy. Political transition occurred when most of the changes in the model had already been achieved by the "ancient regime": opening of the economy to foreign capital and goods (including the signing of the North American Free Trade Agreement [NAFTA]), the reduction of state intervention and expenditure, privatizations, and labor flexibility, among others.

This distinct trajectory of the Mexican case has had important consequences. In the first place, the reforms in Mexico were among the most radical and orthodox in comparison with those of other countries, precisely because they were undertaken by the authoritarian government in conditions of a strict control of civil organizations. The Salinas government introduced both institutional (the constitutional reforms) and economic reforms (the opening of the Mexican economy and the signing of NAFTA). The regime was civil, inclusionary (through corporatism), with a semidemocratic face (elections were held regularly; there was freedom of civil rights) and a high level of legitimacy that helped hold labor and peasant organizations under tight control. In the countries where authoritarian governments tried to implement these same measures under a more exclusionary regime, the result was an upsurge of the labor movement—the appearance of independent currents within the controlled trade unions—that took over the unions or created new ones, which eventually signified their demise. On the other hand, new democratic governments have had a much more difficult time introducing liberal reforms because they are confronted with the interests of the groups that profited from the old economic model (national entrepreneurs strongly linked to state expenditure and investments, labor and peasant unions in state enterprises) and to alternative projects supported by the social sectors that are excluded from the new enterprise.

Although the Mexican political regime suffered important transformations that affected it (and eventually made the transition possible), they were, paradoxically, functional to the authoritarian imposition of the economic model in that they weakened the old social forces while they prevented the creation of new ones. To understand this paradox, we have to take into consideration that from 1982 on, the governing elite made certain decisions that were neither ineluctably determined by the external circumstances, by the financial crisis, or by the agreement reached with the International Monetary Fund (IMF), nor determined by an ideological coherence of the elites among themselves, but that were defined by the specific manner in which they chose to change the relationship of the state with the regime. The governmental elites took a fundamental political position that was supposedly intended to "depoliticize" the state, but that was in reality a political decision. They wished to recuperate the autonomy of the state by disengaging it from the corporatist engagements that had linked it to different sectors of society, either directly through the organizations representing these social sectors or indirectly through different institutions and public policies (Theret 2001). The new governing elites that led the country from 1982 on, the so-called technocrats, wanted to disengage the state from the corporatist pact that was the basis of the inclusionary political regime. This, in sum, implied separating the state from its party, the Partido Revolucionario Institucional (PRI).

This is what, at least in part, determined the manner in which the three post-1982 technocratic governments (de la Madrid, Salinas, and Zedillo) privatized, decentralized, and eliminated all sorts of subsidies and regulations on the economy. It was not only an economic rationality that determined the proclaimed "reduction of the weight of the State," but also a political rationality directed at cutting the links between the state and the popular organizations of the corporatist or populist pact that ensured the stability of the ancient regime, wherein the state was the main agent of development and rewarded, through redistribution, the support of the popular organizations. In fact, in 1983 President Miguel de la Madrid declared that his objective was "to strengthen the capacity of the State by focalizing his energies toward the integral development of the Nation" (de la Madrid 1999: 137). The objective was to strengthen state intervention rather than simply to reduce its weight.

Apart from the objective of reducing the costs of the economic enterprises on the finances of the state, the privatizations served the purpose of hitting the nodal center of the relationship between the state and the organized labor movement, one of the pillars of the regime. In fact, the best organized and most active unions were situated in state-owned enterprises. These latter were the first ones privatized (Ross Schneider 1990). From this moment on, privatization worked as a "sword of Damocles" on the unions of both state enterprises that the government could not or did not want to privatize, and a more diffused threat toward the private sector. This pressure translated into the generalized weakening of unions and of collective contracts; the majority of the collective contracts were modified, eliminating the attributions of the unions and reducing their intervention at the plant level. This resulted in the downgrading of work conditions and salaries in the majority of the enterprises.

Nevertheless, this situation did not result in the opening of new spaces for the independent unions or in the creation of new, more democratic, institutional forms designed to solve labor conflicts that substituted those that worked on clientelistic exchange mechanisms. The government cut off the bases of corporatist control, but at the same time did all it could to prevent the emergence of independent social actors, because its main objective was to implement the new economic model with as little resistance as possible on the part of the trade union movement. It arrived at a political truce with the officialist labor movement, although it was weakening its basis of control at the socioeconomic level. On the other hand, it did not yield its capacity to intervene in union affairs and in the industrial-relations system. The federal labor law that sanctioned a broad overseeing capacity of the state in these affairs was not modified. In this manner, labor flexibility and deunionization were achieved in the same authoritarian manner that, decades before, installed unionization and union control.

In the case of the peasant sector, another pillar of the political regime, the end of agrarian reform—subsidies, price controls, and financing—and less privatizations reduced the intervention of the state in that sector and dried up the resources of clientelist control. The governments of de la Madrid and Salinas not only drastically reduced subsidies, but also ended the regulation of agricultural prices, which meant the end of indirect subsidies. This latter was accomplished through the dismantling of the Comisión Nacional de Subsistencias Populares (National Commission of Popular Means of Consumption, CONASUPO). In the 1990s, this agency retreated from most products, excepting maize and beans. As it continued managing these two products, in 1993–1994, at the summit of its intervention, it bought 23 percent of the total production of maize; in 1998 it bought a mere 12 percent. There was nonetheless a very important privatization: that of the state-owned fertilizer company, Fertimex, that sold its products at subsidized prices to the peasants.

But it was the reform of Article 27 of the constitution, accomplished in

1992, that was crucial to weakening peasant corporatism, not only because this article regulated the distribution of land, but because it also defined that manner in which the peasantry would be organized. Since the reform, the peasants have the possibility of selling their land if the majority of the *ejido* owners so decide (something that was strictly prohibited beforehand). On the other hand, the fact that the *ejido* assemblies received this power of deciding whether to sell or not sell their collective property, and the fact that there are less and less subsidies and financial aids channeled to the *ejidos*, has had as a secondary consequence: that the main state functionary of the *ejido*, the *ejido* commissar, is slowly losing ground.

Decentralization also had a double rationale. In addition to the search for greater efficacy of social services, such as education and health, when these are partially decided upon and administered at the local level, the new governmental elite used its control to weaken corporatist organizations. In the Mexican case, the traditional weakness of local actors (even though they had gained power since the 1980s with more and more local governments falling into the hands of the opposition) has led specialists to say that decentralization was basically decided from above in order to maintain the authoritarian regime; it was needed in order to modernize the local and regional structures and to control the "natural" process of decentralization as a consequence of globalization (Cabrero Mendoza 1998). But one of the main nondeclared purposes was action against the corporatist unions of the central administrative apparatus that it was not able to privatize. Beginning in the second half of the  1970s, under the presidency of López Portillo (1976–1982), the government sought to weaken one of the pillars of corporatist control, the elementary-education teachers' union. On the one hand, this union opposed the governmental educational reforms, while on the other hand it was being eroded by an important internal dissident movement that threatened at the medium term to develop into an opposition against the government itself if it succeeded in winning over popular support for the organization.

Although both privatizations and decentralization were partly used against corporatist mechanisms, these actions were not followed by a will to liberalize the political and social scenarios. On the contrary, although the government went on eroding corporatist control in order to liberate itself from such engagements and assure its capacity to regain autonomy and impose unilaterally a new economic model, liberalization of both the social and the political scenarios was more difficult. Labor and peasant organizations were maintained as an organic part of the PRI (although the state tried to distance itself from the party). On the other hand, the mechanisms through which the state controlled the unions did not change; although the Salinas government modified most of the more important articles in the constitution, it stopped short of the labor law. This clearly meant that although the government was weakening the official unions, it was doing everything to prevent the appearance of an independent union movement. The result was the weakening of the existing social mediations without the emergence of more representative ones. It tried to prevent the devolution of the corporatist system from undermining the political regime. It also had the idea that government had to impose the new economic model unilaterally, in that it drastically lowered the contract conditions of most workers and peasants.

The continuation of state control mechanisms and the "pact" between the technocrats and the corporatist unions—which was accepted by the latter with the idea that although the government continued to impose measures that would weaken the unions, they would not question the leadership—allowed the government not only to impose the new economic model with little resistance on the part of unions, but to radically loosen the industrial-relations system. The old system had given unions a great deal of say about the situation inside their enterprises, as a means to assure their clientelistic control. The government allowed the enterprises to radically modify the collective contracts in order to impose a situation where the employers gained the capacity of deciding on the day-to-day labor administration of their enterprises, including the internal organization of production as well as hiring and promotion of workers within the job hierarchy.

But this was not all. The traditional authoritarian mechanisms, in the hands of the Ministry of Labor, allowed and promoted deunionization and undermined the existence of "protection" unions. The government allowed many *maquiladoras* in the north to exist without unions at all. Whereas, until the 1980s, it had promoted the policy that most industrial plants would have unions affiliated with the officialist federations it controlled, from the mid-1980s on the government promoted that these federations come to terms with the idea that these enterprises were not to unionize. In most of these cases, although we cannot know for sure because the collective contract information is secret, there probably still exists a union, although the workers do not know of its existence, probably signed with one of the officialist federations or more recently with makeshift federations directed by lawyers, all with the complicity of labor authorities. This is deemed necessary because, in case workers try to organize in an independent union, this would not be technically possible because a union already exists.

Social politics have also been drastically transformed. The corporatist regime was not only based on the control of the popular organizations, but also on an active policy of creating what the regulation school names the "wage society." The Mexican state promoted the inclusion of workers in a social-security system through job creation and its agencies of the welfare state. The system of social security dates from 1943, when a law was promulgated in order to ensure health services and retirement benefits to workers. During the government of López Mateos (1958–1964) the Social Security Institute for state workers was created, as well as other more particular instances that covered petroleum workers and the members of the army. In the early 1970s, the Ministry of Social Security began to offer health services to the rest of the population that was not covered by any of the other systems; these were directed toward those who held a formal job, but had very restricted financial means.

The Mexican welfare system was much more restricted than those that existed in Europe, which were the basis of the fordist model; while the latter included most of the population, in Mexico the population covered by both health services and retirement never attained 50 percent. Nevertheless, even this very restricted welfare state has been radically constrained since the 1980s. The main change has been that social policy has shifted from a universal design to a localized one directed exclusively to the poorest (Gordon 1999). On the other hand, the government has tended to dismantle the social institutions it created until the end of the 1970s. There is recurrent talk of privatizing health services in view of the incapacity of the state to continue offering health services through its institutions. Retirement funds have been individualized; each worker has a particular account that accumulates his or her retirement funds and is managed by private banks. The state is also focusing its social policy on programs such as Progresa, which gives a minimum revenue to the poorest if they can prove that their children go to school and go to medical exams regularly. The idea behind such a project is not one of creating a salaried society that constitutes the internal market of the product they help produce, but rather of helping out the poorest in order that they can eventually integrate with the productive sector and stop depending upon the state for assistance.

In terms of our theoretical perspective, this evolution of the sociopolitical regime has important consequences. It created a situation in which the new economic model was imposed by the government, without generating a consensus on what kind of a model would be most desirable. Meanwhile, the government has been dismantling the existing welfare state that constituted one of the key consensual elements of the corporatist regime, its main source of legitimacy. The second proposition of a consensual political order is not fulfilled either: because political decisions are imposed unilaterally, the scope is very great.

Peasants and workers did not have authoritative organizations that represented their interests in the old regime, and they do not have them in the new regime that resulted from the transformations of the technocrats and the presidency, because the old organizations continue to subsist and the new organizations are still a minority. The old tripartite institutions that allowed the state to impose its decisions have been substituted by a vacuum. There are no institutions to mediate the interests of those that are losing with the changes of globalization, and there is thus no possibility of creating a minimal consensus. In fact, the dismantling of the old economic model and the welfare state was used to weaken the existing organizations. At the same time, the existing authoritarian control mechanisms were used to prevent the emergence of independent social organizations that might threaten to endanger the unilateral decisions taken by the government elites. The new model is thus being imposed with almost no mediation mechanisms, with no regard to its legitimacy.

In this manner, the new economic model is lacking what the regulation school calls the regulatory mechanisms that ensure social cohesion and the coherence between the economic, social, and political spheres of the regime. The model is being imposed with minimal social-cohesion measures that are limited to social assistance to the poorest. There are no mechanisms that temper class warfare, that ensure that the dynamism of capital helps to better the conditions of the salaried class and creates a wage society. This may be finally achieved through the action of only the market forces; nevertheless, until the present time the conditions of most workers have worsened; we have seen less job security, social coverage, which is accentuated by the weakness of union representation, which in turn increases the feeling of insecurity among workers.

According to the institutional school, these types of politics vis-à-vis the economic model (i.e., those that lack political consensus) mean that a greater part of the economic energies will go toward inflaming social and political strife and toward the goal of gaining more decisionmaking capacity. For the regulation school, lack of political legitimacy of an economic model means lack of coherence of the model and thus lack of a crucial factor that stabilizes it. Finally, it also impinges on what Streeck calls "beneficial constraints." Constraints on socioeconomic actors allow them to adjust their behavior according to the attitude of each other. This helps each of the actors to attune their actions and to increase their capacity of responding to new situations. The fact that a specific group of employers has to confront active and combative labor unions allows employers to become better prepared to respond to the risks of concurrence. It is also significant that while most active and representative unions have the capacity to raise demands when the situation of the enterprise is good, they also have the capacity to come to terms with the entrepreneurs when their jobs are at risk. They also have the legitimacy to make their members comply with unfavorable decisions in unfavorable times.

From all this we can conclude that the politics of the economic transition in Mexico have not only weakened social mediations, but very probably also undermined the bases of the performance of the Mexican economy. They have also introduced some very specific deformations on the economic integration of Mexico, which I analyze in the next section.

**The New Economic Model**

The new economic model imposed by the Mexican state has absolutely transformed the Mexican economy. Mexico was a very weak exporter at the beginning of the 1980s. At the present time, exports lead the economy if one recognizes that between 1986 and 1993 exports always grew faster than the gross national product (GNP).[1] Mexico has become the eighth-highest exporting country in the world and the first in Latin America. Exports have grown steadily as part of GNP. In 1981 they were a mere 6.5 percent; by 1990 they were already at 27 percent, and in 1996 they were an impressive 66 percent (Katz 1998).[2] Mexico has ceased to be a primary goods exporter and has greatly reduced the weight of oil exports. Manufactured goods represented 33.8 percent and, in 1993, they already represented 71.9 percent (including *maquiladora* exports) (Vega 2004). Even manufactured exports have diversified; while in 1986 50 percent of exports were concentrated in seven products, in 1993 there were already twelve products. Productivity has increased very significantly since the opening of the Mexican economy; while at the beginning of the 1980s it was decreasing at a rate of 0.7 percent and 0.8 percent, in 1982 and 1983 respectively, in 1987, 1988, and 1989 it started growing at rates of 2.5, 3.2, and 4.1 percent, and it was reaching rates of 9.0, 2.7, 8.7 percent in 1994, 1995 and 1997 respectively (Katz 1998).

The change of the economic model has had important regional effects. Whereas the import-substitution model basically concentrated industry and services in three large cities—Mexico, Guadalajara, and Monterrey—the tendency has been the contrary since the opening of the Mexican economy. Between 1985 and 1998, the participation of the population dedicated to manufacturing activities has decreased by almost 10 percent in the central region (the Federal District, State of Mexico, Guanajuato, Hidalgo, Morelos, Puebla, Querétaro, and Tlaxcala), while that of the border states has increased by almost 11 percent. This has meant that the regional industrial structure has changed; the center-periphery structure has shifted to a bipolar structure: while in 1985 the border states participated with little less than 23 percent of the manufacturing labor, and ones in the center had more than 50 percent, in 1998 these percentages shifted to 33.4 and 40.3, respectively (Chamboux-Leroux 2001).

The regional participation in GNP has also increased in the center and north of the country, while that of the Federal District and adjacent states has decreased. While this latter region produced 39.01 percent of the total GNP in 1980, it produced 37.8 percent in 1993. The northern states produced 17.8 percent in 1980 and 18.9 percent in 1993. Finally, the center states produced 6.72 percent in 1980 and 8.35 in 1993 (Katz 1998: table 7, p. 58). Industrial parks and enterprises have been established in different parts of the country, with the concentration of industrial parks in the border regions. There is thus sufficient proof that one of the important effects of the opening of the Mexican economy has been a certain redistribution of Mexican industry, mainly toward the north, but also to some states of central Mexico such as Aguascalientes, Guanajuato, Querétaro, San Luis Potosí, and Zacatecas. Nevertheless, what is also clear is that there are regions of Mexico that are totally marginalized from this process, such as Chiapas, Oaxaca, and Guerrero, among others.

Nevertheless, it is less clear if the fact that some regions have received a greater proportion of the manufacturing sector has also meant a redistribution of wealth, measured, for example, by GNP per person. When we look at the index of relative rates of growth of the regional GNP per person (the rate of regional GNP per person divided by the rate of regional population growth), we can see that in effect certain border states such as Chihuahua, Coahuila, and Tamaulipas have a positive rate (1.11, 1.06, and 1.11, respectively), while other border states such as Baja California, Nuevo León, and Sonora have rates under unity. In the central region, some states such as Aguascalientes, Querétaro, and Guanajuato have rates above unity, while others such as San Luis Potosí and Zacatecas show a negative relation between both indexes. Finally, very poor states such as Chiapas, Oaxaca, and Guerrero have shown a "positive" relationship. This has led the author of the analysis to state that this index is highly influenced by migration. Even if a state's GNP per person does not increase in terms of GNP, if there is enough migration of nonemployed or underemployed persons, without a decrease in production, this enhances an increase in the index. The contrary is also true: states with increased production attract nonproductive migrant populations, which makes the index descend (Chamboux-Leroux 2001).

This observation is further supported by Katz's data, though not by region, as he uses it, but by state. The GNP per person does not seem to follow the distribution of manufacturing production. Baja California decreased its GNP per person from 1980 to 1993, while it augmented very strongly from 1970 to 1980. In Coahuila, Chihuahua, and Tamaulipas, something similar happened. The only border state that escapes this trend is Sonora, which goes from 69.8 to 77.2 pesos of 1970 (Katz 1998: table 6, p. 55). Thus even though there seems to be a relationship between the opening of the Mexican economy and a redistribution of manufacturing industry, this is not followed by an increase in wealth per person. The regions of the north that have become the main manufacturing/exporting centers, the original industrialization centers such as Mexico City, Guadalajara, and Monterrey, and the petrol-exporting zones have the best living-conditions indexes. The worst off are the regions of the country that have traditionally produced for the internal market, either through agricultural or other goods.

Although these diversifications in productivity have been surely important successes of the new economic model, they have also developed very significant deformations. It is my perspective that the particularities of these deformations can be, in the last resort, interpreted as a consequence of path dependency on the constitutional order[3] that has existed in Mexico.

## The Tendency to Monetarism and the Internal Absorption of the Costs of Crises

Although the Mexican state promoted important structural modifications of the economy during the years when it was its main agent (between 1936 and 1982), there were already some crucial indications that it also had a great tendency toward monetarist policies, which went so far as to greatly limit the import-substitution model. Since the beginning of the 1960s, the Mexican government shifted from an economic policy that intended to effect the structural transformation of the economy to another that focused on price stability, both of the goods produced internally and on the exchange rate. Many Mexican economists agree that the import-substitution model was just partly successful in Mexico, because it only succeeded in substituting final consumer goods and failed to substitute intermediary and capital goods. If we compare Mexico with Brazil, for example, we can see that while Mexico imported 13 percent of the total of intermediary products and 66 percent of its capital goods in 1950, these percentages in 1960 were 10.4 percent and 54.9 percent respectively. In Brazil, however, the percentage of intermediary goods imported went from 26 percent to 6.6 percent, while that of capital goods went from 63.7 percent to 10 percent between 1949 and 1964 (Gollas 2004: 7). According to most authors, this dichotomy was due to the monetarist policies adopted by the Mexican government, such as the overvaluation of the Mexican peso, which made imports of intermediary and capital goods more attractive than their production in Mexico. The only reason why consumer goods resisted this overvaluation of the peso was the protection of the Mexican internal market.

The reason for this decision, which gave the Mexican substitution process a definite character, was political. The Mexican political regime entered a moment of intense questioning on the part of the labor and peasant organizations that had supported it and the first industrialization effort, from 1940 to the mid-1950s. There was increasing dissatisfaction with a model based on moderate inflation, around 14 percent, but also on real salaries that were always lagging behind. This situation was greatly accentuated with the devaluation of 1956. The social movements that emerged during 1958–1959 were the consequence of the conjuncture created by the effect on the prices of the products that were produced by the internal market, and the longer-term loss of buying power of salaries was perceived as a serious threat for the Mexican political regime. The diagnosis of the government was that in order to prevent such an event from reproducing itself it had to forestall devaluation and inflation. From this moment on, a new epoch of the economic model was inaugurated, "stabilizing development," which achieved economic growth with price stability.

This decision can be explained in less conjunctural and more structural, although also political, terms. The Mexican state, created in the wake of the revolution, was very closely linked to the regime that emerged in its aftermath. The revolution had as its main effect the destruction of the old ruling classes, the great landowners, and the constitution of a new class of small peasants, government bureaucrats, and industrial workers organized by the state in centralized and hierarchical organizations that were incorporated into the party of the state, the PRI. These organizations gave rise to an authoritarian-corporatist regime very closely linked to the state, which, though its social and political policies helped the emergence of these new social sectors, closely related to its economic policies and to its political policies designed to create a tightly knit social and political construction that assured its political control. This strict control paradoxically determined that the result of the corporatist control of the state upon social forces was to reduce its autonomy, in that it led it to become the warrant of the regime. This explains why, when the regime confronted its first serious threat with the social movement, the Mexican state gave a priority to monetary policies over structural ones. This situation contrasts with other cases, such as the Brazilian[4] one, where in contrast with Presidents Calles (1924–1928) and Cardenas (1934–1940), Brazilian president Vargas (1930–1945 and again 1951–1954) was not as successful in creating a corporatist regime, and the Brazilian political regime had less stability than the Mexican regime created by Calles and Cardenas, as can be seen by the fact that President Goulart was overthrown by a military coup in 1964. Nevertheless, this situation permitted the Brazilian state to be a more autonomous agent with regard to the regime, and it would act under different political regimes and thus be freer to choose between applying structural or monetary policies (Bizberg 2002; Marques-Pereira and Theret 2004).

On the other hand, the application of monetary policies in Mexico was also determined by an institutional configuration. The Mexican state had the institutional capacity to base an economic policy on the control of inflation and the rate of change because the corporatist institutions allowed it. The authoritarian-corporatist regime had an ample legitimacy due to its revolutionary origins and by the fact that it was based upon a national and popular pact that included the most relevant social actors. This gave the regime the capacity to control the demands of the different sectors of society through inclusion rather that through repression. This meant that the state had the capacity to solve the redistribution conflicts *ex-ante*, rather than reacting to them (Marques-Pereira and Theret 2004). Because the Mexican state controlled the trade unions, the peasant organizations, and the entrepreneurial chambers, it could define the main economic variables: salaries and prices. The rest of the prices were set by a state that produced many of the intermediary products in its own enterprises. An additional fact was that the regime was very centralized and based on the hegemony of a political party that had under its control all the regional and local governments. This allowed the federal government to exert a strict monetary control through restrictions of the monetary supply expansion and debt engagement (both were prohibited for local state governments).

This situation contrasts with Brazil, where this "redistribution conflict" was not at all controlled. In the first place, Brazil has a strong federal structure, where each state and region uses its power to emit money directly or through debt. On the other hand, only during a short time under the military junta were salaries strictly controlled. In addition, the state had a limited capacity to control prices. Because it lacked the capacity to exert strict monetary control and stability, the Brazilian state privileged structural policies and economic growth. This situation is closely related to another factor: whereas the legitimacy of the Mexican regime depended upon the alliance of the state with the popular sectors, which obliged it to proceed to a continuously controlled redistributive process, the Brazilian state was on the one hand more autonomous of the regime, and on the other had less control over redistribution. This obliged the state to act as a more coherent agent of development. In addition, each new regime through which Brazil produced had to legitimize itself anew, and it did so through economic growth, obliging it to be more structuralist (Marques-Pereira and Theret 2004).

Until the beginning of the 1980s, this policy played in favor of redistribution and a growth of real salaries, although it affected the evolution of the import-substitution model and did not permit the shift toward another model in the early 1970s, when it was absolutely clear that the model was exhausted. The governments of Echeverría (1970–1976) and López Portillo (1976–1982) used the abundance of external credits and the expansion of the Mexican petroleum industry to postpone structural decisions, and continued trying to maintain an exchange rate favorable to the peso and also continued redistributing resources through the corporatist organizations. Nevertheless, this policy led the Mexican government to a profound financial crisis in 1982. From this point on, monetarist politics, based on the social and political control of all socioeconomic agents, has permitted the government to impose a very strict policy of inflation control based on orthodox monetary measures. This, coupled with a complete change in the economic model from a protectionist and inward-looking model to an open and export-oriented one, has produced an export economy based on a large differential of costs between the Mexican economy and the economies that invest in Mexico in enterprises that are designed specifically for export, mainly the *maquiladora* industries of the north. This large differential of costs is based on low salaries (the decrease in the minimum wage since 1982 has been more than 50 percent), and their maintenance through the strict control of inflation and the stability of the exchange rate.

As a result of these policies, salaries have been continuously falling in real terms since the 1980s. Although minimum salaries are not a very good indicator of real income, because in the formal sector there are increasingly fewer people who live on such a basis (although from 1991 to 1997 the proportion of workers who got less than the minimum salary—another indicator of informality—has gone from 18.1 percent to 20.8 percent of the total working force [García 2001]), they are nevertheless an indicator of how salaries have evolved. From a high in 1977, minimum salaries had decreased to almost one-third of their value in 1996, attaining the level of the mid-1950s (Alba 2000). In the formal sector, salaries have gone from an index of 113.1 in 1980, to 88.1 in 1990, to 114.9 in 1994, 90.1 in 1996, and 98.0 in 2000 (Stallings and Weller 2001: 199). What also happened in the last decade is that the proportion of workers without social benefits has increased, passing from 21 percent to 24.7 percent of the total (García 2001). We also have to consider what has happened with the conditions in the badly known and difficult to evaluate informal sector. In terms of earnings, García has found that at the beginning of the 1990s, the real earnings per hour of the self-employed were higher than that of those working in the private sector. In contrast, at the end of the decade (1998) the tendency has inverted, due to a clear reduction of the earnings of the informal sector versus an increase of the salaries in the private sector (p. 16).

All this has had an impact on income distribution. While during the import-substitution epoch, income distribution bettered slowly but surely, which probably meant that poverty fell, the contrary tendency has been occurring during the last twenty years. In 1984 (just after the crisis and before the opening of the Mexican economy) the poorest 20 percent of the population held a mere 3.9 percent of the total income, and in 1992 this population had only 3.1 percent, while in the year 2000, it got 3.2 percent. On the other hand, the richest 20 percent concentrated 53.6 percent of the wealth in 1984, 59.5 percent in 1992, and 58.7 percent in 2000 (Cortés 2004). In this manner, the richest deciles of the population concentrate ever more resources, while the poorest and the middle classes have less income. As a result, consumption in real terms has reduced its participation in the aggregate demand from 64 percent to 56 percent in the last years (Urquidi 1999: 52). This, in part, explains why the internal market has stagnated.

The fact that the internal market has stagnated has also been the result of the fact that the Mexican government has recurrently chosen to absorb the costs of each of the crises (1982, 1987, and 1994–1995) internally, rather than sharing its costs with the external economic actors (basically, its creditors and investors). This situation is also explained by the institutional configuration of the Mexican regime. Mexico has always been the example for the IMF, and has always adopted its recommendations. The authoritarian-corporatist structure of the regime, and the fact that this configuration implies that the state controls the main social actors, explains why it was faster and easier to absorb the costs of the financial crisis internally, imposing them upon the Mexican society rather than going into long and complicated negotiations with its creditors. In fact, the orthodox stabilization measures were taken with the formal acceptance of workers and entrepreneurs, in the *pactos* inaugurated in 1987 that lasted until the year 2000, although with decreasing efficacy. This same factor explains why the Mexican government could apply the neoliberal model in such a radical manner. As has been mentioned by many authors, the opening of the Mexican economy was done in an extremely rapid and drastic manner; in fact, the Mexican government took almost no action to protect some areas of its economy. The implementation of the new economic model had almost no open defiance: the official workers' movement was subordinated to the state, and the entrepreneurial and peasant organizations had no capacity to resist the way in which the Mexican economy was opening. This latter is only happening nowadays, in the face of a new government of the Partido Acción Nacional (PAN) under Vicente Fox, as the peasantry (both those of the PRI and those that have been more autonomous from the government) are rejecting the opening of certain agricultural products that have taken effect beginning in 2003.

This has resulted in the fact that, although exports have grown enormously in the last twenty years, from 1982 to 2000 the average growth of GNP has been a mere 2.24 percent, which has meant that GNP per person has virtually stagnated; it grew a mere 0.17 percent per year during this period. From 1981 to 1990, GNP per person growth has been less than the population growth, and from 1991 to 1995 it has been even lower due to the 1995 crisis, at 0.84 percent. It had recuperated during the last few years before the 2001 stagnation: from 1996 to 2000, GNP grew at a rate of 4.81, which has meant a GNP per person of almost 3 percent per year. Nevertheless, there hasn't been a really important growth, equivalent to that of exports, and more importantly, this growth has not been continuous, something which is crucial if one expects to see a reduction of poverty and an increase of wealth such as Mexico experienced from 1951 to 1980, when GNP grew at a rate of 6.41 and GNP per person grew at a rate of 3.33. In the last twenty years, only during 1996 and 1997 did the country grow at an equivalent rate (Urquidi 1999: table 1).

This has resulted in the fact that public as well as private investments (except foreign ones) fell in real terms. This in turn has led to the present incapacity to absorb the Mexican labor force, and in the tendency of informal activities to maintain their participation in the economy, thus increasing unemployment and underemployment. Because unemployment is a bad indicator in a country with no unemployment insurance, I prefer to consider the indicator of underemployment, or informality. In the last ten years, the relative importance of nonsalaried workers has increased from 36.6 percent of the total working force in 1991 to 37.2 percent in 1997; those working in small enterprises with less than five employees went from 53.4 percent to 56.6 percent; and finally, those without income went from 12.1 percent to 15.0 percent (García 2001). Thus, unqualified, nonsalaried workers continue to represent about one-fourth of the labor force. If one adds to this percentage the salaried workers and the heads of small enterprises (mostly informal ones), we attain the proportion of 44 percent of people employed in this sector in the sixteen most important cities of the country (García and de Oliveira 2001).

### Betting on Low Costs and Low
### Human Capital Implies Low Productivity Gains

We have seen that the corporatist structure of the regime made it not only possible but far easier to insert the Mexican economy into the international context on the basis of the deregulation of the wages and working conditions of the labor force. The offensive against the trade unions, the end of agrarian reform, the weakening of the social state (especially the privatization of pension funds), and the increased flexibility of labor relations in general have permitted and in a sense made it "natural" for Mexico to insert itself into the world economy on the basis of lower wages. And this configuration has, in turn, conformed the vicious cycle that I describe below.

Neoliberal reforms have imposed on Mexico low levels of growth in productivity. Although productivity increased importantly during the 1980s, if one compares the Mexican situation to other countries one can see that these productivity gains are not quite so impressive. While Mexico's productivity (measured through value added per worker in manufacturing) was US$25,931 per year from 1995 to 1999, Brazil's productivity was $61,595, Argentina's was $37,480, Chile's was $32,977, Bolivia's was $26,282, Korea's was $40,916, and Turkey's was $32,961 (World Bank 2001). If we now compare labor productivity in a few selected countries to that of the United States, we can see that the relative productivity of Mexico was 28.7 percent in 1970, 25.5 percent in 1980, 20.3 percent in 1990, and 17.6 percent in 1998; in the last eight years, relative productivity has not only not increased but has diminished. On the other hand, relative productivity in countries such as Argentina (36.4 percent in 1990, 46.9 percent in 1998), Brazil (21.7 percent and 25 percent), and Uruguay (1.7 percent and 17.3 percent) has increased, although in all these cases it fell sharply from 1970 to 1990. In Mexico, this situation is explained by the fact that only the *maquiladora* industries (and probably the exporting sector as a whole) have increased their productivity, while the rest of the economy did not follow suit (Katz and Stumpo 2001).

Although part of the Mexican economy is able to absorb technology (hard and supple technology per se and new forms of production and work organization), another part is incapable of doing so. A study by López Acevedo found that the enterprises that are able to absorb technology are the "big" ones, i.e., those oriented toward exports, that have foreign investment, that have training for their employees, that finance research and development, and that are located in the north (López Acevedo 2002a). In another study, this same author finds that the enterprises that adopt technology employ workers with a higher educational level and pay them better salaries. This increase in human capital and technology has an impact on higher productivity and earnings (López Acevedo 2002b).

This is also why there is such a low capacity among other Mexican companies to become providers of the exporting companies. Fifty-four percent of the exporting enterprises declared that high prices and low capacities of production were the main problems of the national providers. Other problems mentioned were low or inconsistent quality and the rates of delivery (López Acevedo 2002a). But these reasons are probably the consequence of something else: a gap in human transformation and technology absorption that determine the quality of the work, of the products, their timing, etc. This technological gap makes it impossible for these enterprises to export themselves, and extremely difficult for them to even become the internal purveyors of exporting companies; thus these companies either import those products, or call upon their providers to install themselves in the country.

This technological gap is also what defines the disconnect between the export-oriented and the internal market–oriented sectors, and the fact that the impressive growth of exports seems to be almost completely disconnected from the rest of the Mexican economy. This is demonstrated by the relationship between the rate of growth of exports and that of GNP, which has been negative in the last eighteen years (Romero 2004). While the external market has grown at the rates I have already mentioned, between 1998 and 1994 the internal market has fallen by a third (32.8 percent). On the other hand, exports have a very reduced national content. In 1983, exports had 86 percent of national content on average, but in 1996 they only had 42 percent.

This situation is radicalized if we take into account that almost half of the exports are *maquila* products. In fact, the growth of the *maquiladora* industry has been more rapid than that of other exports between 1990 and 2000; the *maquiladora* industry almost tripled, from 3.9 percent of GNP to

10.2 percent of GNP, while other exports went from 11.9 percent to 19 percent (Romero 2004: 78). But the *maquiladora* industry integrates a negligible part of national production, less that 2 percent. In this manner, the national value added is very small and the impact on the internal economy is minimal (Arroyo Picard 2000). This situation has remained unchanged in contrast to what has happened in the East Asian countries that also started being the assemblers or producers of the spare parts more dependent on their internal labor force. While in 1980 this industry consumed 1.7 percent of its total inputs from the Mexican national economy, in November 2004 this percentage increased to a mere 3.0 percent.[5] More significant with regard to future perspectives is a case where we would expect more integration: the electronics industry in Jalisco. This industry has been very dynamic in the last ten years. It has an ever-greater participation in the national electronics industry, and the regional impact of its exports and labor have been spectacular. A very significant number of enterprises producing computers and electronic products, such as IBM, NEC, Motorola, Siemens, Philips, Compac, Hewlett Packard, Intel, and Telmex, have been installed in the metropolitan area of Guadalajara, in El Salto. In 1997, these enterprises generated around 100,000 direct or indirect jobs, and more than US$2.707 billion, representing more than 53 percent of the total exports in Jalisco (Dussel 1999: 29). Nonetheless, even in this case there is a minimal integration of micro- and small enterprises, and a great dependency on imported parts, with a very small potential to generate value-added chains in the future. The degree of national integration of the electronics industry in Jalisco is thus still very low. Dussel calculates that less than 5 percent of the value added of this sector is of national and regional origin. This is due to the fact that there are few national and regional providers and that most of the providers are foreign-owned. In many cases, the providing enterprises install themselves in Jalisco under a contract with the main enterprise. From this case, Dussel concludes that the situation of the electronics industry in Jalisco is very similar to that of the *maquiladora* industry in general, and that subcontracting in Mexico is just at its beginnings. This is so, although 29 percent of the enterprises have some program to stimulate national providers and there exists a number of government institutions such as NAFIN, Bancomext, Crece, and Secofi that try to foment subcontracting schemes; although these institutions exist, there is no cooperation between them, and their programs duplicate and compete among each other. Thus these enterprises prefer to attract an important number of subcontracting enterprises from their home countries.

As a result, Mexico's export success obliges the country to continuously increase its imports, either through the *maquiladora* industry or through other semi-*maquila* industries (such as Urquidi categorizes the automotive and auto-parts industry, where there is total import freedom and the linkages to national industry are very weak) (Urquidi 1999: 54). Thus, while in 1993 exports represented 12.9 percent of Mexico's GNP, imports of intermediary goods linked to exports represented 6.1 percent of GNP, which signifies an export value added of 6.8 percent of GNP. In 2000, exports more than doubled, to an impressive 28.2 percent of GNP, but imports related to exports almost tripled, rising to 16.3 percent of GNP, resulting in an aggregate product of exports that barely doubled, to 11.9 percent. Another significant fact is that imports associated with exported goods have gone from 6.1 percent in 1993 to 16.3 percent, while imports not associated with exported goods have almost stagnated (they have only grown from 5.5 percent to 6.3 percent) (Romero 2004: 78). Finally, the foreign content of investments has also significantly increased. An increasing proportion of investments are imported, a development that translates the multiplicative effect toward the outside. In 1988, 80 percent of the fixed capital formation was national and 20 percent imported; in 2000, the national part was 67 percent, while the foreign one was 33 percent (p. 80).

## The Impact on the Democratization Process

Most of the discussion of the relationship between politics and economics focuses on the difficulties of newly democratic governments in implementing the necessary measures in order to liberalize their economies. The Mexican situation is radically different: although there are some structural reforms that are still being considered (the reform of the labor law,[6] the privatization of the electric and the petroleum industries), these are not central. In contrast to third-wave countries where democratic governments had the political task of dismantling the political alliances that profited from the old model within a democratic context, in Mexico the new government has had to deal with the effects of these changes, rather than with their implementation. The new government raised rather contradictory expectations: the entrepreneurial actors and part of the middle classes that voted for the PAN in 2000 expected the government to continue applying the new economic model and insuring economic stability; another part of the middle and the popular classes that rejected the PRI expected changes in the economic model, especially in its tendency toward the creation of income inequality. Nevertheless, to continue attracting foreign capital and investments and stimulate national investors, while making the necessary changes to the model in order that it be more equitable and integrative for the Mexican population, seems contradictory but necessary.

This is crucial not only for strictly economic reasons but because this contradiction affects the democratization process that did not end with the changes in the presidency of Vicente Fox. The dilemma is an old one, going as far back as modernization theory itself. In fact, analysts such as Maravall accept the idea that economic development engenders conditions for democracy. This is demonstrated by the fact that authoritarian regimes suffer from their economic success in that they create the conditions for their own invalidation. Authoritarian regimes are also more fragile during economic crises because they depend on efficiency rather than on legality; unless they are totally tyrannical, they depend on their ability to deliver economic growth, and are based on a substantive legitimacy, rather than on a formal one—that is, they depend on delivering economic growth and not on the rule of law. Nevertheless, this does not mean that the contrary relation is true: democractic states do not directly depend on the fact that democracy either betters the lot of their people or succumbs. The relationship between both is indirect, because it passes through social organizations.

There is no "prior normative commitment for democracy," and democracy works if those involved in it believe their interests can be channeled through democratic institutions (Przeworski 1995: 42). Thus, rather than asking if democracy betters the conditions of the poor, we must ask if the poor consider that they have "a reasonable chance to advance their objectives within the institutional framework . . . if it is fair" (p. 42). In order that they feel so, they must be able to express their support or rejection of the economic measures applied by their governments; this means that they must be sufficiently organized or that they believe that the existing political parties represent them. If the answer to either question is negative, these majorities will probably be disaffected with democracy and end up calling for a political solution that will restart the cycle of populist and authoritarian regimes.

The situation in Mexico is not clearly positive in this respect. On the one hand, I have already mentioned that some of the population that thought it was represented by the Fox government, in that it raised expectations that it was going to change the economic model, may be deeply dissatisfied by its focus on economic stability, something that continues with the strict application of the neoliberal model. On the other hand, this same propensity of the government to focus on stability has led it to accommodate itself with the old corporatist organizations that traditionally lack legitimacy and representation. Finally, the political parties, at least what we have seen from their action in Congress, seem to be much more interested in their own electoral fate, rather than really representing specific interests. We may thus actually be seeing an upsurge of dissatisfaction with democracy.

Nevertheless, the mere loss of the presidency by the PRI has opened an important space for the action and organization of civil society that did not exist before. It may eventually lead to the strengthening of civil society by removing the constraints established by the old regime. It may also be possible that the new regime will stimulate political and social organization, whereas an open market requires periodic bargaining over wages and labor conditions that "are conducive to the emergence and consolidation of a bargaining culture" (Waisman 1999: 54). Nevertheless, there is also the danger of "a segmentation of society into an organized and autonomous sector that looks very much like a strong civil society and a disorganized or dependent sector susceptible to political marginality or subordination to the state" (p. 55).

## Conclusion: From Theory to Practice—Some Public Policy Recommendations

In Mexico, low salaries have been a crucial obstacle to the generalized absorption of technology, new organizational schemes within the enterprises, the training of workers, and the creation of educational institutions that stimulate a productive interaction between academy and industry. This in turn has also meant low incentives for the inventiveness of entrepreneurs and stimulated their rent-seeking and speculative character. This has affected the Mexican economy not only in that it almost lacked the incentive to become an endogenous technological nucleus, but also that it has inserted itself into the international economy in a passive rather than an active way (Rivera Ríos 2001). This trend has determined that the external drive of the economy has had a low impact on the internal economy.

Although betting on low costs was a natural option for an underdeveloped country, East Asian countries that started this way transcended this moment and succeeded in embarking in a new direction that favors higher salaries, education, and job training—in sum, it favors enhancing human capital. In fact, according to the Asian model, the evolution of subcontracting is a response to the increase in the technological and organizational capacity of national agents, which in turn makes technology economically viable and profitable (Rivera Ríos 2001). A higher level of human capital both requires and is able to adapt to new technologies in order to increase productivity. Only such a policy, accompanied by the coordination of government policies to link exporting enterprises to local purveyors, can eventually close the gap between nationally and externally oriented enterprises.

International agencies, such as the World Bank, have expressed recommendations for Mexico in this regard. They propose increasing the social capacity of accumulation by elevating the educational and training levels of the labor force and the organizational capacity of the enterprises in order to be more able to interact with external agents. They also propose an increase in the general technological knowledge of the country and the enhancement of the infrastructures of communication and transportation, as well as consolidation of the entrepreneurial nets that favor learning (World Bank

2001). Nonetheless, these recommendations have been totally ineffective, in part because the state is less and less capable of exerting the financial capacity and the leadership to endorse them effectively, and also because what has impeded these recommendations is the authoritarian-corporatist regime that implemented a liberal economic model.

I have argued that the manner in which Mexico chose to apply the new economic model was in part determined on an institutional path. And although there has been a change at the level of the presidency that opens up the possibility of dismantling corporatist controls, the fact that most of the institutions that determined the economic path are still in place makes it difficult to transcend this situation. Although the party that controls most of the unions and peasant organizations no longer holds the nation's presidency, it still holds most of the state governments (twenty out of thirty-one) and the majority of the municipal ones, and in most cases continues to exert a clientelistic control over these social organizations. On the other hand, Fox's government seems more preoccupied with maintaining social peace that ensures a favorable context for foreign investments than with democratizing civil society. It has thus not promoted the dismantling of the organizations that are still in the hands of nonrepresentative leaderships. On the contrary, Fox has tried to accommodate the old, still-majoritary organizations, and has blocked the appearance of independent unions and continued to accept the existence of thousands of "protection unions."

In order to reconstruct the Mexican economy, we need greater investment in social capital. Almost as urgently, we also need the dismantling of the old corporatist controls. This should not mean that we should substitute these controls with the forces of the market, as is meant by most government officials. It is instead necessary to implement a different form of regulation that functions as beneficial constraints. This would open the possibility of implementing different public policies that are negotiated and implemented between the government and the social actors.

## Notes

1. This can be interpreted in another manner, as we will see later, as a way of showing how exports have a very weak impact on the Mexican economy as a whole. See Urquidi (1999).

2. This can also be interpreted in a different manner; exports substitute the internal market, which is why we notice, for example, that in 1983 exports (excluding the *maquiladora* industry, which makes this data more relevant) grew 60 percent, but only 28 percent in 1984, while GNP decreased 7.9 percent and grew 5 percent, respectively, at the lowest point of the crisis. During 1987, another crisis year, when the economy decreased 5.7 percent, exports grew by 20.8 percent. Finally, during the great crisis of 1995, the economy decreased by 4.8 percent and exports grew by 46.9 percent.

3. The concept of constitutional order comes from Charles Sabel (1997).

4. The comparison with Brazil is significant in that Brazil managed to go much further in its import-substitution process because its state was very much oriented to structural rather than monetary policies. Even the military followed these kinds of nationalist and protective policies. Even after the opening of the economy during the Cardoso presidency, Brazil's industry and financial system continues to be much more protectionist. In Brazil there still exists an important coalition between entrepreneurs and government elites that favor structuralist measures, state intervention, and regulation in order to develop the economy. This contrasts with Mexico, where the absolutely dominant coalition is for macroeconmomic stability, deregulation, and unrestricted opening of the Mexican economy.

5. Instituto Nacional de Estadística, Geografía e Informática (2005).

6. Although reform of the labor law has not been accomplished, most of the collective contracts have already been modified in the sense in which a new liberal labor law would have it; there has thus already been a de facto labor law reform.

# 8

# Spain: Globalization's Impact on Democracy and Inequality

*Josep Oliver-Alonso and Josep M. Vallés*

This book aims to identify those policies undertaken by a democratic government that can reduce social inequality at a moment when the globalization phenomenon is redefining the autonomy of national states. As a result of an unprecedented increase of capital flow at the international level, the 1990s has been the source of a very intense debate on the relationship between economic growth and the opening up of economies to overseas commerce, and inequality.[1] However, for the majority of developed countries the discussion concerning the advantages of integration into the world economy was already resolved in a positive fashion more than fifty years ago after the negative effects of the beggar-my-neighbor policies in the 1930s. In this context, the case for Spain can be considered as a prime example. Indeed, the Spanish economy and society during the 1950s and 1960s shared many of the characteristics of those countries that today are referred to as "developing countries": economic underdevelopment, extreme social inequality, and a dictatorial political system. In spite of this point of departure, Spain today now finds itself among those countries with the highest level of development at a worldwide level, with a consolidated democracy and a clearly more egalitarian income distribution.

This transformation is due to many factors, some of which have their origins in the decision to open up the Spanish economy to overseas trade, adopted at the end of the 1950s during the Franco dictatorship. From this point of view, it can be said that the Spanish economy received a very positive impact from a better integration into a globalized world. Although the fundamental steps that led to the modernization of Spain were taken at the end of the 1970s in a democratic context, it has to be remembered that some of the previous measures taken by the dictatorship paved the way for the path followed by the Spanish economy from 1977 onward. From the beginning of the twentieth century up until the 1950s, Spanish capitalism had adopted the so-called nationalist route for economic growth, which can be briefly translated as maintaining extraordinary measures to protect the Spanish market.[2]

This nationalist-biased policy reached its peak in the so-called autarchy period, between 1939 and the middle of the 1950s. Following this policy, economic relations with foreign countries had to be limited to the minimum necessary.[3] During this period, the domestic growth model showed evident inherent weaknesses: the lack of foreign currency reserves (a crucial factor for the development of a country lacking in raw materials), no oil, and a very low level of technological development. The debate over the dual equation "domestic growth–opening up of the economy" came to a head at the end of the 1950s in favor of integration into the world economy,[4] as the autarchic model had proved inadequate to promote growth, asphyxiated as much by inevitable inflation as by the collapse of the foreign trade sector.

The economic boom that followed—the Spanish economy grew between 1962 and 1974 at an average rate in real and yearly terms of 7 percent—in the 1960s and up to the first half of the 1970s (the "economic miracle," as it was then called in imitation of the "post-war German economic miracle") can only be explained in terms of this opening up of the Spanish economy, including the massive export of Spanish work force to the European Community (EC) countries.

As regards the purposes of this chapter, the main question is: which were the main measures taken at that time? Basically, the change in direction of economic policies that took place in July 1959 had two basic aims: opening up to overseas markets and liberalizing the domestic economy. Although this last aspect was quickly counteracted, the group of measures that inspired the policies for economic development in the 1960s (the increasing opening up of the Spanish economy to overseas trading) constituted a resounding success. Spain devalued its currency and entered the International Monetary Fund (IMF) agreeing to comply with the measures demanded by this organization, and joined the World Bank. These became primary considerations for decisions taken by Spain from then onward.[5] Spain also became a member of the Organization for Economic Development and Cooperation (OECD), joined the General Agreement on Tariffs and Trade (GATT), and adopted a policy of customs duties that were clearly less protectionist. Although the current "economic globalization" concept and the old "economic opening up" are not identical, it can be said that the Spanish process of that time moved in the same "globalization" direction that it does today.

The combination of this opening up of the Spanish economy along with the expansionist wave in the Western countries during the 1960s and the beginning of the 1970s brought about a dramatic change in the forces that had impaired the growth of the Spanish economy. For the first time since the 1930s, the foreign trading sector ceased to be a restriction to economic growth, and became instead the actual source of it.

The factors that contributed to this change in foreign trade policies are many and varied. In the first place, there was a change in the productive structure of the Spanish economy that significantly increased its industrial exports. This, however, simultaneously increased its intermediary input needs: raw materials, mainly energy, and capital goods. In fact, there was a steady negative trade balance during these years. There were three compensatory mechanisms for this deficit that resulted from the economic successes during these years. First, the balance in services highly improved, thanks to a growing tourist sector. The second was the mass of Spanish workers leaving Spain to work in the Western European labor market, which brought with it currencies in the form of bank transfers that, along with incomes from the tourist sector, generated a foreign currency surplus. Third, Spain became a net receiving country for indirect investments coming from abroad (especially from the United States and Switzerland). These three factors counteracted the goods deficits, allowed for an increase in currency reserves, and closed the gap that traditionally had held back Spanish economic growth.

However, this model brought about several problems that became apparent when international growth slowed down in 1974 as a result of the first oil crisis. Basically, and as far as we are concerned here, there are two aspects that need to be highlighted when considering Spanish social and economic relations during this time. First is the particularly inadequate role of the public sector: public revenue and spending in 1975 accounted for a little less than 25 percent of the gross domestic product (GDP), a figure that was a long way off the average figures for European economies for that period. And second, a highly unequal income distribution plagued the Spanish economy.

These are the two sides of the same coin. In short, a system was in operation under the Franco dictatorship where the absence of social-agreement policies was assured by political repression: it has to be remembered that free-trade unions were banned under Franco's regime. Although Franco's government persisted in its aspiration to become a member of the European Economic Community (EEC),[6] Spain's EEC membership required, in addition to the prerequisite of a democratic government, the adoption of the European economic growth model, mainly based on the concept of a social-contract policy. As we said above, Spain lacked an effective public sector with sufficient resources and was unable to provide a wide range of public and social services. In the period 1973–1977, Spain found itself facing some formidable challenges, when the Franco political regime was coming to its end and the first energy crisis was striking hard on the Spanish economy.[7]

It is in this context that the Spanish experience takes on its particular relevance. As we will try to show in this chapter, success in terms of economic growth, modernization of social services, and improvements in the standard of living and inequality have been impressive. This chapter's aim is to identify the main elements that have allowed for this change and to analyze to what extent this experience can be exported to other countries in a similar situation.

It is important to stress that, in the Spanish case, globalization has had two special features: it has been a long process started at the end of the 1950s, and it has been strongly related to the country's membership in the European Union (EU) since 1986. As we said before, the economic opening up of Spanish society started in 1959, when Spain entered into the GATT, the IMF, the OECD, and the World Bank. From this moment onward, Spain dramatically changed its attitude and its legal background toward foreign investment, replacing the traditional opposition of its economic and political elites with a more friendly attitude. Broadly speaking, the long race toward a more globalized economy that started at the late 1950s ended almost forty years later when the Spanish peseta was replaced by the euro in 1999.

It has to be remembered what it meant for Spain to become an EU member. The Treaty of Rome (1956) was, and still is, extremely clear about the relationship between European candidates to the European Union and its political system. A democratic system was then, as it is today, a prerequisite to beginning negotiations to become a full EU member. From this point of view, when Spain tried to start this process in 1962, the answer was clearly negative. As a result, Spanish political, business, and financial rulers in the 1970s—encompassing from a nonnegligible part of the old political class to the new political parties—identified the full integration into the EU with a stable democratic system. In the same way, the relationship between democratic legitimacy and inequality reduction was clear from the beginning of the Spanish transition. If Spain had to become a stable democracy, it was necessary to build up a totally new social network, increasing public expenditure in social goods and services (health care, education, and pensions).

Summing up all these factors, it can be said that at the end of the 1970s Spain faced a difficult problem. In a context of a deep economic crisis, it had to build up a new welfare-state system as a basis for the legitimation of the new democratic situation. In spite of the clear steps taken during the 1960s and 1970s toward a deeper integration into the international economy, to go further at the end of the 1970s asked for full EU membership. This meant that democracy, economic growth, less inequality, and full membership in the EU were different parts of the same project. In the Spanish case, globalization and social and political transformations were part of the same process.

Thus this chapter will deal with three major questions: To what extent is Spain a consolidated democracy and, if so, how has this consolidation been brought about? To what degree has a democratic Spain, as full member of the EU, managed to be successful in combining economic growth and reducing inequality? What policies or decisions adopted by democratic governments were at the origin of this result? In a final section, we offer some conclusions concerning the possibility of "exporting" the Spanish experience to other countries.

## Consolidating Democracy in Spain: The Main Changes

In June 1977, democratic elections were called in Spain for the first time since those held forty years earlier in February 1936. Between 1936 and 1977, Spain had lived through a military coup, a bloody civil war (1936–1939), and a prolonged dictatorship under General Francisco Franco (1939–1975). For almost half a century Spain was deprived of the main institutions associated with democracy: freedom of the press, freedom to form political parties and trade unions, a democratically elected parliament, and an independent judiciary. Almost two generations of Spaniards had grown up under the pressure of a political ideology clearly opposed to the basic freedoms and institutions of democratic regimes. Political repression and official propaganda played in favor of the social, cultural, and economic principles of a socially conservative and politically authoritarian system.

One foreseeable development from the prolonged individual dictatorship of General Franco—grounded on the combined interests of the dominant economic sectors, the armed forces, and the most intransigent sectors within the Catholic Church—could have been a slow transition toward a "limited democracy," with a reduced set of political rights and a strong conservative government.[8] However, only five years after the first democratic elections, the left-wing Spanish Workers' Socialist Party (PSOE) came to power after obtaining an absolute parliamentary majority in the 1982 elections. These peaceful changes are the reason why the Spanish case has been described as a success story by political scientists in several works dealing with transition processes to democracy.[9]

### Explaining the Spanish Transition to Democracy

Analysts have regarded several structural and strategic factors as determining elements in the Spanish transition processes.

Some explanations emphasize the emergence of some favorable "structural factors" (economic and social) as favorable conditions toward bringing about the consolidation of institutions and democratic behavior. Among these factors, the Spanish case can show the relative modernization of the Spanish economy between 1960 and 1970, particularly in industry and tourism. As we said above, this modernization implied a gradual integration into the European and Western world economy and its institutions (OECD, IMF, the World Bank, and GATT).

At the same time, large-scale urban development involving the most dynamic sectors of the population (urban workers in industries and services, small businesses, technically skilled workers and professionals) had also taken place during these years, with deep changes in the country's social and cultural mores. But these positive structural factors were to some extent counterbalanced by the fact that the end of Franco's dictatorship and the subsequent transition to democracy coincided with a serious depression resulting from the major impact of the 1973 oil crisis.

Other explanations stress the importance of the "strategic options" of the main players in the transition processes. In Spain, the main players came from politically opposed areas, loosely organized in two groups. The first group included the business and finance sectors, political leaders, and high-ranking civil servants of Franco's regime and the armed forces. The second group included the underground political parties and trade unions, a large section of the intellectual and university elites, and the nationalist movements in Catalonia and in the Basque Provinces.

These different players were considering three possible scenarios after General Franco's disappearance from the political stage: continuity, reform, and rupture. An important section of the political elite who supported the dictatorship believed that a "dictatorship without Franco" was still a viable option.[10] Very soon it was clear that the real alternatives would be "rupture or reform." An evaluation of the potential of the democratic opposition forces and the "reformist" section of the Francoist elites led both of them to the conclusion that neither of the two was strong enough to impose its own option.[11] This explains why the outcome of this situation was an "agreed rupture." This outcome included not only political reforms, but also deep social changes, as we will see later.[12]

We can talk of an "agreed rupture" because it produced radical changes in the institutions and legal foundations of authority, according to the demands of the democratic opposition. But it was "agreed" because these changes came about through the reform of the laws and institutions of the dictatorship in a process that was mainly led by the evolutionist sector of the Franco regime itself.[13]

This transition model was reinforced—or rather spurred on—by two other factors: the majority opinion of Spanish citizens and the Western European political context. The feeling among the majority of Spanish people was in favor of a nontraumatic evolution toward a democratic system with which a significant part of the Spanish population had become acquainted during the latter part of the Franco regime, through the phenomena of social migrations and mass tourism.[14] On the other hand, the collective memory of the suffering induced by the Civil War (1936–1939) also had a strong influence on Spanish public opinion, which seemed ready to reject any kind of excessive confrontation between political positions and to tend toward nonviolent solutions.

At the same time, the European setting also favorably influenced a peaceful transition toward democracy in Spain.[15] The leading members of the European Community—France and Germany—were also important partners for the Spanish economy and their financial, business, and political elites kept close relations with Spanish political and economic elites. At the same time, political parties and trade unions of these European countries had established a permanent relationship with the democratic opposition parties and trade unions in Spain and provided them political guidance and financial support.

Therefore, the European factor, from an economic and political perspective, was extremely important for the success of the democratic transition. Membership in the EC was an aspiration largely shared by the evolutionist or reformist groups of the Franco regime, by the democratic opposition, and by the general public. This is why the European factor represented a strong incentive to undertake the process of making Spain a democracy and, at the same time, acted as a guarantee that the key elements of this process would be protected by political powers from outside.[16] Thus, this international context helped the nonconflictive transformation of the Spanish dictatorship into a democratic system that was acceptable to the EC.[17]

### New Political Institutions and Basic Social Agreements

From 1978 to 1980, negotiations between the Francoist-reformist elite and representatives of the democratic opposition resulted in decisions that gave a solid ground to the buildup of a pluralist democracy. These decisions concerned the institutional arena and the pattern of socioeconomic relations.

With regard to the institutional arena and in a relatively short span of time (1976–1978), the Spanish political system was grounded on the main rules of democratic regimes:

1. Freedom of the press for both print and audio-visual media
2. Freedom to organize trade unions, legalizing the preexisting clandestine organizations, among which the most important were and still are the Comisiones Obreras (CCOO) and Unión General de Trabajadores (UGT)[18]
3. Freedom to organize political parties, legalizing the already existing underground parties such as the PSOE (socialist) or the PCE (Spanish Communist Party)[19]

4. The end of the criminal prosecution of all political activity, along with a general amnesty for all the so-called political and opinion crimes, including the right to return to the country for all political exiles
5. The gradual submission of the armed forces to civil authority, avoiding the risk of an autonomous military power that might have turned Spain into a democracy under the control of the armed forces
6. A deep territorial decentralization policy in order to answer the historical claims of Catalan and Basque populations, that at the end extended this decentralization to all regions of the Spanish state to the point of creating a parafederal structure
7. The democratization of local governments after free local elections were held in 1979

All of these decisions answered the main and basic claims of the democratic opposition movements. The price paid by the opposition was to accept the king as head of state and abandon its historical demand for a referendum on this issue. In the same way, the opposition gave up its demand of taking legal action against any of the political leaders and bureaucrats—magistrates, police, or military officers—of the dictatorship. This is why a rather rapid transition was assured, yet at the same time without a formal rupture with the previous regime.

These institutional changes as a whole were condensed and reaffirmed in the drawing up and passing of a new constitution in 1978. The constitution established "un Estado social y democrático de derecho," that is, a state based on the rule of law, democratic pluralism, and social rights. In addition, the constitution defined Spain as a constitutional monarchy. The constitution was passed in Parliament by a large majority—including the most important political forces—and was ratified in a referendum in December 1978.[20] The 1978 constitution can be seen as the formal and final step of a peaceful process by which the foundations of political legitimacy radically changed from the dictator's sole and autonomous power—who, in his own words, held himself accountable "only to God and history"—to a democratic authority grounded on the people's will, bound by law, and accountable to the electorate.

Concerning the pattern of socioeconomic relations, changes were also produced by way of three general agreements when it came to tackling the serious economic crisis that Spain was experiencing at that time. These agreements had an effect on tax reforms, salary increases, working conditions, unemployment benefits, and other social-security benefits. In spite of this transaction-oriented atmosphere, not all the agreements received the full support of the relevant actors, since those who signed the socioeconomic pacts between 1977 and 1981 varied in each case.

Table 8.1 shows these variations in signing parties: agreements between political parties without the presence of social actors (trade unions or business organizations); agreements between trade unions and the Confederación Española de Organizaciones Empresariales (CEOE, the main Spanish business association) and trilateral agreements between the government, trade unions, and the CEOE. All these agreements had, however, an effect on economic and social policies of the time, as will be seen in the next sections.

## Political Attitudes and Behavior

This transition process and the resulting institutional and social framework developed under the influence of some prevalent political attitudes and behavior patterns among the Spanish people and the political elites. It is useful to give some attention to the main features of the new democratic political culture in Spain because this culture will appear as an important variable when explaining other economic and social changes.

Electoral behavior has produced a moderate multiparty system. Between 1977 and 2000, there have been eight parliamentary elections.[21] The results of these elections are given in Table 8.2. This table shows two phases in electoral trends. In the first period (1977–1979) the Unión de Centro Democrático (UCD) and the Partido Socialista Obrero Española (PSOE) appear as the main political parties. In the second phase (1982–2000), the UCD has now been replaced by the Alianza Popular and the Partido Popular (PP) as the main center-right political party.[22] In addition to these three political parties, there are other nationalist or regional parties that have also won seats in the Spanish Parliament.[23] During some of the terms of government, these minority parties have given decisive support to the statewide parties when they had to form a government and lacked the necessary parliamentary working majority (in 1993 for the PSOE, and in 1996 for the PP). It should also be noted that up to now the Spanish electorate has not given any significant support to extreme

**Table 8.1  Socioeconomic Agreements During the Transition Period, 1977–1981**

| Year | Agreement | Participating Groups |
| --- | --- | --- |
| 1977 | Pactos de la Moncloa | Government and all political parties |
| 1980 | Acuerdo-marco interconfederal | UGT and CEOE[a] |
| 1981 | Acuerdo nacional de empleo | Government, UGT, CCOO and CEOE |

*Note:* a. The CEOE is the national employer's association, reorganized in 1977 on the basis of the association existing during Franco's regime.

left or extreme right-wing forces that might have acted as "antisystem" parties.[24]

Consequently, a moderate pluralist model has taken shape in which two major national parties compete for the center voting space within the political spectrum. It is winning in this center space that has allowed the PSOE (a social-democrat party) to stay in government between 1982 and 1996 and to implement the set of social and economic policies that can be considered as essential factors in the evolution of Spanish economy and society.

A large majority of Spanish voters tend toward center-left political positions and clearly favor socioeconomic reforms. Electoral behavior described above reflects in a way how Spaniards define themselves when answering the question, "Where do you place yourself on a Left-Right scale?" The average self-placement is located in the center-left position of the political spectrum. This average position has remained stable throughout the entire period, as can be seen in Table 8.3.

Other data related to social and political attitudes confirm this ideological self-placement. Thus, for example, when faced with the dilemma of choosing between social change or maintaining the status quo, a large majority clearly tends to favor gradual reforms, while only a minority show themselves in favor of preserving the existing order.

Table 8.2    **Spanish Electoral Results in the Lower Chamber (Congreso de los Diputados), 1977–2000 (percentage of the total vote)**

|  | 1977 | 1979 | 1982 | 1986 | 1989 | 1993 | 1996 | 2000 |
|---|---|---|---|---|---|---|---|---|
| Parties |  |  |  |  |  |  |  |  |
| UCD | 34.6 | 35.0 | 6.8 | — | — | — | — | — |
| PSOE | 29.3 | 30.5 | 48.4 | 44.2 | 39.6 | 38.8 | 37.5 | 34.1 |
| IU (PCE) | 9.4 | 10.8 | 4.0 | 4.6 | 9.1 | 9.6 | 10.6 | 5.4 |
| PP (AP/CP) | 8.3 | 6.0 | 26.5 | 26.2 | 25.8 | 34.8 | 38.9 | 44.5 |
| CDS | — | — | 2.9 | 9.1 | 8.0 | 1.8 | — | — |
| CIU | 2.8 | 2.7 | 3.7 | 5.0 | 5.1 | 4.9 | 4.6 | 4.2 |
| PNV | 1.7 | 1.5 | 1.9 | 1.6 | 1.3 | 1.2 | 1.3 | 1.5 |
| Others | 13.9 | 13.5 | 5.8 | 9.3 | 11.1 | 8.9 | 7.1 | 10.3 |
| Total | 100.0 | 100.0 | 100.0 | 100.0 | 100.0 | 100.0 | 100.0 | 100.0 |
| Electoral turnout | 79.1 | 68.3 | 79.8 | 70.6 | 69.7 | 76.4 | 78.1 | 68.7 |

*Notes:*
UCD (center-right): Unión de Centro Democrático
PSOE (social democrats): Partido Socialista Obrero Español
IU (former communists and greens): Izquierda Unida
PP (center-right): Partido Popular
CDS (center-right): Centro Democrático y Social
CIU (Catalan center-right nationalists): Convergencia i Unió
PNV (Basque center-right nationalists): Partido Nacionalista Vasco

**Table 8.3    Ideological Self-Placement of the Spanish Electorate, 1977–2002**

|                  | 1977 | 1982 | 1989 | 1993 | 1996 | 2002 |
|------------------|------|------|------|------|------|------|
| Average position | 5.6  | 4.8  | 4.7  | 4.7  | 4.7  | 4.8  |

*Source:* Centro de Investigaciones Sociológicas (CIS), authors' compilation from various years.
*Note:* Respondents placed themselves along a scale of 1–10, 1 being the value that corresponds to the extreme left and 10 being the value that corresponds to the extreme right.

At the same time, almost half of the Spanish electorate declares that government (or the state, in the European sense) should assume more responsibilities in socioeconomic affairs. This tendency toward gradual reforms appears to be based on giving priority to social equality, as opposed to individual freedom, when it comes to prioritizing one value over the other.[25] This trend in public opinion may be seen as an explanatory factor for the support given to the social and economic policies of the period that will be analyzed in the next sections.

Spanish citizens show a very limited degree of active involvement in political parties or trade unions. The election results place Spain among the European political systems with the lowest level of electoral turnout (see Table 8.2). This high electoral abstention goes together with a low rate of direct involvement with or membership in parties and trade unions. Spanish parties have been from their very beginning "voters parties" and not "mass parties," according to the well-known typology used in parties and party-systems analysis.[26] One can explain this fact by examining the role of the mass media—mainly, TV and radio—as the basic communication tools between the political class and the citizenry. It has often been said that Spain ranks high among European countries where television takes precedence over the direct message of political parties when it comes to political information.

Trade unions also have fairly modest membership rates when compared with those for other European countries.[27] This does not mean that private and public wage-earning employees disregard the claims and negotiating role of the major trade unions. On the contrary, the major unions do have the support of the wage-earning population from both private and public sectors when it comes to negotiating working conditions with their respective employers.[28] Some analysts have explained this limited tendency toward active involvement by the very same process of transition to democracy, when political elites stressed the importance of their agreements and did not deliberately appeal to mass mobilization as a pressure resource.

A strongly professional party system has been built up by the political elite. Spaniards' resistance to getting involved in any permanent manner with party organizations has been paralleled by the tendency among the political elite to transform their parties into highly professionalized structures, very hierarchical and mainly dependent on state financing. One can state that the bureaucratizing of political parties in Spain has developed in a short period of time: a large part of their active members hold elected positions at the different levels of government (local, regional, or state) or are associated with public institutions in managerial positions or as employees.

At the same time, political parties act in a very centralized way, by which the leader or person holding the highest-ranking position and his/her immediate collaborators have a decisive influence. Party financing basically comes from state funding, making them closer to state institutions than to other social organizations. As has happened in other European countries (Italy, France, Belgium, or Germany), there have been some reported cases of illegal financing in parties that have used their local or national power to raise contributions from private companies and the private sector in exchange for favors or privileges in their relations with the administration. All of this has contributed to political parties losing prestige among the Spanish populace and reinforcing its tendency to keep some distance from them, even though they still see parties as necessary instruments for an operative democracy.[29]

As in the Philippines (see Chapter 5), mass media have made politics into something of an entertainment business. As stated above, the transition to democracy took place within a media context where radio and television reached a wider audience and were more influential than the print press.[30] All in all, it can be said that the role of mass media helped the peaceful transition to a democratic system. With a few exceptions, the young generation of journalists and newspaper editors did belong either to the democratic opposition groups or to the Francoist reformist sector. The success of the transition process helped to stress the role of the media, which became since then very prominent actors on the public scene. Politics is therefore developed mainly under the pressure of mass media and, especially, of audio-visual media.

But this pressure has put politics under the rules of the audio-visual show business, in which party leaders and the so-called opinion leaders are the main actors. Representative institutions such as governments and parliaments are often perceived as being far too unconcerned with the daily problems faced by the population and far too obsessed with circumstantial disputes where the only persons taking part are the political leaders and the aforementioned opinion leaders, seen as members of the same "political class" and separate from the average person in the street.

Public opinion aligns its support to the Spanish democracy, but has developed a high degree of political disaffection. The five phenomena mentioned so far (moderate party pluralism, center-oriented political attitudes, low membership in parties and trade unions, parties' bureaucratization, and the role of audio-visual media) have evolved and consolidated themselves in the twenty-five-year period since a polyarchy—according to Robert Dahl's paradigm—was established in Spain. This polyarchy is, in essence, comparable to other political systems in Western Europe and North America. But to what degree do these five characteristics weaken or reinforce the consolidation of this polyarchy? Do they affect its legitimacy in some way or another?

Some observers relate the acceptance or legitimacy of a democratic system to the degree in which people perceive its effectiveness and yield in terms of economic and social progress, i.e., its capacity to respond to important collective demands such as economic growth, social equality, welfare, etc. This is the meaning of legitimacy that has been qualified as "functional—or instrumental—legitimacy" because it is conditioned by the political system's output. This functional or instrumental legitimacy can be distinguished from a second kind, a "substantive—or unconditional—legitimacy" that would suggest a strong adherence to the democratic system even when its political results are not seen to be satisfactory.

Can one discern these two faces of democratic legitimacy in Spanish public opinion? Since democracy was established (1975–1977) until today, Spanish society has lived through a wide range of economic and political changes: economic crises, political instability, terrorism, corruption, to name but a few. These changes have all had an impact on how effective the democratic system is seen to be when it comes to solving collective problems. But these changes have at no point altered the substantial support for a democratic system of government, as is illustrated in Table 8.4.[31]

The statement "democracy is better than any other form of government" is supported by 70–80 percent of the polled population, while somewhere around 20 percent claim to be indifferent or would prefer "under certain circumstances" an authoritarian system. The same percentage distribution is confirmed when they respond to the statement "democracy is

**Table 8.4 The Legitimacy of Spain's Democratic Political System, 1978–1994**
(percentage of the polled population who agreed with the statement, "Democracy is the best political system for a country like ours")

| 1978 | 1980 | 1981 | 1982 | 1983 | 1988 | 1993 | 1994 |
|------|------|------|------|------|------|------|------|
| 77 | 69 | 81 | 74 | 73 | 87 | 79 | 82 |

*Source:* Centro de Investigaciones Sociológicas (various years) and Montero, Gunther, and Torcal (1997).

the best political system for a country like ours," wherein 70–80 percent of those polled also agreed with this statement.[32]

But the studies available point out that present-day Spanish society is capable of endowing its democratic system with a high degree of legitimacy and yet at the same time distancing itself from it or expressing a certain degree of estrangement with regard to democratic politics. In this sense, an open support for democracy and its institutions is compatible with negative indicators such as low electoral turnout, resistance to becoming active members of political parties or trade unions, little apparent interest in politics, lack of confidence in their own ability to influence politics, lack of trust in parties and the political class in general, etc.[33]

When these social symptoms are combined together, they can be defined, according to some observers, as the "political disaffection syndrome." This political syndrome can also be seen in other countries with democratic systems of government that have been around for longer than the Spanish system.[34] These shared political attitudes have hardly changed since democracy and democratic institutions were first set up in the early years of the democratic transition. It appears, therefore, as some sort of chronic and long-term feature of the dominant political culture that shows itself rather immune to changes in economic cycles, political majorities, or any other factors.

## Economic Changes in Democratic Spain: Economic Growth and Inequality Reduction

In the previous sections we have described the transformation of Spanish political institutions and the attitudes and behavior that have supported this transformation during the last twenty-five years. However, there have also been some deep socioeconomic changes during this period that have allowed Spain to position itself among the most-developed countries. In this section we will describe the evolution of the Spanish economy in terms of the main indicators that explain this transformation and its impact on the distribution of income. First, we will offer a summary of the evolution of Spain's gross domestic product (GDP). Second, we will summarize the main structural changes to the Spanish economy and their impact on the job market. Finally, we will describe some indicators concerning social welfare, which show to what degree the economic growth achieved has translated into general improvements in social welfare.

### Economic Growth: 1975–2001

If we begin with an appraisal of economic growth and employment figures for the last twenty-five years of the twentieth century, the first thing that stands out is the remarkable progress in Spain's GDP, despite the fact that this progress has not been linear nor, and this is important to remember, free from major crises. Table 8.5 offers a summary of the growth of the Spanish GDP during this lengthy period, with an average increase of 2.8 percent for the twenty-year period 1981–2000. This figure is greater than averages achieved by other countries—for example: France (2.1 percent), Italy (1.9 percent), and Japan (2.7 percent). In fact, only the United States (3.2 percent) has recorded a figure greater than Spain's.

However, this increase in GDP has taken place during moments of changing economic fortunes where one can distinguish, from a broad perspective, two periods of recession (the first half of the 1980s and during the period 1993–1994), and two periods of expansion (the second half of the 1980s and the second during the 1990s). These cyclical changes in the Spanish economy are partly due to the impact of economic shock waves coming from abroad. In some cases these have had a particularly negative impact on the Spanish economy, such as those resulting from the second oil

**Table 8.5    Growth of GDP, Exports, and Employment in Spain and Other OECD Countries, 1981–2000, percentages**

|  | Germany | France | Italy | U.S. | Japan | Spain |
|---|---|---|---|---|---|---|
| **GDP** | | | | | | |
| Average 1981–1985 | n.a. | 1.5 | 1.7 | 3.2 | 3.3 | 1.4 |
| Average 1986–1991 | n.a. | 2.8 | 2.6 | 2.6 | 4.6 | 4.2 |
| Average 1992–1995 | 1.3 | 1.1 | 1.3 | 3.1 | 1.0 | 1.3 |
| Average 1996–2000 | 1.8 | 2.6 | 1.9 | 4.1 | 1.3 | 3.8 |
| Average 1981–2000 | n.a. | 2.1 | 1.9 | 3.2 | 2.7 | 2.8 |
| **Exports** | | | | | | |
| Average 1981–1985 | n.a. | 3.6 | 4.0 | 0.5 | 7.7 | 7.8 |
| Average 1986–1991 | n.a. | 5.3 | 4.0 | 10.3 | 3.3 | 3.9 |
| Average 1992–1995 | 1.8 | 5.2 | 9.7 | 7.2 | 2.8 | 10.4 |
| Average 1996–2000 | 8.4 | 8.1 | 4.2 | 7.1 | 5.8 | 10.2 |
| Average 1981–2000 | n.a. | 5.5 | 5.2 | 6.4 | 4.9 | 7.8 |
| **Employment** | | | | | | |
| Average 1981–1985 | −0.3 | −0.4 | 0.2 | 1.5 | 1.0 | −1.7 |
| Average 1986–1991 | 6.4 | 0.9 | 0.6 | 1.5 | 1.6 | 2.7 |
| Average 1992–1995 | −0.7 | −0.3 | −1.7 | 1.4 | 0.4 | −1.3 |
| Average 1996–2000 | 0.3 | 1.6 | 1.0 | n.a. | n.a. | 3.7 |
| Average 1981–2000 | 0.5 | 0.5 | 0.2 | n.a. | n.a. | 0.9 |

*Source:* Organization for Economic Cooperation and Development, National Annual Accounts, various years.

crisis (1981) or that of the European Monetary System (EMS) at the end of 1992 and during 1993. In contrast, other events have had a positive impact on the Spanish economy—for example, during the 1980s the signing of the Treaty of Accession to the EU (1986) and entry into the EMS (1989); then again, during the second half of the 1990s, as a result of the nominal convergence effort that led to Spain entering the European Monetary System (1999).

Within this complex and changing context, the principal characteristic features for this period, all of them with important consequences for the distribution of income, can be summarized as follows. During the final years of the 1970s and the first half of the 1980s, the Spanish economy had to cope with various supply shocks that had a very significant effect on its capacity to generate income and translated into both very low increases in the GDP (1.4 percent between 1980–1985) and a particularly harsh effect on levels of employment.

Consequently, the rate of unemployment, which in 1975 was running at some 2 percent, began to rise steadily, finally reaching 22 percent in 1985 with a net loss of more than 2 million jobs (mainly in industry), and at the same time, a fall in the percentage of the working-age population. This important change in the Spanish economy was a response to the shock caused by the second oil crisis and, in particular, to those proposed reforms in response to the first oil crisis (1973–1974) that had not been carried out.

Perhaps the clearest indication of the accumulation of economic imbalances is the rate of inflation that, in May and June of 1977, rose to a level higher than 30 percent in yearly terms. As one might expect, such a high level of domestic inflation was a reflection, at the same time, of a considerable loss of overseas competitiveness, with a current account balance showing enormous deficits in 1974, 1975, 1976, and 1977. We have shown above that the downward spiral was finally tackled after the first democratic elections were held in June 1977.

This came in the form of an agreement or pact between all the emerging political parties of the transition. The objective was to stabilize the Spanish economy and was formally expressed in October 1977 in what was called the Pactos de la Moncloa (the Moncloa Pacts), and later, in the major agreement that led to the Spanish constitution of 1978. Probably, the magnitude of this profound economic crisis is best illustrated by looking at investment that, during the lengthy period between 1975 and 1985, showed a negative yearly growth rate: in 1974 it accounted for 25.5 percent of the GDP, but by 1985 had fallen to 18.1 percent.

This crisis experienced by the industrial-production apparatus,[35] and the corresponding rise in unemployment, did not have such a profound effect on available household income since the public sector partially compensated for this negative trend.[36] This period of streamlining and restructuring came to an end around 1984. By then Spanish companies had reorganized their profit margins and potentially were in the situation of being able to increase investment, which had not grown for a number of years. Consumption at the household level had, for the same reasons, been seriously restricted, and had accumulated deficits that were going to be covered as the economic cycle changed. As regards the overseas sector during the same period, this had shown a significant recovery, precisely as a result of the major adjustment in demand at a national level, so much so that surpluses had been accumulated in the early 1980s. The budget deficit, although it continued at a rate of approximately 5 percent of the GDP, had ceased to increase and was beginning to finance itself by appealing to the capital markets.

In short, from a national perspective, the scene was set for a new period of expansion. The necessary spark for this came, logically, from the changes in conditioning factors from overseas, in the form of the important fall in petroleum prices and the dollar (after the Acuerdos Plaza of 1985), and particularly, as a result of the positive effects of Spain's entry into the EU on 1 January 1986. From this moment forward the Spanish economy exhibited very significant rates of increase in its GDP, accompanied by no less spectacular increases in employment (in net terms, between 1987 and 1991, an increase of 1,157,300 jobs).

Although the dismantling of customs barriers had negative repercussions on the foreign trade balance of payments (the current account balance changed from a surplus of 1.6 percent of the GDP in 1985 to a deficit of 3.1 percent of the GDP in 1991), domestic demand, driven by the previous deficits in consumption and investment and the important change in expectations, more than compensated for the drainage abroad. In addition, the incorporation of the peseta into the European Monetary System (1988), although to the detriment of exporters due to the high exchange rate, contributed to creating the belief that Spain had emerged from a long process of adjustment. This phase of expansion, however, was cut short in 1992, as much due to overseas factors (the important high interest rates in Germany that created the EMS crisis) as to domestic factors (an increase in national demand higher than supply that was impossible to maintain on a long-term basis).

However, the state of the Spanish markets, and particularly the labor market, had changed significantly. In contrast to the ten-year period 1975–1985, the adaptation of the Spanish economy to the new conditions was almost instantaneous, to the degree that unemployment figures rose to around 900,000 in approximately one year. This response by companies was the direct result of the greater flexibility within the job market from 1984, when seasonal hiring was introduced into Spanish legislation.[37]

Finally, one should note the important progress made during the years 1994–2001, with an average increase in the GDP of 3.4 percent in real terms, a good deal higher than the average for the European Union (2.5 percent) or Japan (1.2 percent); only the United States showed a higher increase (3.6 percent).

One of the most important lessons learned from this process is the positive link between the opening up of the economy and economic growth, and, indirectly, an improvement in the distribution of income. Indeed, from our perspective, Spain's categorical entry into the European and international markets has been one of the most decisive factors resulting in improvements in the Spanish economy in the last twenty-five years. If we accept this line of thinking, the Spanish experience suggests that, for a relatively small country like Spain, there is no better alternative to long-term sustained growth than complete integration into international trading and, beyond this, into supranational organizations such as the European Union or the European Monetary System. During this time Spain has been able to see for itself how its response to shocks from abroad differed depending on whether it was isolated from, or part of, the European Union. An example of the first of these, isolation, were the two energy crises in the 1970s and the early 1980s that resulted in a series of consequences that took Spain years to rectify.

In fact, these crises had a greater effect on the Spanish economy and in a comparatively different manner than other EC countries. Inflation rates, unemployment, budget deficits, and imbalances in overseas trade were systematically higher than rates for the same areas in other member countries of the European Economic Community at that time. In contrast, competition with other countries changed surprisingly as a result of dismantling customs duties to comply with Spain's entry into the EU (begun in 1986 and ended in 1993), the signing of the Single European Act (which freed up almost completely the movement of capital among member countries of the EU), Spain's accession to the EMS (1988), and finally Spain's acceptance of forming part of the European Monetary Union (after signing the Treaty of Maastricht in 1991).

It is well known that the growth of the Spanish economy during most of the twentieth century was strongly hindered by trading restrictions with other countries. A small country such as Spain, and one lacking the most important raw materials for growth, showed a tendency toward inflation rates that were higher than its neighboring trading countries, and chronic deficits in its foreign balance. In addition, Spain's dependency on foreign trading meant that the Spanish economy was much more vulnerable to shocks from abroad, as illustrated by the energy crises. Consequently, Spain's economic growth was held back by its paltry exporting capacity and the limitations imposed by the overseas sector. This was the basic problem of the Spanish economy during the 1940s and 1950s, as well as during the 1960s and 1970s, although with better results.

Turning to Spain's performance as part of the EU and from a more structural perspective, one of the main features of the remarkable progress made between 1980 and 2001 is due to no less than the opening up of the Spanish economy. That is to say that the Spanish economy has made this strong progress in terms of production and employment at the same time that exports of Spanish products and services proportionally increased their share of domestic supply (see Table 8.5). While in 1980 exports of goods and services represented around 12 percent of the Spanish GDP (9.2 percent for the sale of products alone), by 2000 these had dramatically increased, reaching 30.5 percent as a whole for sales overseas (of which 20.2 percent were sales of products).

In comparison with other OECD countries, this progress has been quite surprising, with a growth rate higher than 150 percent and above any other advanced economy. (In 1980, Italy and France showed a degree of opening up similar to Spain's, close to 30 percent, yet had begun from much more advantageous positions twenty years earlier.) This enormous push of Spanish exports is paralleled by an even greater increase for imports, which have risen from 10.2 percent to 32.5 percent of Spain's GDP between 1980 and 2000, registering a surprising growth of more than 200 percent for this period.

Since Spain entered the EU, this growth model changed appreciably. From this point of view one can conclude that the shocks originating from the world economy, in particular from the second half of the 1990s, have had practically no effect on Spain's growth. So, while a very significant part of the world GDP fell heavily after the crisis in the major countries of Southeast Asia in October 1997, the Spanish economy continued to grow steadily. The same can be said of the impact of later financial crises (Russia, Brazil, and Argentina) and economic crises (recession in the United States and in Germany in 2001).

In fact, within these contexts of such unstable economic growth, Spain registered surprising growth rates with respect to GDP during these years, as mentioned earlier. The underlying reasons for such a favorable behavior are all related precisely to Spain's joining the EU and in the last phase, the European Monetary Union (EMU). Although Spain registered a significant deterioration in its overseas balance of payments in the second half of the 1980s (partially due to the dismantling of its customs barriers, which was aggravated further by its incorporation into the EMS at a highly unfavorable exchange rate), the finalizing of the process of dismantling customs barriers and the return to a parity of the peseta in the EMS in 1992–1993 to a value more in accordance with Spain's relative situation of prices and costs implied a radical change in Spain's ability to compete in overseas trade.

In addition, the Maastricht Treaty of 1991 obliged Spain, in order to enter the EMU in 1998, to adopt a group of tax measures for prices and costs that, when seen in perspective, resulted in a very favorable change in Spain's ability to compete in the overseas trade market.[38]

The official interest rates that in 1993 (at the height of the monetary crisis) had risen to figures above 12 percent then began to decrease steadily from 1995 onward as required by the Maastricht Treaty, with figures lower than 3 percent in the spring of 1999 (Spain was then part of the EMU). Furthermore, given that Spain's inflation differential was much higher than that required for entry into the EMU,[39] this meant that Spain had to make greater efforts to contain costs and prices. Another aspect to be considered here is that during this period the trade unions followed a policy that permitted a significant reduction in labor costs, likewise contributing to meeting the requirements of the Maastricht agreement regarding inflation. Finally, the reduction of Spain's budget deficit also contributed to releasing resources for the overseas sector.

This transformation of the Spanish economy and society has come about simultaneously with Spain's full entry into the EU in 1986, beginning with dismantling customs barriers, and followed by its adherence to the EMS in 1988 and the signing of the Single European Act. Finally, in 1991, Spain signed the Maastricht Treaty that led to its entering the EMU from 1999 onward. Therefore, in the case of economic growth in Spain, an improved distribution of income and opening up its economy (see Table 8.6) are three sides of the same triangle, where the triangle cannot be seen unless all sides are comprehended as a whole. In fact Spain's success is inconceivable without its decisions to join the EU and the EMU.[40]

### Structural Change and Transformations in the Employment Market

This panoramic view of structural changes in the Spanish economy and society during the last twenty-five years would be incomplete without taking into consideration the profound modifications to the productive apparatus, employment levels, and job openings. In short, and as regards modifications to the productive apparatus, the Spanish economy has shown a strong development toward tertiary industries, and this is most apparent when one looks at the issue of employment. While in 1977 the services sector employed 41.8 percent of the total, by 2000 this percentage had risen as high as 62.4 percent. This significant increase brought with it a progressive fall in the percentage of people employed in the primary sector (from 20.8 percent to 6.9 percent for the same period) and in the industrial sector (falling from 27.6 percent to 19.8 percent).

For the purpose of this discussion, it should be pointed out that a fairly appreciable number of jobs created in the tertiary sector and, in particular,

**Table 8.6    Opening up of Spain's Economy and the Economies of Other OECD Countries, 1980–2000 (Real rates of annual growth, percentages)**

|  | Germany | France | Italy | U.S. | Japan | Spain |
|---|---|---|---|---|---|---|
| Exports of goods and services |  |  |  |  |  |  |
| 1980 | n.a. | 15.1 | 16.2 | 6.8 | 7.5 | 12.0 |
| 1985 | n.a. | 16.7 | 18.1 | 6.0 | 9.2 | 16.3 |
| 1990 | n.a. | 18.3 | 20.2 | 8.6 | 8.4 | 15.2 |
| 1995 | 24.5 | 22.5 | 27.0 | 10.7 | 9.1 | 22.6 |
| 2000 | 33.5 | 29.2 | 30.1 | 12.3 | 11.2 | 30.5 |
| Change 1980–2000 |  |  |  |  |  |  |
| In percentage points | n.a. | 14.1 | 13.9 | 5.5 | 3.7 | 18.5 |
| In percentage | n.a. | 93.4 | 85.8 | 80.9 | 49.3 | 154.2 |
| Imports of goods and services |  |  |  |  |  |  |
| 1980 | n.a. | 15.1 | 15.4 | 6.6 | 6.0 | 10.2 |
| 1985 | n.a. | 15.6 | 16.2 | 8.6 | 5.2 | 10.1 |
| 1990 | n.a. | 18.9 | 21.1 | 9.4 | 7.0 | 17.8 |
| 1995 | 23.8 | 21.1 | 23.0 | 11.8 | 7.7 | 22.8 |
| 2000 | 31.6 | 27.1 | 28.5 | 16.6 | 8.7 | 32.5 |
| Change 1980–2000 |  |  |  |  |  |  |
| In percentage points | n.a. | 12.0 | 13.1 | 10.0 | 2.7 | 22.3 |
| In percentage | n.a. | 79.5 | 85.1 | 151.5 | 45.0 | 218.6 |

*Source:* Organization for Economic Cooperation and Development, National Annual Accounts, various years.

more qualified labor, have been demanded by the public sector itself, which at this time was going through a profound transformation as much in terms of how it operated (a significant process of decentralization) as its structure (acquiring a weight much higher than its initial weight).

Total employment in public services (general administration and public and private health and education) increased from 1.1 million in 1977 to 2.6 million in 2000, an increase of 1.5 million job positions, which explains most of the progress made in employment in Spain for this period (which was, in total and in net terms, 2.1 million). These characteristics as a whole are summarized in Table 8.7.

Alongside these modifications in the production and demand for labor, the Spanish experience offers one peculiar characteristic in reference to job offers. Throughout most of the period since Spain has become a democracy, one of the main problems that has affected the Spanish economy and society has been unemployment. Other minor factors aside, the causes of unemployment have been due to the productive changes mentioned above, and particularly to the changes in labor supply, namely the entry into the labor

**Table 8.7   Stylized Features of the Job Market in Spain, 1978–2000**

Absolute values in percentages. Decreasing order by subsector according to rates of change.

|  | 1977 | 1985 | 1991 | 1994 | 2000 | Change 2000–1977 |
|---|---|---|---|---|---|---|
| Absolute values |  |  |  |  |  |  |
| Primary | 2,565 | 1,950 | 1,372 | 1,161 | 992 | −1,573 |
| Industrial | 3,395 | 2,592 | 2,900 | 2,462 | 2,868 | −527 |
| Construction | 1,205 | 768 | 1,273 | 1,060 | 1.578 | 374 |
| Services[a] | 5,141 | 5,240 | 7,048 | 7,015 | 9,011 | 3,869 |
| Pub. services | 1,113 | 1,406 | 1,996 | 2,020 | 2,589 | 1,476 |
| Priv. services | 4,028 | 3,834 | 5,051 | 4,996 | 6,422 | 2,394 |
| Total | 12,306 | 10,551 | 12,592 | 11,698 | 14,450 | 2,144 |
| Relative structure |  |  |  |  |  |  |
| Primary | 20.8 | 18.5 | 10.9 | 9.9 | 6.9 | −73.4 |
| Industrial | 27.6 | 24.6 | 23.0 | 21.0 | 19.8 | −24.6 |
| Construction | 9.8 | 7.3 | 10.1 | 9.1 | 10.9 | 17.4 |
| Services[a] | 41.8 | 49.7 | 56.0 | 60.0 | 62.4 | 180.5 |
| Pub. services | 9.0 | 13.3 | 15.9 | 17.3 | 17.9 | 68.8 |
| Priv. services | 32.7 | 36.3 | 40.1 | 42.7 | 44.4 | 111.7 |
| Total | 100.0 | 100.0 | 100.0 | 100.0 | 100.0 | 100.0 |

*Source:* Instituto Nacional de Estadística (INE), *Encuesta de población active* (EPA) for the second trimester of each year.
*Note:* a. Public Administrations' general services, education, and health (private and public).

market of workers from the postwar baby boom and the large-scale incorporation of women.

Beginning with purely demographic aspects, what needs to be emphasized here is the impact of the dynamics of the Spanish population on both the level of unemployment and on the welfare of the elderly. With this perspective in mind (see Table 8.8), two stylized facts need to be pointed out: the change in the proportion of young people, and the progressively larger proportion of the population of people older than sixty-five.

As regards the impact of young people on the job market, during the 1980s and the first half of the 1990s, young people from the baby boom had a major impact on the rise of unemployment. In contrast, the young people of today, born from 1975 onward, have had the contrary effect since the mid-1990s,[41] contributing to a decrease in absolute terms that is drastically reducing the rate of unemployment.

In contrast, and with totally different implications for welfare and pension systems, one needs to highlight the increasing number of people older than sixty-five. Figures show an increase running from approximately 12

**Table 8.8    Population in Spain, by Age Groups, 1971–2001**

| Age groups | 1971 | 1981 | 1991 | 2001 |
|---|---|---|---|---|
| Less than 16 years | 29.5% | 27.2% | 20.8% | 16.0% |
| From 16 to 19 years | 6.3 | 6.9 | 6.8 | 5.0 |
| From 20 to 24 years | 7.4 | 7.8 | 8.3 | 7.7 |
| From 25 to 29 years | 6.8 | 6.8 | 8.0 | 8.4 |
| From 30 to 34 years | 6.0 | 6.5 | 7.4 | 8.2 |
| From 35 to 39 years | 6.9 | 6.0 | 6.5 | 7.9 |
| From 40 to 44 years | 6.7 | 5.4 | 6.2 | 7.2 |
| From 45 to 49 years | 6.3 | 6.2 | 5.7 | 6.4 |
| From 50 to 54 years | 5.2 | 6.0 | 5.0 | 6.0 |
| From 55 to 59 years | 4.7 | 5.4 | 5.7 | 5.4 |
| From 60 to 64 years | 4.4 | 4.3 | 5.4 | 4.7 |
| From 65 to 69 years | 3.8 | 3.8 | 4.7 | 5.1 |
| More than 70 years | 6.0 | 7.5 | 9.2 | 11.9 |
| Total | 100.0 | 100.0 | 100.0 | 100.0 |
| Total population, millions | 34.2 | 37.7 | 38.9 | 39.5 |

*Source:* Instituto Nacional de Estadística (INE), *Encuesta de población active (EPA)* for the second trimester of each year.
*Note:* INE projections for 2001.

percent in 1978 to close to 19 percent in 2001, an increase in real terms of close to 3 million people (from 4.4 million in 1978 to 7.3 million in 2001).

The second aspect that needs to be highlighted is the importance of the incorporation of women into the job market and their impact on the falling birth rate. Traditionally in Spain, as often is the case in underdeveloped societies, the presence of women in the job market was basically limited to the age range prior to marriage. This meant that the rates for actively employed women aged twenty-five and older fell quite significantly. The end of the Franco era and the transition to democracy produced a major change in this trend, with a strong tendency for women workers to remain actively employed.[42] This feature is one of the most important contributions to the social and economic modernization of Spain, since one of the things that most differentiated Spanish society from other more developed European countries had been precisely the minor presence of women in the job market.[43]

## Welfare, Income Distribution, and Growth

The consequences for this structural transformation and the growth of the GDP to the welfare of Spanish citizens have been substantial. A brief summary of the main welfare indicators illustrate this point. Take for example the figures for students in education beyond the obligatory age. The enrollment rate of people sixteen to seventeen years old has increased from 43 percent in the academic year 1974–1975 to 85.4 percent in the academic year 2001–2002. Similar increases can be found in enrollment rates of other young people. Similarly, the GDP per person (measured in dollars) has risen very significantly, increasing from US$7,562 (purchasing power parity, PPP) to US$18,361 (PPP) between 1985 and 2000. From this perspective, the real convergence of the Spanish economy (measured in terms of the GDP per person in Spain compared to the average of the EMU) has also made remarkable progress, cutting back on differences from 71.1 percent in 1985 to 81.6 percent in 2000.

Other indicators of social welfare also point in a similar direction. Examples of this are those for actively employed women in the job market and the proportion of public expenditure destined for providing collective services (health care, pensions, and education). In both cases the improvements registered in Spain go beyond what could be expected of a country such as Spain during the mid-1970s. While in 1980 the proportion of actively employed women in the labor market was only 36 percent of the total potential active female work force (those between the ages of sixteen and sixty-four), twenty years later this proportion had already risen to 52 percent, an increase that is representative of one of the most relevant transformations in Spain's social network. Finally, and thanks to policies undertaken by the socialist governments in the period 1982–1996, public expenditure grew from approximately 25 percent of the GDP in 1975 to close to 40 percent in 2001, mainly in education, health care, and pensions. Thus, social public expenditure has steadily increased up to figures more in accordance with the average welfare level for Europe.

The process of economic growth during the opening up of the Spanish economy has been accompanied by an appreciable modification in the distribution of income. In short, two features define this. First, an absolute level of inequality higher in Spain than the average for the countries of the EU and others from the OECD. Second, a significant lowering of inequality in the last twenty-five years, particularly noticeable up to the beginning of the 1990s and maintained afterwards.

This tendency takes on special importance when contrasted with the international context, since the majority of OECD countries have shown a different tendency,[44] although this development has not been so clear-cut in recent years.[45] Beginning with its relative position, the classifying of Spain among the main Western countries with the highest degree of inequality when it comes to the distribution of income is commonplace in the literature on this matter (see Table 8.9). Recent studies suggest that this relative position tended to be maintained in the second half of the 1990s.[46] Within

**Table 8.9    Inequality in the European Union Countries, 1994–1996**

Average values from the Gini index for three fiscal years[a]

| | |
|---|---|
| Portugal | 39.7 |
| Belgium | 37.3 |
| Greece | 37.0 |
| Ireland | 35.2 |
| **Spain** | **34.8** |
| UK | 33.6 |
| Germany | 33.5 |
| Italy | 32.8 |
| Luxembourg | 31.8 |
| France | 31.7 |
| Holland | 31.3 |
| Austria | 28.9 |
| Sweden | 24.5 |
| Finland | 23.8 |
| Denmark | 23.8 |

*Source:* Oliver, Ramos, and Raymond (2002).
*Note:* a. Except for Austria (average 1995–1997), Finland (average 1996–1997), Luxembourg (average 1994–1996), and Sweden (1997).

the EU, Spain rates among the countries with the highest level of inequality, with an average value of 34.8 on the Gini index for the period 1994–1997, with only Ireland, Greece, Belgium, and Portugal rating worse. In 1997 Spain was positioned thirteenth as regards GDP per capita and the same position as regards level of inequality. In this sense, Spain does not appear to that be that far away from what would be the EC norm.

## A New Democracy's Social and Economic Policies

The lessening of inequality and improvements in social welfare discussed above have come about as a result of a wide range of factors. Some of these have nothing to do, except indirectly, with the role of the public sector,[47] and for this reason will not be dealt with here. However, what is of interest here is to determine those policies that have contributed most to economic growth and improvements in welfare, because of their value as "exportable items" to other countries. One of these, and perhaps the most important, is the opening up of the Spanish economy and Spain's entry into the EU and EMS. Alongside this first factor, the second is the role played by the public sector in the policies defined and executed by the first governments of the democracy.

In light of the process of fiscal consolidation carried out in the 1990s, the particularly positive role played by the expansion of the public sector might seem surprising. In fact, today Spain finds itself bound by a policy of tax stabilization that originates from the Pacto por la Estabilidad (Pact for Stability) signed in 1996 to guarantee the feasibility of the common currency. In fact, in 2003 Spain presented a surplus budget for the first time since 1976 (0.3 percent of the GDP). The case for Spain demonstrates that an underdeveloped country, with a deficient public sector, procyclical, and with an unequal distribution of the tax burden, cannot develop. Put another way, the growth of the Spanish economy during the last twenty-five years, and the importance of its balanced budget and social transformation, cannot be understood without taking into account the growth of the public sector, as much in terms of revenue as for spending.

The wide-ranging consensus of opinion regarding the redistributive role of public spending that emerges from studies of inequality in Spain in the 1980s is a common feature.[48] Thus the following discussion offers a summary of the evolution of the Spanish public sector from the transition to democracy onwards. After having explained the major changes in income, expenditure, budget deficit, and national debt, the discussion continues by offering a review of their impact on the education of the Spanish population and work force. Finally, there is a review of some of the indicators that reflect on this increase in public expenditure over other social expenditure categories.

### The Public Sector's Structural Changes

Our starting hypothesis is that the circumstances surrounding national debt differ radically depending on how one approaches the weight that public expenditure (and income) have on a national economy, and Spain is no exception. Here once again one has to mention the Pactos de la Moncloa and the major social contract agreements of the 1980s. If there is one point that needs to be highlighted for the Spanish case, it is the redistributing role in the public sector, without which it would have been difficult to produce the necessary transformation and the opening up of the Spanish economy.

One can get an idea of this increase in public income from the fact that current revenues for the public sector in Spain increased their participation in GDP by 18.7 percent, rising from 23.1 percent of the GDP in 1970 to 41.4 percent in 1999. In other words, during a period of some twenty years the relatively small size of the Spanish public sector almost doubled. During this time, Spain was a country with a collection of unsatisfied social demands linked to certain expectancies regarding taxation. The advent of democracy brought with it a significant increase in public spending as well as the tax burden, even though Spanish society may not have clearly identified the public-sector deficit with the need for higher future taxation.

The figures in the Table 8.10 show what we want to point out. At the beginning of the transition to democracy in 1975, Spain's weight of rev-

**Table 8.10    Current Incomes and Taxation System in Spain, 1975–1999**

Income as percentages of GDP

|  | Current incomes | Total taxes | Taxes on income and property | Taxes on household income | Other taxes: /on inc. /prop. | Soc. Sec. payments | Taxes on capital | Taxes on production and imports |
|---|---|---|---|---|---|---|---|---|
| 1975 | 25.5 | 21.4 | 4.4 | 2.8 | 1.5 | 10.3 | 0.3 | 6.5 |
| 1985 | 35.4 | 31.3 | 8.5 | 6.5 | 2.0 | 13.2 | 0.2 | 9.5 |
| 1995 | 39.3 | 35.4 | 11.5 | 9.1 | 2.4 | 13.6 | 0.3 | 10.1 |
| 1996 | 40.1 | 36.0 | 11.6 | 9.1 | 2.5 | 14.0 | 0.3 | 10.2 |
| 1997 | 40.7 | 36.6 | 11.9 | 8.6 | 3.3 | 14.0 | 0.3 | 10.5 |
| 1998 | 41.1 | 37.0 | 11.6 | 8.3 | 3.3 | 14.0 | 0.3 | 11.2 |
| 1999 | 41.4 | 37.6 | 11.6 | 7.8 | 3.9 | 13.9 | 0.3 | 11.7 |

*Source:* Banco Bilbao Vizcaya Argentaria (2000).

enues (and public expenditure) over the GDP was, to all appearances, insufficient when compared to European figures for the same period. This low weight (hardly 25 percent of the GDP) was not reflected in the budget deficit given that the low levels of public expenditure allowed for surplus resources. Already by 1976, there was a veritable revolution in Spain's public finances, to such a degree that total expenditure increased from approximately 25 percent over the GDP in 1975 to close to 45 percent in 1985. This represents an annual increase of close to two points of the GDP, unheard of elsewhere at an international level. In spite of the fact that the increase in public revenue and a more equal distribution of the tax burden were the dominating policies since the beginning of the transition period,[49] this increase was accompanied by a lower increase of current revenue. So, a constant feature for these years is the progressive rising of public deficit. Finally, the accumulation of these deficits brought in its wake a progressive and significant increase in Spain's national debt, running at rates close to 65 percent of the GDP in the mid 1990s, when the process of fiscal consolidation began. In addition, one has to highlight that the growth of the level of taxation has been mainly due to the increase in the aggregate taxes on income/property and social-security contributions, having risen from 3.4 percent to 11.6 percent and from 7.8 percent to 13.9 percent, respectively. Also, indirect taxation has increased with regard to the total GDP, rising from 7.8 percent to 11.7 percent. The growing tax burden (close to 18 percent of the GDP) was mainly due to the increasing importance of taxes on income and property (8.2 percent) and social-security contributions (6.2 percent) that explain almost 80 percent of the increase of all taxes for the entire period (see Table 8.10). Finally, the redistributive impact of a progressive income tax for households was also important. All of the studies on the distribution of income in Spain confirm this progressive nature of taxation; all measures taken have resulted in a significant improvement in the distribution of income.

### Education, Technological Change, and Economic Growth

Along with the redistributive function of the tax system itself, another area where the public sector has had an impact on the distribution of income and economic growth is the expansion in public education and improvements in the distribution of human capital throughout the Spanish population.[50] Although the level of education in Spain at the end of the 1990s was still one of the lowest in the EU, the increase in the level of education during the last twenty years has been exceptional. In 1977, close to 9 million working people had no education or only basic schooling (approximately 80 percent of the total number of working people). This has now fallen to a figure slightly higher than 4 million (29.4 percent of the total working population). Furthermore, the sector of the working population with some university education has increased from 5.6 percent of the total working population in 1977 to 18.7 percent (from approximately 600,000 to some 2.7 million). Finally, the most marked transformation in education is in the area of secondary education and postobligatory education, with an increase running from 14.8 percent to 52.2 percent (from 1.7 million to close to 7.5 million between 1977 and 2001).

This impressive increase in the level of education of the working population (and, logically, of those of working age) is also reflected in the average number of years that the working Spanish population are in education. This has increased from 8.2 years to 11.4 years between 1977 and 1999 (see Figure 8.1).

This represents an increase of close to 40 percent and illustrates the profound transformation that is taking place in Spain in this area. Nevertheless, there are still important differences between Spain and the average for other European countries. Basically these figures show that while Spain has cut back the gap in higher education since the beginning of the 1980s, in secondary education the differences continue to be quite pronounced.[51]

The reasons for this successful upward trend are as much a result of the supply as the demand for education. In addition, at least up until the mid-1990s, this growing supply of more qualified workers has not meant a relative fall in salaries for these workers.[52] At first sight, it is certain that the very significant increase in free (or partially free) opportunities in the public school system at all levels of education is the basis for this significant improvement in the level of education.[53] In contrast, and from the perspec-

**Figure 8.1    Average Number of Years of Education for Working Age Persons in Spain, 1977–1999**

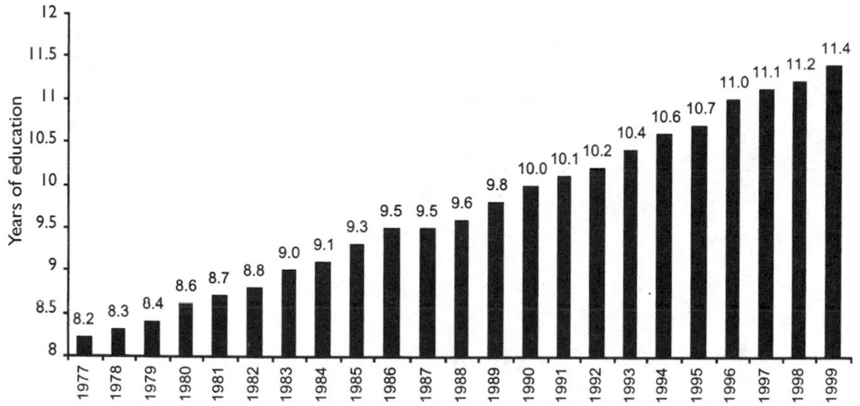

*Source:* Barceinas, Oliver, Raymond, and Roig (2000).

tive of demand, two elements have influenced this rising tendency: the incorporation of women into the job market and the very high levels of young unemployed. In fact there is a close correlation between the level of education and economic activity, particularly noticeable in the case of women (Bover and Arellano 1995; Bover 1997).

In addition, the fact that a higher level of education is associated with less likelihood of being unemployed appears to have played a relevant role in the average training of the Spanish work force that has even led to excesses of "overeducation."[54] In spite of this, one cannot overlook the very important transformation in Spanish higher education, which has increased from some 666,550 students at the end of the 1970s to more than 1.5 million. Despite the existing problems associated with overeducation and the correlation between family background and access to university, access to higher education has become the primary example of social mobility in democratic Spain.

This improvement in human capital in Spain, and its impact on the distribution of income, has pros and cons. On the plus side, is the way in which, at least potentially, an active working population with a higher level of education has to generate greater value-added units per work unit. Since this process of improvement of human capital stock has been biased toward those families with the most limited financial means, we should be able to see a better distribution of income, considering that the remaining influencing factors are constants. Nevertheless, alongside this aspect, there are also some not-so-positive extremes. All of these point to the fact that part of this process may have translated into overeducation, at least provisionally, of certain groups, with a corresponding waste of public and private resources.

Apart from the temporary phenomenon of overeducation, one has to highlight the role of public expenditure on education invested in research and development. Although the proportions of this variable over the GDP are lower than those for other more advanced countries, it is difficult to understand the growth of this expenditure (which has increased from 4.7 percent[55] to 5.7 percent[56] of the GDP between 1980 and 2000) without taking into account the formidable increase in public spending on university education.

## Increasing Social Spending

Finally, in this review of the principal factors that underlie the changes in the distribution of income, we turn to some of the profound changes in the social-security system and, particularly, the subsystem of pensions and health care.[57] The advances seen in Spain are reflected in Table 8.11, where we have reproduced some of the most relevant items referring to pensions, unemployment, and health for Spain and some of the other OECD countries.

As can been seen from these figures—although some of the absolute levels of public spending are below those for the principal countries of the EU—the rate of increase in the last twenty years has been quite exceptional. With regard to pensions, we have already pointed out that part of the costs incurred with the restructuring process during the first half of the 1980s was absorbed by the pension systems resulting from the expedient measure of early retirements. In addition, during those years one subgroup of pensioners also increased due to recognition of compensations linked to the Spanish Civil War.

During those years, the results of the measures adopted when the system was in its early stages (in the 1970s) started to become evident, in particular the recognition of the pension rights for widows of earlier contributors. Whatever the case, the number of pensioners in real terms has grown steadily during the last twenty years, increasing from close to 3 million pensioners covered by the public pension plan in 1977 to more than 7 million today.

Given that in the Spanish public pension system there is a limit to contributions, and also a ceiling on pensions, the disparity between the highest and lowest pensions is significantly lower than the disparity between salaries at both ends of the scale of the distribution of income. For this reason, as indicated further on, it comes as no surprise that the increase in the number of pensioners appears as an element that has had an appreciable impact on the distribution of income. In addition, around the mid-1980s, Spanish society established a minimum pension to all people older than sixty-five without incomes and who had not contributed to the state pension

**Table 8.11   Indicators for Public Spending on Pensions, Unemployment, and Health in Spain and in Other OECD Countries, 1975–1997, in percentage of GDP and variation in percentage**

|  | France | Italy | U.S. | Japan | Spain |
|---|---|---|---|---|---|
| Health expenditure |  |  |  |  |  |
| 1980 | 5.8 | 5.6 | 3.7 | 4.5 | 4.3 |
| 1990 | 6.7 | 6.3 | 4.6 | 4.6 | 5.3 |
| 1997 | 7.3 | 5.6 | 5.9 | 5.6 | 5.4 |
| Variation 1980–1997 | 25.9 | 0.0 | 59.5 | 24.4 | 25.6 |
| Unemployment expenditure |  |  |  |  |  |
| 1980 | 1.3 | 0.6 | 0.7 | 0.5 | 2.0 |
| 1990 | 1.8 | 0.8 | 0.4 | 0.3 | 2.5 |
| 1997 | 1.8 | 0.8 | 0.3 | 0.5 | 1.8 |
| Variation 1980–1997 | 38.5 | 33.3 | -57.1 | 0.0 | -10.0 |
| Pensions expenditure |  |  |  |  |  |
| 1980 | 7.6 | 7.4 | 5.1 | 2.9 | 4.7 |
| 1990 | 9.2 | 11.0 | 4.9 | 4.0 | 7.0 |
| 1997 | 10.6 | 13.0 | 5.1 | 5.4 | 8.2 |
| Variation 1980–1997 | 39.5 | 75.7 | 0.0 | 86.2 | 74.5 |
| Total social expenditure |  |  |  |  |  |
| 1980 | 22.9 | 18.4 | 13.2 | 10.4 | 15.8 |
| 1990 | 26.5 | 23.8 | 12.8 | 11.1 | 19.3 |
| 1997 | 29.4 | 26.4 | 14.6 | 14.1 | 19.8 |
| Variation 1980–1997 | 28.4 | 43.5 | 10.6 | 35.6 | 25.3 |

*Source:* Organization for Economic Cooperation and Development (National Annual Accounts, various years).

scheme (or were not fully paid up), which added a further dimension to the redistribution of income.

The other major factor regarding spending on social services of a redistributive nature has been health care. In effect, everyone residing in Spain has access to public health care (including illegal immigrants). Given that making use of public health care is not uniform along the income scale (those with greater available economic resources tend to make less use of it), the expansion of free public health care and universal access has contributed to lessening the effects of income inequality (Bandrés 1990).

## Conclusion

The main conclusion of this chapter is that—in the Spanish experience—there seems to exist a "virtuous circle" that encompasses economic globalization, economic growth, reduction of social and economic inequality, and democratic legitimization. In the Spanish case, it is very difficult to distinguish the impact of economic globalization on economic growth from the one that it has had on the process of democratic legitimation.

We have seen that today's Spain can be considered a consolidated democracy. Its political institutions and behavior patterns follow the main criteria that we find in older Western European or North American polyarchies. These criteria were a formal condition to gaining full access to the European Union. Since its peaceful change from a dictatorial regime to a democratic system, Spain has been able to count on massive public support, as the public looks at this democratic form of government as preferable to any other.

This "substantive or unconditioned" legitimization of the democratic system is related to the reduction of social and economic inequalities, while policies that have made possible this reduction are a consequence of decisions taken by democratic governments and the role and orientation given to the public sector in this transformation process. Most of these policies were undertaken by the social-democratic governments of 1982–1989, which, under the pressure and with the participation of all social partners, gave the Spanish public sector a stronger role than it had had in the past.

This means that, without the consolidation and legitimization of an efficient and fair taxation system, countries with markedly insufficient public capital resources (as was the case for Spain in 1975) will hardly attain the optimum conditions for development that require a certain amount of public spending. Spain's increase in public spending in education, along with the revenue set aside for health care, pensions, and unemployment benefits, act as a "compensatory social salary" that its trade unions thought to be a necessary and sufficient return for moderating their wage claims, giving the economy a better capacity to compete in the world scene.

Again, the opportunity to build up the necessary conditions for this far-reaching social contract—by which workers accept a reduction in their real wages in exchange for the offer of a "social salary bonus"—arises from the existence of a free and open negotiation between social actors in a fully democratic atmosphere.

In the Spanish experience, therefore, we can see how inequality reductions are the result of a combination of factors that includes democratic legitimacy, economic growth, and redistribution of income through the public sector. These factors are related to globalization or opening up to the world economy. In this sense, it can be said that Spain has benefited from its integration into the globalization process.

But in Western Europe this globalization process has had a particular accent. In addition to the general meaning that it has in any other part of the world—i.e., gradual opening up of national economies to the competition of foreign countries by the way of free commerce, free financial transactions, and unrestricted movement of people—the European version of globalization has been accompanied by democratic legitimacy and a public responsibility for the reduction of social and economic inequalities. This is the "European model" of the globalization process that is embedded in EU tradition and policies.

This European model of globalization—open economies, democratic legitimacy and a politically active public sector—is one that has allowed Spain to become a successful experiment by which economic growth has been made compatible with better income distribution. The enduring "vicious circle" of lack of public revenue, insufficient public spending, underdevelopment, income inequality, and social and political instability has been replaced by the "virtuous circle" of stable democracy, economic growth, and inequality reduction.

## Notes

1. Figures for international financial investment in developing countries increased from a total close to $200 billion in the 1980s to a yearly average of the same amount in the 1990s (up until the crisis in Asia in the autumn of 1997).

2. It has to be remembered that Spain lost in 1898 its last overseas colonies (Cuba, Puerto Rico, and the Philippines).

3. This economic policy was essentially based on that developed in fascist Italy in the 1930s.

4. After the so-called Plan de Estabilización (Stabilization Plan) in 1959, Spain joined the OECD, IMF, and GATT, and even got as far as applying for membership to the European Economic Community in 1962 (the application was denied on the basis of Spain being a dictatorship).

5. Legal and administrative reforms were also adopted as complementary measures taken to this change in economic policy. This set of measures was embodied in the Planes de Desarrollo Económico y Social, inspired by the five-year plans set up by the French governments during the 1950s and 1960s.

6. Seventy percent of foreign commerce in goods was, and still is, with EU countries, both exports and imports.

7. In 1974 the Spanish economy was the most dependent on oil from abroad of any of the principal European countries, with close to 65 percent of its primary energy dependent on this resource.

8. Turkey, Chile, or to a certain degree Brazil, would be examples of a "controlled democracy." Other observers hoped that the authoritarian Franco regime would become a moderately tolerant authoritarian system. This hoped-for transition was described as a change from a "dicta-dura" (harsh dictate) to a "dicta-blanda" (soft dictate), thus playing on the Spanish words (*dura* = harsh, *blanda* = soft).

9. The Spanish transition was part of a wave of transitions to democracy taking place in southern Europe between 1975 and 1979 (Portugal, Greece, and Spain), before those that took place in Latin America (Argentina, Uruguay, Chile, and Brazil), East Asia (South Korea, Taiwan), and in the 1990s in central and eastern Europe.

10. The first attempt at "continuity" from the most intransigent sector of the Franco regime failed in the early months of 1976 (the Arias government).

11. According to Diamond (1998), the Franco reformist elite calculated that the cost of a political "opening up" was less than the cost of repression. So, the combination of pressures from the opposition and concessions from the side of the Franco regime resulted in an "agreed rupture."

12. Basically, these transformations involved setting up a proportional income tax on wages and the progressive adaptation of real salaries to provide contingencies for unemployment and pension contributions.

13. A strategic analysis cannot ignore the push for the transaction by some leaders, both those from the authoritarian regime as well as those from the opposition. Among the first one should not forget King Juan Carlos himself, the prime minister, Adolfo Suárez, or Cardinal Enrique Tarancón, president of the Spanish bishops. Among the opposition one should note the position of Santiago Carrillo, the long-serving leader of the Spanish Communist Party, along with leaders of social-democratic parties, Christian democrats, and Basque and Catalan nationalists. Some analyses from the press have stressed the role of these leaders and left aside the consideration of other factors.

14. The waves of migration of Spanish workers between 1960 and 1970 to other EC countries, and the massive wave of tourists coming from the same countries, allowed many Spaniards to come into contact with social values and political institutions in pluralist democracies.

15. This favorable context contrasts with the experience in Spain in the previous attempts to construct a democracy during the Liberal Republic of 1931–1936. Europe at that time was a stage where there were struggles between the liberal democracies, the nazi-fascist regimes, and the left-wing social-revolution movements. This struggle also moved to republican Spain and contributed to aggravating internal conflicts that finally led to the Spanish Civil War.

16. Spain finally joined the European Community in 1986, after difficult negotiations on the economic aspects of Spain's entry.

17. In 1962, the European Parliament had established the prerequisites for admitting new countries into the European Community. These conditions were effectively a veto against membership by authoritarian or dictatorial regimes and provided a powerful argument for those who supported an evolution toward democracy.

18. CCOO had been originally linked to the Spanish Communist Party (PCE). The UGT was historically associated to the Spanish Socialist Party (PSOE). Since the middle of the 1980s both of these trade unions have taken a completely autonomous path with respect to the political parties.

19. The Franco regime had made the Spanish Communist Party (PCE) its main ideological adversary, often qualifying as "communist" all democratic opposition to the dictatorship. At the same time the PCE was the clandestine organization that had the most widespread support, albeit limited in its operations. This explains why the legalization of the PCE would be strongly opposed by the Franco regime elite and why the decision to legalize the PCE taken by the government led by Suárez in April 1977 was seen as a critical step in the process of political reform.

20. This referendum (6 December 1978) returned a vote of 87 percent in favor of the proposed constitution, 8 percent against, and 4 percent of the votes left blank.

21. During the same period (1977–2000), six local elections have also been held, five regional elections, and four European elections. The support given to political parties in these other elections sometimes differs substantially from support for political parties at the statewide level.

22. AP (Alianza Popular) became the PP (Partido Popular) as of 1989.

23. Among these, the CiU (center-right Catalan national party) and the PNV (centre-right Basque nationalist party) are the most important due to the strong support they have within their own regions.

24. The only exception is the HB, the Basque party for independence, which politically supports the terrorist organization ETA.

25. Compare with F.A. Andrés Orizo (1996: 223 and following). This preference for equality is expressed in the 1990s, while individual freedom appeared as the preferred value in the early years of the transition to democracy.

26. The ratio between the aggregate number of affiliated members of political parties and the total number of voters is around 1:40, below that found in other Western European countries.

27. Affiliated membership of trade unions is around 15 percent of the wage-earning population. The majority of trade union members belong to the two major unions: the CCOO and the UGT.

28. The issue of low membership also applies to social, cultural, religious, or sports associations. One can discern in this phenomenon an indication of a low level of "social capital" in the Spanish democracy. Up until now, only the persistence of strong family links seem to counterbalance the lack of participation in associations.

29. According to opinion polls, around 65 percent of Spanish people persist in the belief that "there can be no democracy without political parties." Fifteen percent of the remainder of those polled do not share this belief in the relationship between democracy and political parties. The remaining 20 percent did not express an opinion on this matter.

30. This is partly explained by the fact that levels of literacy in Spanish society were still rather low when, at the end of the nineteenth century, written press was becoming the main vehicle for political communication in other countries. The advent of radio and television therefore meant that they found themselves operating at a time when the written press was limited to a readership from elite classes. Consequently, radio and television were able to transform themselves with ease into the principal instruments for communicating politics in the new democracy.

31. In contrast to the Spanish case, legitimacy in other recent democracies appears to have been more vulnerable to the outcome of social and economic circumstances.

32. This degree of support for the democratic system is comparable to support within other countries of the European Union with a longer tradition of democracy, and higher than that shown in Latin American countries or in central and eastern Europe where polyarchies were established in the 1980s and 1990s.

33. Forty percent of the population state that they are not interested in politics and a further 40 percent express little interest.

34. This resilient syndrome of "political disaffection" in an established democracy questions the thesis that the stability of democracies goes hand in hand with the predominance of a "civic culture," with high rates of citizens' active participation in public affairs. One of the main questions raised here would be the relationship that analysts themselves establish between the interest and involvement in policies and interest and direct involvement by citizens in party politics. The incongruence between the high rate of support for the legitimacy of democracy and the falling rate of direct involvement by citizens is perhaps due to the fact that party politics are perceived by people as being less and less relevant when it comes to issues that directly affect their daily life.

35. And, consequently, a major bank crisis that affected more than 50 credit

entities. Also for the construction sector, there was a loss of 296,200 jobs between 1977 and 1982, 23.9 percent of the total jobs in this sector.

36. Logically taking on the responsibility for these costs was only possible through the expedient measure of significantly increasing the national debt. One of the mechanisms employed so that the public sector could absorb part of the welfare costs of the crisis was to offer early retirement plans as a means to making the necessary adjustments in the labor market. These early retirements had a double impact on social-security finances (less income from contributions and an increase in its liabilities).

37. In 1992, approximately one-third of salaried workers had seasonal contracts, a surprising figure taking into account the brief period of time that had transpired since the reform of hiring laws.

38. The Maastricht Agreement (1991), which opened the way to the European Monetary Union, and the creation of the Central European Bank in 1999, required those countries wishing to opt for joining the European Monetary Union in 1999 to comply with a set of very demanding tax and price prerequisites. The most relevant measures were the adoption of autonomy statutes for the issuing bank (for Spain, this was done in January 1995), and that the treasury was prohibited from requesting loans from the Bank of Spain. In addition, in spring of 1998, the exchange rate for the peseta had to remain completely fixed to the other EMS currencies during the last two years. Inflation could not exceed a maximum of 1.5 percent of that of the three member states with the need for improvement in the areas of prices. Long-term nominal interest rates could not be higher than a maximum of 2 percent compared to those of the three member states with the need for improvements in the area of stabilizing prices. The budget deficit could not exceed 3 percent of the GDP, and the national debt had to be below 60 percent of the GDP.

39. In 1995 the Spanish consumer price index had increased to a yearly rate of 4.7 percent compared to 1.8 percent for France and 1.7 percent for Germany.

40. By way of example, one should note the remarkable stability of the European currency in relation to the dollar during the period 1999–2001. Given this stability, it would be difficult to imagine that the peseta would have fared in the same way in the context of the major financial and exchange crises in Southeast Asia (1997), the foreign bankruptcy in Russia (1998), the floating and devaluation of the Brazilian real (1999), or, finally, the crises of the Turkish lira and the Argentinean peso (2001).

41. This major reduction is unprecedented; while Spain had the highest birth rates in Europe at the beginning of the 1970s, with close to 19 births per 1,000 inhabitants, in 1980 this had reduced to 15.5, to 10.2 in 1990, and lower than 10 in 2000.

42. In fact, today there are two coexisting groups of women in Spanish society, differentiated exclusively by age: women younger than forty to forty-five and who began working as of the end of the 1970s have maintained very high levels of active participation in the labor market. In 1999, the figures for women between the ages thirty and thirty-four was 68.5 percent; and for thirty-five to thirty-nine, 63.9 percent, compared to 1976 when respective figures were 27.7 percent and 27.3 percent of actively employed women for the same age groups. In contrast, women aged from fifty to fifty-four has varied to a much lesser degree, rising from 28.2 percent in 1976 to 38.8 percent in 1999.

43. In absolute terms, this increase is even more spectacular. While in 1976 the total number of men actively employed in the labor market reached a figure of 9.2 million as opposed to 3.2 million women, in 1999 the figure for male workers

had hardly changed (a total of 9.9 million), while the number of women actively employed in the labor market had increased by an extraodrinary amount (up to 6.5 million). This accounts for most of the total increase in the actively employed Spanish population.

44. See Smeeding and Gottschalk (1995), Gottschalk and Smeeding (1999), and Zaidi and de Vos (1998).

45. For a complete review of the state of studies on inequality (and poverty) in Spain, see Cantó, del Río, and Gradín (2000). The study by Imedio, Parrado, and, Sarrión (1997) is the only one that also includes the period 1985–1996.

46. See Oliver, Ramos, and Raymond (2002).

47. This would be the case for the fall in birth rates and smaller average number of family members (much greater for the lowest income brackets).

48. See the studies by Medel, Molina, and Sánchez (1988), Bandrés (1990; 1993), and Gimeno (1993).

49. The first law passed by the new Parliament in 1977 was precisely one which introduced a modern income tax system.

50. In studies on the factors that most influence improvements in income after taxes (Oliver, Ramos, and Raymond, 2001a and 2001b) human capital appears as the most relevant variable among those that can be measured.

51. In 1999, and going by the Eurostat three division classification of levels of education, Spain showed a level higher than 21.9 percent compared to the simple European average of 21.3 percent, while the lowest level reached a total of 61 percent, a figure that has to be compared with the European average of 37 percent (see Barceinas, Oliver, Raymond, and Roig 2000).

52. This remarkable change has been coupled with an even more remarkable stability in the yield from investment in education, at least for the period 1985–1992. This would indicate that, in spite of increases in supply, the demand for higher qualifications has grown at a similar rate, so much so that its price has been maintained. Nevertheless, as of 1992 there has been an increase in the yield per academic year. While in 1990 the yield rate per additional year of studies for a male head of the household was 7 percent, this rate had risen to 8 percent in 1995. In addition, there is growing empirical evidence that suggests that this technical change is influencing demand for higher-qualified labor, to the degree the wages they would be earning are on the increase (Barceinas, Oliver, Raymond, and Roig 2001).

53. So, for example, the total number of those in pre- and post-obligatory secondary education has risen from 1,979,918 in 1980 to 3,171,308 in 2000. Similarly, the increase in university students can also be classified as spectacular, increasing from 639,288 to 1,547,331, respectively.

54. There is no consensus of opinion on the permanent or temporary nature of overeducation in Spain. While Dolado, Felgueroso, and Jimeno (2000) argue that this is temporary, recent research into overeducation in Spain indicates that when this is integrated into the demographic decrease, this produces a double process of permanent overeducation for an appreciable number of workers (some 1.5 million in 2001). Alternatively, overeducation will tend to diminish and disappear, approximately over the next ten years (Oliver, Raymond, Mañé, and Sala 2002).

55. Uriel, et al. (1997)

56. "Datos básicos de la Educación en España en el curso 2001/2002," Ministerio de Educación y Ciencia, Madrid.

57. The redistributive impact of unemployment insurance is nil.

# 9

# Inequalities and
# the Globalization Debate

*Joseph S. Tulchin and Gary Bland*

## External and Internal Factors

Factors influencing the impact of globalization include, most importantly, the full institutional context within which any change is occurring in a given country. Generally, countries with an effective institutional base appear to do better in the globalized world than countries where the rule of law is weak, corruption is rampant, property rights are unprotected, and civil society is not able to force accountability from government. On the other hand, vulnerabilities to international factors, such as textile and agriculture protectionism in the industrialized world, are a particularly glaring impediment to efforts to take advantage of global interconnectedness.

All of the chapters in this volume demonstrate in fairly dramatic fashion the interplay of external (or international) and internal (or domestic) influences on each of the countries under consideration. Bizberg, writing about Mexico, emphasizes that the effects of global integration are not simply endured by the state but, rather, must pass through the institutional mediations of the country. In Mexico, globalization has been instrumentalized by government elites who, under the preceding authoritarian system, had the wherewithal to dismantle the constraints on capitalism. Friedman makes the strongest argument for the importance of domestic factors, which he sees as predominant in South Africa. He writes that "globalization, to the extent that it influences prospects for democratic egalitarianism in South Africa, merely builds on domestic trends—the chief constraints and opportunities exist largely independent of it" (p. 46). Conversely, for Spain, the influence of the European Union on the country's globalization and political transition was powerful. It is safe to say that, in the Spanish case, even conservative governments felt compelled to enact progressive social policies to deal with unemployment and inequality.

In assessing the interrelationships between globalization and inequality, it is best to view each country as facing an international and national combination of facilitating factors and barriers to progress. As our authors illustrate, the challenge is to identify the most salient, accurately measure their relative impacts, and then devise and implement policies to respond to them.

## The Role of Democratic Institutions

The so-called third wave of democracy of recent decades and continuing international pressure—most recently in the Middle East—for representative and accountable governance reflect the strong influence of political globalization around the world today. It must be noted that political globalization is not necessarily complementary with other types of global change. The global integration of telecommunications and information technology can be prodemocratic, for example, because it promotes transparency and citizen access to public information; but it raises questions of access, which are anything but equitable. The institution of a market-based, internationally competitive economy, however, presents potential pitfalls for a democratic regime.

The authors of this volume make it clear that the democratic institutions of their respective countries face significant challenges from the vagaries of the global system. That is, they directly address the concern that democracy and globalization can be in conflict. With the important exception of the Turkish and Korean cases, however, the authors view globalization not as something that must be endured by the state, as Bizberg puts it, but rather as a force that must be mediated or filtered through the social, economic, and political institutions of the country. In the end, it is the functioning of these institutions and the decisions of political and economic elites that significantly determine the ability of the country to respond with an effective social policy for the furtherance of democratic stability.

The global context sets the limits and has other effects, as Schwartzman points out, but it is on the domestic side that the battle for equity is won or lost. On the other hand, Yang and Moon see the impact of globalization on inequality as negative; indeed, social-safety nets have been sacrificed on the altar of employment growth and conservative fiscal policy. In this case, the implication is that growing inequality is at odds with the consolidation of democracy. Keyman, addressing the Turkish case, makes a similar argument, namely that market liberalization is directly associated with increasing inequality and that rising distributive injustice is a barrier to democratic governance. These arguments sharpen the case made by Dani Rodrik and others that democratic institutions matter in the impact of globalization on domestic social and economic conditions (Rodrik and Rigobon 2004).[1]

Signifying the importance of democracy, each author in this volume pays heed to the role of democratic institutions or politics in considering the question of globalization and inequality. The discussion centers on economic reform within a democratic system as opposed to an authoritarian regime; on valuing democratic institutions at the expense, if need be, of economic integration into the world economy; and on globalization's ability, intentionally or otherwise, to bolster or generate political demands within a democratic system for poverty reduction and increased equality.

Spain is viewed by the authors as a case in which "globalization and social and political transformation are part of the same process." The central goal of globalization—Spain's entrance into the European Union—could not be accomplished without democratization. In fact, the democratic side of the equation could not progress until the end of the Franco regime. Bizberg argues that Mexico is fundamentally different than many cases precisely because the authoritarian-corporatist regime implemented the new economic model. The Fox administration, rather than having to implement reforms, has had to deal with the effects of them, which is problematic because many of the old institutions have not been dismantled (p. 177).[2]

Laquian identifies the strong influence of globalization in the Philippines as primarily political. The practice of liberal democracy—democratic elections, thriving civil-society participation in public affairs, and a rambunctious free press—is the result of global influences beginning in the colonial era. For him, the economic changes that globalization normally implies were less relevant in the Philippines, since it has been a country that has been deeply integrated into the world economy for centuries.

Keyman finds that in Turkey, the February 2001 financial crisis, which was tied to the globalization of the economy, had such a strong impact on societal and political actors that the hitherto ignored question of democratic governance—especially social justice and poverty—could no longer be set aside. Democratic governance cannot be achieved in Turkey without progress on social justice. For Yang and Moon, South Korea is a clear example of an attempt, in the midst of crisis, to balance the IMF conditionality with the imperative created by democratic politics of providing social-safety nets for the labor sector. Friedman argues that the South African poor lack a political voice and that democratic representative institutions need to become more accessible. Yet, he adds, the current international trend toward public debate and participation mechanisms will not work because they tend to benefit only the politically organized segments of society. For all of the authors, political institutions play a vital role in determining how globalization will affect each society; they determine how broadly the population will have access to the benefits of globalization and they determine whether the opening of the economy will have a negative impact on the population.

In terms of understanding the political processes that constitute globalization and the responses to it, Ulrich Beck has argued that globalization actually occurs within a society, and that it creates links between the local and the global. Beck refers to a concept of "disembedded individualization" to explain how people are becoming more and more involved in international things while at the same time maintaining their local ties. He argues that people are becoming detached from traditional categories, such as class, while remaining tied to local institutions or groups at the same time that they are becoming linked to international networks or professional identities. While Beck is focused on the industrialized societies of Western Europe, he implies that other, less developed societies are evolving in the same manner (Beck and Willms 2004).

## Historical Developments: Globalization over Time

If globalization is the "thickening" of international interdependence over time, as some have argued (Nye and Donahue 2000), then the concept is clearly linked to past developments, institutional, cultural, political, and otherwise. Globalization, which has existed in one form or another for hundreds of years, cannot be appropriately examined without placing the country within the proper historical context. All of the authors of this volume clearly recognize that history matters. It is important to mention here that about a century ago, most of the developing countries of the world made a conscious decision to enter the international trading system and to open themselves to foreign investment. That episode of export-led development also produced a ferocious debate about the linkages between economic growth and inequality. Without revisiting that debate, it is sufficient to point out that the earlier episode is different from the current experience with globalization in at least two critical dimensions: the earlier experience did not involve democratic government and popular participation in decisionmaking, and the insertion of primary product exporters into the international market did not involve significant transfers of technology and information (Cardoso and Faletto 1979).[3]

Laquian traces the impact of globalization to the colonial era in the Philippines, while Oliver-Alonso and Vallés examine a quarter century of developments in Spain, beginning with a detailed examination of socioeconomic and institutional changes in the mid-1970s. Schwartzman traces the global integration of Brazil to the Portuguese empire and notes that internationalization has been linked to poverty and social inequity from the start. Friedman, for his part, begins the story of globalization in South Africa with a political history of apartheid, starting in the 1920s. Addressing influences on the South Korean labor market, Yang and Moon, citing others, point out that "constructing a viable welfare state to cope with income and power inequalities from market forces has been at the center of intellectual debates on a new social contract in Western European countries since World War II" (p. 71).

It should not come as a surprise that historical developments, both domestic and international, exert considerable influence on any assessment of the impact associated with globalization today. One should remain aware, however, that assessing such effects, especially with respect to inequality, can be considerably determined by the time period covered by the analysis. Shortening the period of analysis or leaving out important historical influences, for example, can easily lead to a distorted or biased view of contemporary globalization.

## Institutions of International Governance

In an interdependent world, effective institutions of global governance are required to improve opportunities for the poor, reduce inequality, and protect against rejection of an international system based on political democracy and market economics, which would increase the potential for interstate conflict. In practice, improved global governance may merely involve movement toward interstate cooperation or the establishment of mechanisms for collaboration on critical national-policy issues. Existing multilateral institutions could be the target of improvements as well. In other words, international governance plays an important role in determining whether globalization will benefit nations or hurt them.

As Robert Keohane has discussed, regional or global institutions should be called on to play five key roles (Keohane 2001: 2–3). First, they should limit the use of large-scale violence or warfare. Second, global governance institutions can serve to limit the opportunities for one state actor to externalize the costs of its actions to another state actor. Examples of externalized costs include failure to control air pollution or the harboring of terrorists. Third, according to Keohane, global institutions can provide "focal points" for coordinated action such as, for example, agreeing on single standards for measurement or for language usage. Fourth, as systemic risk increases, these institutions can deal with disruptions, as is done to a degree today by the United Nations. Finally, governance institutions must be used to guard against the worst forms of abuse, such as violence and deprivation.

The chapters in this volume provide some evidence of the potential impact of effective institutions of global governance. The obvious example, Spain, has enjoyed the tremendous political and economic influence of the European Union in setting standards for collaborative interaction. "The European version of globalization," Oliver-Alonso and Vallés write, "has been accompanied by democratic legitimacy and a public responsibility for the reduction of social and economic inequalities." Spain's entrance into the EU bears further consideration for the substantial financial payments it has brought not only Spain, but other entrants such as Ireland, Greece, and Portugal. The EU long ago made economic and social cohesion a central policy of the union. The intention is to narrow the gaps in development—income and employment—among the neighbors of the region and members of the union. A variety of financing mechanisms, especially the investment funds, have been created to support the aim of balanced development. Each year, the EU now publishes progress reports on the status of the recipient countries and the policy as a whole. Intra-EU income disparity continues to be considerable, for example, but the EU reported in 2001 that the average per capita income in Greece, Spain, and Portugal (the three poorest states) rose from 68 percent of the EU average to 79 percent from 1988 to 1999. With respect to globalization and poverty, the impact of cohesion policy in counteracting the turbulence of the global economy is considerable, perhaps especially from the Turkish viewpoint. It is of little practical relevance in the developing world outside of the EU orbit. NAFTA and other trade agreements have hardly broached topics beyond the free movement of trade within their geographic areas. The idea of creating a NAFTA common market, which was raised by Mexico's president Vicente Fox, is really no more than an idea—and the income and employment gaps within North America are much larger than those seen in Europe.[4]

On the other hand, existing institutions may prove to be a less-than-ideal source of globalization (or in this case, free trade) pressure on a country such as South Korea. In the early 1990s, in a major shift in economic management, the South Koreans turned in rapid succession to joining the OECD and the Uruguay and subsequent rounds of trade negotiations. The eventual result was an ineffective labor reform and rising social inequality. For the Philippines, the Asia Pacific Economic Cooperation (the Philippines was a cofounder) and ASEAN Free Trade Area are notably important to global integration. In both cases, the international context shaped the national response to globalization.

In its website on globalization, the World Bank emphasizes the positive impact of international cooperation in such areas as women's rights, the opposition to child labor, and other forms of gross discrimination. These advances suggest that international governance is making progress in the area of shared values, even if multinational institutions are not always effective or if they are rejected as modes of international cooperation by individual nation-states. The chapters in this volume also point to the internationalization of these and other values as part of the democratization process, further strengthening the linkages between democracy and positive globalization. As the awareness of shared values increases, it becomes increasingly possible for the developing nations of the world to appreciate their role as members of an international community and to define for themselves roles in that community. At the same time, individuals within countries come to have stronger ties to this emerging international community, to feel themselves embedded in the global community, while preserving their identity as citizens of individual countries.[5]

## Policy Insights

A case-study approach, such as the one used in this volume, is advantageous in that the experience of each country serves as a source of policy implications or recommendations for use in cross-country comparisons. Each of the authors in this volume has examined the policy lessons to be learned from the experiences of their respective countries.

The central policy issue of this volume is the need to balance economic progress, which is typically attributed to globalization, and the imperative of addressing social inequity. With the exception of Spain, each case demonstrates a clear absence of balance—a highly inadequate or regressive approach to the design and effective execution of policies to assist the poor. Counteracting the vicissitudes of the global marketplace requires, the authors find, the ability to generate healthy negotiation among all societal actors for the establishment of effective social policies.

In the case of Brazil, Schwartzman argues that the country's extreme inequality has "less to do with globalization than with the government's inability to redirect social spending and to implement better social policies" (p. 149). Moon and Yang much more directly target neoliberal financial and monetary management as the cause of increased inequality, but they also believe that the government can and should make extraordinary efforts to protect newly vulnerable workers. They advocate a Dutch approach of "flexicurity," which provides for economic growth through labor market flexibility coupled with strong rights for all workers. The Spaniards make the same point, but based on their country's positive experience. The success of Spain's global integration, they argue, is due precisely to the government's strong commitment to compensate, through extraordinary public spending on education, health care, pensions, and unemployment benefits, for the economic sacrifices made to become internationally competitive. Oliver-Alonso and Vallés recommend a consolidated, legitimate, and fair tax system to provide the public resources for investment in the social sector.

In Turkey, Keyman argues, any government attempt to give primacy to social and distributive justice will see its relations with the International Monetary Fund begin to turn sour. The demands of the IMF structural adjustment program tightly restrict the government's options, and the poor are suffering the consequences of an inadequate response to social needs. The government's role has been somewhat different in Mexico. There, Bizberg points out, the model for opening up to the international economy has been predicated on low labor costs, thus removing any incentives for the emergence of an endogenous technological base.

With respect to policy priorities, Laquian adopts a relatively sanguine view of globalization. He indicates that global integration can produce pressure for policy changes that are sorely needed in the Philippines. Anticorruption in particular and electoral reform could be promoted. Corrupt practices can be curtailed to the extent that globalization increases public access to information, increases the demand for transparency in transactions, and forces greater adherence to international standards of conduct in business operations. Similar effects can be seen in South Korea, Turkey, and Brazil.

Addressing the case of South Africa, Friedman approaches the question of policy and poverty alleviation from the perspective of institutional performance. Generally, institutional reforms aimed at improving representative democracy—changes that give a political voice to the poor—are essential. Political-party dominance at all governmental levels, facilitated by the use of closed-list proportional representation as opposed to a constituency-based system, reduces opportunities. Ironically, in Friedman's view, public discussion and public participation processes are exclusionary. Smaller or local government tends to be more accessible to marginalized populations. In this regard, decentralization and an effort to produce more effective local governance seem to be potential remedies.[6]

In all of the cases we have studied, globalization presents challenges to new democracies with fragile institutions and imperfect modes of citizen participation and interest articulation. In every case, we believe, the response is for more democracy, not less. Globalization must be made to serve the interests of people everywhere. It cannot be assumed that it will be neutral or apolitical. It is a political phenomenon and it must be put at the service of all people.

## Notes

1. Dani Rodrik and Jeffrey Sachs have conducted a debate as to whether governance or geography matters more. See Sachs's (2003) answer to Rodrik's "Institutions Rule" (2002a).

2. Similar arguments were made about the Chilean case, where the military dictator, Augusto Pinochet, began the market reforms that allowed the economy to begin to grow several years before the return to democracy in 1989. See Ffrench-Davis (1997).

3. For a good analysis of the earliest period of modernization, market opening, and growth of the export economy in nineteenth-century Hispanic America, see

Cortés Conde (1974). Also see, for Brazil: Furtado (1963); for Chile: Pinto Santa Cruz (1962); for Peru: Cotler (1978; 1991); and for Mexico: Cosio Villegas (1959).

4. It might be noted in passing that the bilateral discussions between the United States and Mexico over migration may well have similar long-term effects to social cohesion policy in the EU. See Tulchin and Selee (2003) and Edgar, Meissner, and Cochairs (2004).

5. On the importance of shared values in assuming roles in the international community, see Tulchin and Espach (2004). On the concept of embeddedness, see Beck (2000).

6. Friedman and others make this point in Oxhorn, Tulchin, and Selee (2004).

# Bibliography

Abedian, Iraj. 2001. "Do Redistributive Politics in South Africa Defy Economic Gravity?" Presentation to the Centre for Policy Studies, 6 September, Johannesburg, Standard Bank Economics Division.

Abreu, Marcelo de Paiva, ed. 1990. *A Ordem do progresso—cem anos de política econômica republicana, 1889–1989* (Rio de Janeiro: Editora Campus).

African National Congress. 1994. *The Reconstruction and Development Programme* (Johannesburg: Unyamo Publications).

Aglietta, Michel. 1997. "Postface: Le capitalisme au tournant du siècle. La théorie de la regulation a l'épreucve de la crise," in *Regulation et Crises du capitalisme* (Paris: Odile Jacob).

Ahn, Joyup. 2001. "What Have We Learned About Alternative Employment Arrangement in Korea: Definition, Trends, and Their Characteristics." Paper presented at the KLI-CALSS workshop on "Non-standard Workers and Policy Directions." October.

Alba, Carlos. 2000. "México después del TLCAN," in Barbara Klauke, ed., *México y sus perspectivas para el Siglo XXI* (Munster, Germany: CELA-LIT Verlag).

Almonte, Jose. 1996. "The Philippine Framework for Policy Reform," in W. Scott Thompson and Wilfrido V. Villacorta, eds., *The Philippine Road to NICHood* (Manila: De la Salle University and Social Weather Stations Inc.).

Amadeo, Edward J., Indermit S. Gill, and Marcelo C. Neri. 2000. "Brazil: The Pressure Points in Labor Legislation," in *Ensaios Econômicos* (Rio de Janeiro: Fundação Getúlio Vargas Escola de Pós-Graduação em Economia).

Amsberg, Joachim von, Peter Lanjuow, and Kimberly Nead. 2000. "A focalização do gasto social sobre a pobreze no Brasil," in R. Henriques, ed., *Desigualdade e pobreza no Brasil* (Rio de Janeiro: IPEA).

Andrés Orizo, F. A. 1996. *Sistemas de valores en la España de los 90* (Madrid: Centro de Investigaciones Sociológicas).

Arroyo Picard, Alberto. 2000. "El TLCAN: Balance de sus resultados y propuesta para una inserción diferente en la economía mundial," in Jorge A. Calderón Salazar, ed., *Estudios de Evaluación del Tratado de Libre Comercio de América del Norte* (México: Senado de la República).

Bağımsız Sosyal Bilimciler İktisad Grubu. 2001. *Güçlü Ekonomiye Geçis Programı Üzerine Degerlendirmeler* (Remarks on the Programme for Strong Economy) (Ankara: Türk Mühendis ve Mimar Odalar Birligi).

Balisacan, Arsenio. 1994. *Poverty: Urbanization and Development Policy, a Philippine Perspective* (Metro Manila: University of the Philippines Press).

Banco Bilbao Vizcaya Argentaria (BBVA). 2000. *Informe económico BBVA* (Madrid).

Bandrés, E. 1990. *Los efectos de los gastos sociales sobre la distribución de la renta en España* (Madrid: Instituto de Estudios Fiscales, Monografía).

———. 1993. "La eficacia redistributiva de los gastos sociales. Una aplicación al caso español (1980–90)," in *I Simposio sobre igualdad y distribución de la renta y la riqueza,* Vol. VII (Madrid: Fundación Argentaria).

Barceinas, F., J. Oliver, J. L. Raymond, and J. L. Roig. n.d. *Rendimientos de la educación y efecto tratamiento: El caso de España* (Barcelona: Universitat Autónoma de Barcelona).

Barceinas Paredes, F., J. Oliver Alonso, J. L. Raymond Bara, and J. L. Roig Sabaté. 2000. "Los rendimientos de la educación y la inserción laboral en España," *Papeles de Economía Española* 86, pp. 128–148.

———. 2001. "Spain," in Colm Harmon, Ian Walker, Niels Westergaard-Nielsen, eds., *Education and Earnings in Europe: A Cross Country Analysis of the Return to Education* (Cheltenham, UK: Edward Elgar Publishing Limited).

Barros, Alexandre Rands, Sandra Correia de Andrade, and Roberto Accioly Perrelli. 2000. "A eficiência do Plano Nacional de Qualificação Profissional como instrumento de combate à pobreza no Brasil: Os casos de Pernambuco e Mato Grosso," in R. Henriques, ed., *Desigualdade e pobreza no Brasil* (Rio de Janeiro: IPEA).

Barros, Ricardo Paes de, and Miguel Nathan Foguel. 2000. "Focalização de gastos públicos sociais e erradicação da pobreza no Brasil," in R. Henriques, ed., *Desigualdade e pobreza no Brasil* (Rio de Janeiro: IPEA).

Baskin, Jeremy. 1991. *Striking Back: A History of COSATU* (Johannesburg: Ravan Press).

Beck, Ulrich. 1997. *The Rethinking of Politics* (Cambridge: Polity Press).

———. 2000. *What Is Globalization?* (Cambridge: Polity Press).

Beck, Ulrich, and Johannes Willms. 2004. *Conversations with Ulrich Beck* (Cambridge: Polity Press).

Beitz, C. 2001. "Does Global Inequality Matter?" *Metaphilosophy* 32, no. 1.

Bethell, Leslie. 1970. *The Abolition of the Brazilian Slave Trade: Britain, Brazil and the Slave Trade Question, 1807–1869,* Cambridge Latin American Studies (Cambridge: Cambridge University Press).

Bethell, Leslie, and José Murilo de Carvalho. 1984. "Brazil, 1822–1850," in Leslie Bethell, ed., *The Cambridge History of Latin America. Volume XI— Bibliographical Essays* (Cambridge and New York: Cambridge University Press).

Bhagwati, Jagdish N. 2003. *In Defense of Globalization* (New York: Oxford University Press).

Bhorat, Haroon. 2003. "The Post-Apartheid Challenge: Labour Demand Trends in the South African Labour Market, 1995–1999." Development Policy Research Unit, University of Cape Town, Working Paper 03/82, August.

Bhorat, Haroon, and Rashaad Cassim. 1999. *Industry and Trade Policy? Is It Job Friendly?* Summary of a seminar held at the Centre for Policy Studies with the support of the Friedrich Ebert Stiftung. (Johannesburg: Centre for Policy Studies).

Birdsall, Nancy. 2002. "From Social Policy to an Open-Economy Social Contract in Latin America," CGD Working Papers 21 (Center for Global Development).

Bizberg, Ilán. 2002. "Trayectorias políticas e institucionales de México y Brasil: El caso de las relaciones industriales," in Carlos Alba and Ilán Bizberg, eds., *Democracia y Globalización: Autonomía del Estado y trayectorias políticas, sociales y geográficas en México y Brasil* (México: El Colegio de México).

Bond, Patrick. 2000. *Elite Transition: From Apartheid to Neo-Liberalism in South Africa* (London: Pluto Press).

Bover, Olympia. 1997. "Cambios en la composición del empleo y actividad laboral femenina," *Papeles de Economíu Española,* pp. 38 51.

Bover, Olympia, and Manuel Arellano. 1995. "Female Labour Force Participation in the 1980s: The Case of Spain," *Investigaciones Economicas* 19, no. 2 (Fundación SEPI), pp. 171–194.

Brasil Ministério da Educação, and Secretaria de Educação Fundamental. 2002. *Políticas de melhora da qualidade da educação: um balanço institucional* (Brasília: MEC/SEF).

Brasil Ministério do Planejamento, Orçamento e Gestão. 2002. *Balanço da reforma do estado no Brasil: a nova gestão pública* (Brasília: MP, SEGES).

Brasil Ministério do Trabalho. 1998. *PLANFOR—Programa Nacional de Qualificação do Trabalhador. Avaliação gerencial. Brasilia: Fundo de Amparo ao Trabalhador (FAT)* (Brasília: Ministério do Trabalho–SEFOR). Online at: http://www.ilo.org/public/spanish/region/ampro/cinterfor/dbase/ret/f_comp/ii/.

Brillantes, Jose. 1998. "The Philippine Overseas Employment Program and Its Effects on Immigration in Canada," in Eleanor R. Laquian, Aprodicio Laquian, and T. G. McGee, eds., *The Silent Debate: Asian Immigration and Racism in Canada* (Vancouver, BC: Institute of Asian Research, University of British Columbia).

Buğra, A. 1999. *Islam in Economic Organizations* (Istanbul: Tesev Publications).

Burtless, G., R. Lawrence, R. Litan, and R. Shapiro. 1998. *Golalphobia: Confronting Fears About Open Trade* (Washington, DC: Brookings Institution).

Cabrero Mendoza, Enrique. 1998. "La ola descentralizadora. Un análisis de tendencias y obstáculos de las políticas descentralizadoras en el ámbito internacional," in E. Cabrero Mendoza, ed., *Las políticas descentralizadoras en México 1983–1993: Logros y desencantos* (Mexico: Porrúa).

Camargo, José Márcio, and Francisco H. G. Ferreira. 2001. "O benefício social único: uma proposta de reforma da política social no Brasil." In *Texto Para Discussão* (Rio de Janeiro: Pontificia Universidade Catolica do Rio De Janeiro). Online at: http://www.puc-rio.br/sobrepuc/depto/economia/.

Camargo, José Márcio, and André Urani. 1996. *Flexibilidade do mercado de trabalho no Brasil* (Rio de Janeiro: Fundação Getúlio Vargas Editora).

Cantó, O., C. del Río, and C. Gradín. 2000. "La situación de los estudios sobre desigualdad y pobreza en España," in I. Bazaga, J. A. Ramos, and M. Tamayo, eds., *Pobreza y Desigualdad en España: Enfoques, Fuentes y Acción Pública, Cuadernos de Gobierno y Administración* 2, pp. 25–94.

Cardoso, Fernando Henrique, and Enzo Faletto. 1969. *Dependencia y desarrollo en América Latina: Ensayo de interpretación sociológica* (México: Siglo Veintiuno Editores).

———. 1979. *Dependency and Development in Latin America* (Berkeley: University of California Press).

Castels, Robert. 2001. "Empleo, exclusion y las nuevas cuestiones sociales," in

*Desigualdad y Globalización: Cinco Conferencias* (Buenos Aires: Ediciones Manantial).

Castells, Manuel. 2002. *The Interet Galaxy: Reflections of the Internet, Business, and Society* (New York: Oxford University Press).

Cawson, Alan. 1986. *Corporatism and Political Theory* (London: Basil Blackwell).

Central Bank of the Republic of Turkey. 2002. *The Impact of Globalization on the Turkish Economy* (Ankara).

Centre for Policy Studies. 2000. *South Africa Update* 2, no. 2 (March) (Johannesburg: Centre for Policy Studies).

Centro de Investigaciones Sociológicas (CIS). various years. *Indicadores de autodefinición ideológica* (Madrid: Ministerio de la Presidencia).

————. various years. *Barómetros de opinión* (Madrid: Ministerio de la Presidencia).

Chamboux-Leroux, Jean-Ives. 2001. "Efectos de la apertura comercial en las regiones y la localización industrial en México," *Comercio Exterior* 51, no. 7 (July) (México: Banco Nacional de Comercio Exterior).

Charney, Craig. 1995. *Voices of a New Democracy: African Expectations in the New South Africa*. (Johannesburg: Centre for Policy Studies).

Cohen, Michael. 2004. "Reframing Urban Assistance: Scale, Ambition, and Possibility." *Urban Update,* no. 5 (February).

Conde, Roberto Cortés. 1974. *The First Stages of Modernization in Spanish America* (New York: Harper & Row).

Constable, Nicole. 1997. *Maid to Order in Hong Kong: Stories of Filipino Workers* (Ithaca, NY: Cornell University Press).

Cortés, Fernando Cortés. 2004. "Casi cuarenta años de desigualdad de la distribución del ingreso en México," in Ilán Bizberg and Lorenzo Meyer, eds., *Una Historia Contemporánea de México*. Vol. 1: *Transformaciones y permanencias* (México: Océano).

Cotler, Julio. 1978. *Clases, Estado y Nación en Perú* (Lima: Instituto de Estudios Peruanos).

————. 1991. "Perú Since 1960," in Leslie Bethell, ed., *The Cambridge History of Latin America* (Cambridge: Cambridge University Press).

Cox, Robert. 1997. "Structural Issues of Global Governance: Implications for Europe," in Richard Falk and Tamás Szentes, eds., *A New Europe in the Changing Global System* (New York: United Nations University Press).

Crespo, Manuel, José Francisco Soares, and Alberto Mello e Souza. 2000. "The Brazilian National Evaluation System of Basic Education: Context, Process, and Impact." *Studies in Educational Evaluation* 26, no. 2.

Crouch, C. 1993. *Industrial Relations and European State Traditions* (Oxford: Clarendon Press).

Dahlman, Carl J., and Francisco C. Sercovich. 1984. "Exports of Technology from Semi-Industrial Economies and Local Technological Development." *Journal of Development Economics* 16.

Dean, Warren. 1969. *The Industrialization of São Paulo, 1880–1945*. Latin American monographs. (Austin: University of Texas Press).

de la Madrid, Miguel. 1999. *Plan Nacional de Desarrollo,* cited in Isabelle Rousseau, *Mexique: Une revolution silencieuse? Elites gouvernamentales et projet de modernisation* (Paris: L'Harmattan).

Departamento Intersindical de Estatística e Estudos Sócio-Econômicos (DIEESE). 2002. *Anuário dos trabalhadores 2000–2001* (São Paulo: DIEESE). Online at: http://www.dieese.org.br/anu/2001/anu2001-1.html#CAP1

Department of Finance (South Africa). 1996. *Growth, Employment, and Redistribution: A Macroeconomic Strategy for SA* (Pretoria: Government Printer).

Department of Water Affairs and Forestry (South Africa). 2001. *Free Basic Water* (Pretoria: Government Printer).

Derviş, Kemal. 2001. "Turkey's Crises: Causes, Consequences and Solutions." *Insight Turkey* 3, no. 1.

de Soto, Hernando. 1989. *The Other Path* (London: I.B. Tauris).

———. 2000. *The Mystery of Capital: Why Capitalism Triumphs in the West and Fails Everywhere Else* (New York: Basic Books).

Deyo, Frederic. 1989. *The Political Economy of the New Asian Industrialism* (Ithaca, NY: Cornell University Press).

Diamond, L. 1998. *Political Culture and Democratic Consolidation*. Working Paper 1998/18 (Madrid: Instituto Juan March).

Dolado, J. J., F. Felgueroso, and J. F. Jimeno. 2000. "Explaining Youth Labor Market Problems in Spain: Crowing-Out, Institutions, or Technology Shifts?" *Documento de Trabajo 2000-09* (Madrid: FEDEA).

Dollar, David, and Aart Kraay. 2002. "Response," in "Point/Counterpoint: Making Globalization Work for the Poor," *Finance and Development* (International Monetary Fund, March).

Dornbusch, Rudiger, and Eliana Cardoso. 1988. "Brazilian Debt: A Requiem for Muddling Through." *CEPR Discussion Papers* 243.

Drache, D., and M. Froese. 2003. "The Great Global Poverty Debate." Roberts Centre Research Papers, Toronto.

Dussel, Enrique. 1999. "La subcontratación como proceso de aprendizaje: El caso de la electrónica de Jalisco en la década de los noventa." Serie Desarrollo Productivo, Santiago de Chile, CEPAL-ECLAC.

Edgar, Jim, Doris Meissner, and Alejandro Silva Cochairs. 2004. *Keeping the Promise: Immigration Proposals from the Heartland*. Report of an Independent Task Force (Chicago: Chicago Council on Foreign Relations).

Elliot Armijo, Leslie. 1999. "Balance Sheet or Ballot Box?" in Philip Oxhorn and Pamela K. Starr, *Markets and Democracy in Latin America* (London and Boulder, CO: Lynne Rienner Pubishers).

Esping-Andersen, Gøsta. 1985. *Politics Against Market* (Princeton, NJ: Princeton University Press, 1985).

———. 1990. *The Three Worlds of Welfare Capitalism* (Princeton, NJ: Princeton University Press).

———. 1996. *Welfare States in Transition: National States in Global Economics* (London: Sage).

———. 1999. *Social Foundations of Postindustrial Economies* (New York: Oxford University Press).

Esping-Andersen, Gøsta, and Marino Regini. 2000. *Why Deregulate Labor Markets?* (New York: Oxford University Press).

Fabella, Raul V. 1996. "Features of the Emerging World Economic Order: Implications on Growth Policy," in Cayetano W. Paderanga Jr., ed., *The Philippines in the Emerging World Environment: Globalization at a Glance* (Metro Manila: University of the Philippines Center for Integrative and Development Studies and University of the Philippines Press).

Falk, R. 2000. *Predatory Globalization* (London: Pinter).

Fanon, Frantz. 1961. *Les damnés de la terre*, 2nd ed. (Paris: F. Maspero).

Faux, J., and L. Michel. 2001. "Inequality and the Global Economy," in W. Hutton and A. Giddens, eds., *On the Edge* (London: Vintage).

Fernandes, Maria Alice da Cunha, Denise C. Correa da Rocha, Margarida Maria Sousa de Oliveira, José Aparecido Carlos Ribeiro, and Luseni Maria Cordeiro de Aquino. 1998. "Gasto social das três esferas de governo—1995." *Texto para Discussão* (Brasília: IPEA). Online at: http://www.ipea.gov.br/pub/td/td_598.pdf.

Fernandes, Maria Alice da Cunha, Margarida Maria Sousa Oliveira, Denise C. Correa da Rocha, Nyedja da Silva Marinho, and José Aparecido Carlos Ribeiro. 1998. "Dimensionamento e acompanhamento do gasto social federal." *Texto para Discussão* (Brasília: IPEA). Online at: http://www.ipea.gov.br/pub/td/td_547.pdf.

Ffrench-Davis, Ricardo. 1997. *Coping with Capital Surges: The Return of Finance to Latin America.* (Boulder, CO: Lynne Rienner Publishers).

Fishlow, Albert. 2000. "Brazil and Economic Realities." *Daedalus (Proceedings of the American Academy of Arts and Sciences)* 129, no. 2.

*Foreign Policy.* 2004. "Measuring Economic Reversals: Forward Momentum Globalization," no. 141 (March–April), p. 54.

Franco, Maria Sylvia de Carvalho. 1969. *Homens livres na ordem escravocrata* (São Paulo: Instituto de Estudos Brasileiros Universidade de São Paulo).

Frank, Andre Gunder. 1967. *Capitalism and Underdevelopment in Latin America: Historical Studies of Chile and Brazil* (New York: Monthly Review Press).

Fraser, N. 2000. "Recognition Without Ethics," in M. Garber et al., eds., *The Turn to Ethics* (London: Routledge).

Frieden, J. 1981. "Third World Indebted Industrialization: International Finance and State Capitalism in Mexico, Brazil, Algeria, and South Korea." *International Organization* 35.

Friedman, Steven. 1987. *Building Tomorrow Today: African Workers in Trade Unions, 1970–1984* (Johannesburg: Ravan Press).

———. 1999a. "Who We Are: Voter Participation, Rationality and the 1999 Election." *Politikon* 26, no. 2.

———. 1999b. "South Africa: Entering the Post-Mandela Era." *Journal of Democracy* 10, no. 4 (October).

———. 2001a. *Free but Unequal: Democracy, Inequality and the State in Latin America and Africa* (Johannesburg: Centre for Policy Studies).

———. 2001b. "A Quest for Control: High Modernism and Its Discontents in Johannesburg South Africa," in Blair A. Ruble, Richard E. Stren, Joseph S. Tulchin, and Diana H. Varat, eds., *Urban Governance Around the World* (Washington, DC: Woodrow Wilson International Center for Scholars, Comparative Urban Studies Project).

———. 2002. "Democracy, Inequality and the Reconstitution of Politics," in Joseph S. Tulchin (with Amelia Brown), eds., *Democratic Governance and Social Inequality* (Boulder, CO: Lynne Rienner), pp.13–40.

———. (forthcoming). "An End in Itself: Democracy and the Building of Post-Apartheid South Africa." Paper prepared for Gulbenkian Foundation conference on New Democracies, June 2000.

Friedman, Steven, and Ivor Chipkin. 2001. *A Poor Voice? The Politics of Inequality in South Africa* (Johannesburg: Centre for Policy Studies).

Friedman, Steven, and Richard Humphries, eds. 1993. *Federalism and Its Foes* (Johannesburg: Centre for Policy Studies, May). Developed from proceedings of a joint Institute for Multi-Party Democracy/CPS workshop entitled "The

Politics and Economics of Federalism: A South African Debate," held in August 1992.

Friedman, Steven, and Caroline Kihato. (forthcoming). "Decentralization, Civil Society, and Democratic Governance." Woodrow Wilson Center.

Friedman, Steven, Joel Barkan, Claude Kabemba, Chris Landsberg, and Khehla Shubane. 1998. *Assessing the USAID Governance Sector Programme* (Johannesburg: Centre for Policy Studies).

Friedman, Thomas. 2000. *Understanding Globalization: The Lexus and the Olive Tree* (New York: Random House).

Furtado, Celso. 1963. *The Economic Growth of Brazil: A Survey from Colonial to Modern Times.* Translated by A.R.W. and E. C. Drysdale (Berkeley: University of California Press).

———. 1985. *A fantasia organizada: Coleão Estudos brasileiros (Paz e Terra [Firm])* (Rio de Janeiro: Paz e Terra).

García, Brigida. 2001. "Reestructuración económica y feminización del mercado de trabajo en México." *Papeles de Población* (Toluca, México), no. 27 (January-March).

García, Brigida, and Orlandina de Oliveira. 2001. "Heterogeneidad laboral y calidad de los empleos en las principales áreas urbanas de México." Unpublished manuscript.

Garrett, Geoffrey. 1998. *Partisan Politics in the Global Economy* (Cambridge: Cambridge University Press).

Gazier, Bernard, and Remy Herrera. 2000. "Escaping from the Crisis and Activating Labor Market Policies in Asia: Some Lessons from European and French Experience with a Special Focus on South Korea." Paper presented at an international conference on "Flexibility vs. Security?: Social Policy and the Labor Market in Europe and East Asia." 30 November–1 December, Seoul, South Korea.

George, Susan. 2002. "Globalofóbicos no, ciudadanos globales sí." *Foreign Affairs en Español* 2, no. 1 (spring).

Germani, Gino. 1972. *Aspectos teóricos de la marginalidad* (Asunción, Paraguay: Centro Paraguayo de Estudios Sociológicos).

Gilbert, Alan. 2002. "On the Mystery of Capital and the Myths of Hernando de Soto: What Difference Does Legal Title Make?" *IDPR* 24, no. 1.

Gimeno, J. A. 1993. "Incidencia del gasto público por niveles de renta (España 1990 vs. 1980)." *I Simposio sobre Igualdad y Distribución de la Renta y la Riqueza,* vol. VII (Madrid: Fundación Argentaria).

Göle, N. 2000. *Melez Desenler* (Hybrid Designs) (Istanbul: Metis).

Gollas, Manuel. 2004. "Breve relato de cincuenta años de política económica," in Ilán Bizberg and Lorenzo Meyer, eds., *Una Historia Contemporánea de México.* Vol. 1: *Transformaciones y permanencias* (México: Océano).

Gomes, Angela Maria de Castro, and Maria Celina Soares d'Araújo. 1989. *Getulismo e trabalhismo, Série Princpios* (São Paulo: Editora Atica).

Gordon, Sara. 1999. "Del universalismo estratificado a los programas focalizados," in Martha Schteingart, ed., *Políticas sociales para los pobres en América Latina* (México: Miguel Angel Porrua).

Gottschalk, P., and T. M. Smeeding. 1999. "Empirical Evidence on Income Inequality in Industrialized Countries," in A. B. Atkinson and F. Bourguignon, eds., *Handbook of Income Distribution* (New York: Elsevier-North Holland Publishers).

Gotz, Graeme A. 1997. "The Limits of Community: The Dynamics of Rural Water Provision." Unpublished report for Rand Water, Johannesburg, Centre for Policy Studies.

———. 2000. "Shoot Anything That Flies, Claim Anything That Falls: Labour and the Changing Definition of the Reconstruction and Development Programme," in Glenn Adler and Eddie Webster, eds., *Trade Unions And Democratization in South Africa, 1985–1997* (New York: St Martin's).

Graziano, Xico. 2003a. "O custo da reforma agrária." *O Estado de São Paulo,* 21 January. Online at: http://www.estado.com.br/editorias/2003/01/21/aberto001 .html

———. 2003b. "O desafio da agricultura familiar." *O Estado de São Paulo,* 5 February. Online at: http://www.estado.com.br/editorias/2003/02/05/ abeto001.html.

Gutierrez, Eric. 1994. *The Ties That Bind: A Guide to Family, Business and Other Interests in the Ninth House of Representatives* (Metro Manila: Philippine Center for Investigative Journalism).

Habib, Adam, and Vishnu Padayachee. 2000. "Economic Policy and Power Relations in South Africa's Transition to Democracy." *World Development* 28, no. 2.

Haggard, Stephan, and Robert Kaufman. 1995. *The Political Economy of Democratic Transitions* (Princeton, NJ: Princeton University Press).

Hall, Peter, and David Soskice. 2001. *Varieties of Capitalism: The Institutional Foundations of Comparative Advantage* (New York: Oxford University Press).

Havel, Vaclav. 1999. "Kosovo, Cambridge Mass, London, and the End of the Nation-State." *New York Review* (10 June).

Held, David. 1995. *Democracy and the Global Order: From the Modern State to Cosmopolitan Governance* (Cambridge: Polity Press).

Held, David, et al. 1999. *Global Transformations* (Cambridge: Polity Press).

Heller, Patrick, and Libhongo Ntlokonkulu. 2001. *A Civic Movement, or a Movement of Civics? The South African National Civic Organisation in the post-Apartheid Period* (Johannesburg: Centre for Policy Studies, June).

Henriques, Ricardo, ed. 2000. *Desigualdade e pobreza no Brasil* (Rio de Janeiro: IPEA).

Henwood, Doug. 2003. "Beyond Globophobia." *The Nation,* 1 December 2003, p. 3. Online at: http://www.thenation.com.

Heper, M., and F. Keyman. 1999. "Double-Faced State: Political Patronage and the Consolidation of Democracy in Turkey," in S. Kedourie, ed., *Turkey Before and After Ataturk* (London: Frank Cass).

Hernandez, Carolina G. 1996. "Political Reform for Global Competitiveness: The Philippines in the 1990s," in W. Scott Thompson and Wilfrido V. Villacorta, eds., *The Philippine Road to NIChood* (Manila: De la Salle University and Social Weather Stations Inc.).

Holton, R., 1998. *Globalization and the Nation-State* (London: Macmillan Press).

Huber, Evelyne, and John D. Stephens. 2001. *Development and Crisis of the Welfare State: Parties and Policies in Global Markets* (Chicago and London: University of Chicago Press).

Hudson, Peter. 1986. "The Freedom Charter and the Theory of National Democratic Revolution." *Transformation* 1 (Durban, South Africa: University of Natal).

Humphries, Richard, and Maxine Reitzes, eds. 1995. *Civil Society After Apartheid* (Johannesburg: Centre for Policy Studies, December).

Imedio, L. J., E. M. Parrado, and M. D. Sarrión. 1997. "Evolución de la desigualdad y la pobreza en la distribución de la renta familiar en España en el periodo 1985–1995." *Cuadernos* 32, pp. 93–109.

Instituto Brasileiro de Geografia e Estadística (IBGE). 2002. *Evolução e perspectivas de mortalidade infantil no Brasil,* no. 2 (Rio de Janeiro: IBGE).

———. 1992, 1995, 1999, 2001. *Pesquisa Nacional por Amostra de Domicílios* (Rio de Janeiro: IBGE).

Instituto de Estudos do Trabalho e Sociedade and André Urani. 2002. *Desenvolvimento e distribuição de renda no Brasil* (Rio de Janeiro: IETS).

Instituto Nacional de Estadística (INE). *Encuesta de población activa (EPA)* for the second trimester of each year.

Instituto Nacional de Estadística, Geografía e Informática (INEGI). 2005. *Industria Maquiladora de Exportación* (México: INEGI, January).

International Labour Organization (ILO). 2000. *World Labour Report 2000: Income Security and Social Protection in a Changing World* (Geneva: ILO).

International Monetary Fund. 1994. *World Economic Outlook* (May).

Iversen, Torben, and Anne Wren. 1998. "Equality, Employment, and Budgetary Restraint: The Trilemma of the Service Economy." *World Politics* 50, no. 4.

Jaguaribe, Hélio. 1966. *The Brazilian Nationalism and the Dynamics of Its Political Development.* Studies in Comparative International Development (St. Louis: Social Science Institute, Washington University).

Jones, Catherine. 1990. "Hong Kong, Singapore, South Korea and Taiwan: Oikonomic Welfare States." *Government and Opposition* 25, no. 4.

Kabemba, Claude. 2000. "Failure of RDP Office Holds Important Governance Lessons." *Synopsis* 4, no. 2 (Johannesburg: Centre for Policy Studies).

Kalati, Noushin, and James Manor. n.d. "Elite Perceptions of Poverty and Poor People in South Africa." Unpublished paper, Institute of Development Studies, Sussex University.

Kang, Myung-Sei, and In-Sub Ma. 2001. "Opportunities and Constraints of Tripartism and Welfare Reforms Under the Kim Dae Jung Government." Paper presented at the meetings of the Korean Political Science Association, December.

Karnow, Stanley. 1989. *In Our Own Image: America's Empire in the Philippines* (New York: Ballantine Books).

Katz, Isaac M. 1998. *La apertura comercial y su impacto regional sobre la economía mexicana* (México: Miguel Angel Porrua-ITAM).

Katz, J., and Giovanni Stumpo. 2001. "Regímenes sectoriales, productividad y competitividad internacional." *Revista de la CEPAL* 75 (Santiago de Chile) (November).

Katzman, Martin T. 1977. *Cities and Frontiers in Brazil: Regional Dimensions of Economic Development* (Cambridge, MA: Harvard University Press).

Kearney, A. T./*Foreign Policy* magazine. 2002. "The Globalization Index," in *Global Outlook,* International Urban Research Monitor (Washington, DC: Woodrow Wilson International Center for Scholars and U.S. Department of Housing and Urban Development, April).

Kentridge, Matthew. 1993. *Turning the Tanker: The Economic Debate in South Africa* (Johannesburg: Centre for Policy Studies).

Keohane, Robert O. 2001. "Governance in a Partially Globalized World." Presidential address to the American Political Science Association, 2000. *American Political Science Review* 95, no. 1 (March).

Keyman, E. F. 1997. *Globalization, State, Identity/Difference* (New Jersey: Humanities Press).

————. 2000. "Global Modernity, Identity, and Turkey," in G. Özdoğan, ed., *Rethinking State, Nation, and Citizenship* (Istanbul: Eren Press).

————. 2001. "Globalization, Islam and Civil Society in Turkey," in J. Jenson, ed., *Global Institutions* (London: Ashgate Press).

Keyman, E. F., and A. Içduygu. 2003. "Globalization, Civil Society and Citizenship in Turkey." *Citizenship Studies* 7, no. 2.

Kihato, Caroline. 2001. "Privatisation, What Privatisation?" in *Topical Trends* (Johannesburg: Centre for Policy Studies, November).

Kihato, Caroline, and Thabo Rapoo. 2001. "A Future for the Provinces? New Rethink Needed on Role of Provinces." Johannesburg, Centre for Policy Studies Policy Brief No. 23, June.

Kihato, Caroline, and Tobias Schmitz. 2002. *Enhancing Policy Implementation: Lessons from the Water Sector* (Johannesburg: Centre for Policy Studies).

Kim, Samuel. 2000. "South Korea's *Segyewha* (Globalization): A Framework for Analysis," in Sam Kim, ed., *South Korea and Segyewha (Globalization)* (New York: Cambridge University Press).

Kim, So-Young. 2001. "Social Protection Program and Policy Alternatives for Non-Standard Workers in Korea." Paper presented at the KLI-CALSS workshop on "Non-Standard Workers and Policy Directions," October.

Kim, Yeon-myung. 2000. "The Present State of the Korean Social Insurance System and Its Future Tasks" (in Korean). *Korean Journal of Social Welfare*.

Kingston, Peter. 1999. "Constitutional Reform and Macroeconomic Stability," in Philip Oxhorn and Pamela K. Starr, eds., *Markets and Democracy in Latin America* (London and Boulder, CO: Lynne Rienner Publishers).

Klein, Herbert S. 1999. *The Atlantic Slave Trade: New Approaches to the Americas* (Cambridge and New York: Cambridge University Press).

Koo, Hagen. 2001. *Korean Workers: The Culture and Politics of Class Formation* (Ithaca, NY: Cornell University Press).

Kramer, H. 2000. *A Challenging Turkey: The Challenge to Europe and the United States* (Washinghton, DC: Brookings Institution Press).

Krugman, Paul. 1998. *Pop Internationalism* (Cambridge, MA: MIT Press).

Lambert, Jacques. 1963. *Amerique Latine: Structures sociales et institutions politiques* (Paris: Presses Universitaires de France).

Landes, David S. 1999. *The Wealth and Poverty of Nations: Why Some Are So Rich and Some So Poor* (New York: W. W. Norton).

Lane, Max R. 1990. *The Urban Mass Movement in the Philippines, 1983–1987* (Singapore: Institute of Asian Studies and the Research School of Pacific Studies, Australian National University).

Laquian, Aprodicio A., and Eleanor R. Laquian. 2002. *The Erap Tragedy: Tales from the Snake Pit* (Manila: Anvil Publications Inc.).

Lavinas, Lena, Maria Lígia Barbosa, and Octávio Tourinho. 2001. *Assessing Local Minimum Income Programmes in Brazil: ILO–World Bank Agreement* (Geneva: International Labour Office). Online at: http://www.ilo.org/public/english/protection/ses/info/publ/.

Lee, Byung-hee, and Jae-ho Chung. 2001. "Analysis of Poverty Structure After the Economic Crisis" (in Korean). Paper presented at the conference on "Labor and Industrial Relations in Transitional Period of the Korean Economy," August.

Lee, Ho-Geun. 2001. "The Continuity and Change in Work Arrangements in South Korea: The Development of the Non-Standard Work and Its Regulation Problem." Paper presented at the meetings of the Korean Political Science Association, December.

Leftwich, A. 1993. "Governance, Democracy and Development in the Third World." *Third World Quarterly* 14, no. 3, pp. 605–624.

Lieberman, Evan. 2000. "Payment for Privilege? Race and Space in the Politics of Taxation in Brazil and South Africa." *Political Science* (University of California–Berkeley).

———. 2001. "National Political Community and the Politics of Income Taxation in Brazil and South Africa in the 20th Century." *Politics and Society* 29 no. 4.

Lindert, Peter H., and Jeffrey G. Williamson. 2001. "Does Globalization Make the World More Unequal?" NBER Working Paper No. w8228, April.

Lisboa, Marcos B., ed. 2002. *A Agenda Perdida: Diagnósticos e propostas para a retomada do crescimento com maior justiça social.* Online at: http://www.iets.inf.br/.

Lodovici, Manuela Samek. 2000. "The Dynamics of Labour Market Reform in European Countries," in Gøsta Esping-Andersen and Marino Regini, eds., *Why Deregulate Labor Markets?* (New York: Oxford University Press).

Looney, Robert E. 1975. *Income Distribution Policies and Economic Growth in Semiindustrialized Countries: A Comparative Study of Iran, Mexico, Brazil, and South Korea* (New York: Praeger).

López Acevedo, Gladys. 2002a. "Determinants of Technology Adoption in México," World Bank, *Policy Research Working Paper,* no. WPS2780, February. Online at: http://econ.worldbank.org/view.php?type=5&id=11791.

———. 2002b. "Technology and Skill Demand in México," World Bank, *Policy Rsearch Working Paper,* no. WPS2779, February. Online at: http://econ. worldbank.org/view.php?type=5&id=11790.

Mamdani, Mahmood. 1995. *Citizen and Subject: Contemporary Africa and the Politics of Late Colonialism* (Kampala, Uganda: Fountain).

Manchester, Alan Krebs. 1964. *British Preeminence in Brazil—Its Rise and Decline: A Study in European Expansion* (New York: Octagon Books).

Manuel, Trevor A. 1999. *Budget Speech.* Online at: http://www.finance.gov.za.

———. 2000. *Budget Speech.* 23 February. Online at: http://www.finance.gov.za.

———. 2001. *Address to the National Assembly on the Introduction of the Adjustments Appropriation Bill and the 2001 Medium Term Budget Policy Statement,* 30 October. Online at: http://www.finance.gov.za.

———. 2002. *Budget Speech.* Online at: www.finance.gov.za.

Marais, Hein. 1998. *South Africa Limits to Change: The Political Economy of Transition* (London: Palgrave).

Maravall, J. M. 1997. *Regimes, Politics and Markets* (Cambridge: Oxford University Press).

Marques-Pereira, Jaime, and Bruno Theret. 2004. "Mediaciones institucionales de regulación social y dinámicas macroeconómicas: Los casos de Brasil y México," in Carlos Alba and Ilán Bizberg, eds., *Democracia y Globalización en México y Brasil* (México: El Colegio de México).

Marshall, T. H. 1992. *Citizenship and Social Class* (London: Pluto, reprint).

Mattoso, Kátia M. de Queirós. 1988. *Família e sociedade na Bahia do século XIX, Baianada; 6* (São Paulo: Corrupio).

May, Julian, et al. 1998. *Poverty and Inequality Report* (Durban, South Africa: Praxis Publishers).

Mayende, Gilingwe. 2000. "Media Briefing by the New Director-General of Land Affairs, Dr. Gilingwe Mayende, Sheraton Hotel, Pretoria, 4 July 2000." Online at: http://www.info.gov.za/speeches/2000/0007101010a1007.htm.

Mbeki, Thabo. 2002. *State of the Nation Address by President Mbeki to the Joint*

*Sitting of the Houses of Parliament,* Cape Town, 8 February. Online at: http://www.anc.org.za/ancdocs/history/mbeki/2002/tm0208.html.

Mboweni, T. T. 2003. *Statement of the Monetary Policy Committee, 10 September 2003.* Issued by T. T. Mboweni, governor of the South African Reserve Bank, reproduced in South African Reserve Bank *Quarterly Bulletin,* September 2003, pp. 65–67.

McGrath, Mike, and Andrew Whiteford. 1994. "Disparate Circumstances." *Indicator SA* 11, no 3 (winter).

McGrew, A. 1998. "Globalization: Conceptualizing a Moving Target," in P. Schori, ed., *Understanding Globalization* (Stockholm: Swedish Ministry for Foreign Affairs Publication).

Mdlalana, Membathisi. 2000. *Statement by the Minister of Labour on the Occasion of the Release of Labour Law Amendments,* Pretoria, Department of Labour, 26 July.

Medeiros, Carlos Aguiar. 2002. "Distribuição de renda como política de desenvolvimento," in A. C. Castro, ed., *Desenvolvimento em debate: Painéis do desenvolvimento brasileiro* (Rio de Janeiro: Mauad; Banco Nacional de Desenvolvimento Econômico e Social [BNDES]).

Medel, B., A. Molina, and J. Sánchez. 1988. "Los efectos distributivos del gasto público en España." *FIES Documento de Trabajo,* no. 28/1988.

Médici, André Cezar. 2002. "Los gastos en salud en las familias de Brasil: Algunas evidencias de su carácter regresivo," in *Serie de informes técnicos del Departamento de Desarrollo Sostenible* (Washingtion, DC: Banco Interamericano de Desarrollo).

Melucci, Alberto. 1996. *Challenging Codes: Collective Action in the Information Age* (Cambridge: Cambridge University Press, Cambridge Cultural Social Studies).

Michie, Jonathan, and Vishnu Padayachee. 1998. "Three Years After Apartheid: Growth, Employment and Redistribution." *Cambridge Journal of Economics* 22, no. 5.

Milanovic, Branco. 2002. "Against Globalization as We Know It," in *International Development Economics Associate.* Online at: http://www.networkideas.org/feathm/jun2002/ft24_Against_Globalization.htm.

Ministry of Finance and Economy (South Korea). 2003. *Major Economic Indicators* (Seoul: MOFE).

Ministry of Health and Welfare (South Korea). 2003. "Major Indicators of Health and Welfare." Online at: http://www.mohw.go.kr (accessed 25 June 2003).

Mishra, Ramesh. 1984. *The Welfare State in Crisis* (Brighton, UK: Wheatsheaf Books).

———. 1999. *Globalization and the Welfare State* (Cheltenham: Edward Elgar).

Mittelman, James H., ed. 1996. *Globalization: Theory and Practice* (New York: Frances Pinter).

Montero, J. R., R. Gunther, and M. Torcal. 1997. *Democracy in Spain: Legitimacy, Discontent and Disaffection.* WP 1997/100 (Madrid: Instituto Juan March).

Moon, Chung-in, and Young-Cheol Kim. 2000. "Globalization and Workers in South Korea," in Samuel Kim, ed., *Korea's Globalization* (New York: Cambridge University Press).

Moon, Chung-in, and Jongryn Mo. 2000. *Economic Crisis and Structural Reforms in South Korea.* (Washington, DC: Economic Strategy Institute).

Moon, Chung-in, and Jae-jin Yang. 2002a. "Globalization, Social Inequality, and Democratic Governance in South Korea." In Joseph S. Tulchin, ed.,

*Democratic Governance and Social Inequality.* (Boulder, CO: Lynne Rienner Publishers).

———. 2002b. "The Kim Dae-jung Government and the Productive Welfare Initiative: Ideals and Reality." In Chung-in Moon and David I. Steinberg, eds., *Korea in Transition: Three Years Under the Kim Dae-jung Government* (Seoul: Yonsei University Press).

Moore, Barrington. 1966. *Social Origins of Dictatorship and Democracy: Lord and Peasant in the Making of the Modern World* (Boston: Beacon Press).

Morley, Samuel A. 1995. *Poverty and Inequality in Latin America: The Impact of Adjustment and Recovery in the 1980s* (Baltimore: Johns Hopkins University Press).

Muslim, Macapado Abaton. 1994. *The Moro Armed Struggle in the Philippines: The Nonviolent Autonomy Alternative* (Marawi City: Mindanao State University Press).

National Statistical Office (South Korea). 2002. KOSIS (Online Data Base): http://kosis.nso.go.kr (accessed 25 December 2002).

Nelson, Joan. 1993. "The Politics of Economic Transformation: Is Third World Experience Relevant in Eastern Europe?" *World Politics* 45 (Johns Hopkins University Press, April).

North, Douglass. 1990. *Institutions, Institutional Change and Economic Performance* (Cambridge: Cambridge University Press).

North, Douglass C., William Summerhill, and Barry R. Weingast. 2002. "Orden, Desorden y cambio económico; Latinoamercia vs. Norte América." *Revista Instituciones y desarrollo,* no. 12-13 (Institut Internacional de Governabilitat de Cataluna, Barcelona).

Nye, Joseph D., and John D. Donahue, eds. 2000. *Governance in a Globalizing World* (Washington, DC: Brookings Institution Press).

O'Donnell, Guillermo. 1996. "Illusions About Consolidation." *Journal of Democracy* 7, no. 2 (April).

Office of the President. 2000. *DJ Welfarism: A New Paradigm for Productive Welfare in Korea* (Seoul: Office of the President).

Ohmae, Kenichi. 1990. *The Borderless World.* (New York: HarperCollins).

———. 1996. *The End of the Nation State: The Rise of Regional Economies* (New York: Free Press).

Oliveira, João Batista Araújo e. 1984. *Desburocratização e democracia* (Campinas, Brazil: Papirus Livraria Editora).

Oliver J., X. Ramos, and J. L. Raymond. 2001a. "Anatomía de la distribución de la renta en España, 1985–1996: La continuidad de la mejora," *Papeles de Economía Española* 88, pp. 67–88.

———. 2001b. "Capital humano y desigualdad en España 1985–1996," *Papeles de Economía Española* 88, pp. 240–255.

———. 2002. "La desigualdad en la distribución de la renta en la UE a mediados de los noventa. Evidencia del Panel de Hogares Europeo," *Papeles de Economía Española* 91, pp. 129–150.

Oliver, J., J. L. Raymond, F. Mañé, and H. Sala. 2002. *La sobreeducación en la economía española 1980-2001* (Barcelona: Fundació Empresa i Ciència).

Öniş, Z. 2003. "Domestic Versus Global Dynamics: Towards a Political Economy of the 2000 and 2001 Financial Crises in Turkey." *Turkish Studies* 4, no. 2.

Öniş, Z., and F. Keyman. 2003. "A New Path Emerges." *Journal of Democracy* 14, no. 2.

Organization for Economic Cooperation and Development (OECD). 1999.

*Employment Protection, and Labor Market Performance,* OECD Employment Outlook 1999 (Paris: OECD).

————. 2000. *Pushing Ahead with Reform in Korea: Labor Market and Social Safety-Net Policies* (Paris: OECD).

————. various years. *Annual National Accounts* (Paris: OECD).

Oxhorn, Philip, and G. Ducatenzeiller. 1999. "The Problematic Relationship Between Economic and Political Liberalization: Some Theoretical Considerations," in Philip Oxhorn and Pamela K. Starr, eds., *Markets and Democracy in Latin America* (London and Boulder, CO: Lynne Rienner Publishers).

Oxhorn, Philip, Joseph S. Tulchin, and Andrew Selee, eds. 2004. *Decentralization and Democratic Governance* (Baltimore: Johns Hopkins University Press).

Özbudun, E., and F. Keyman. 2002. "Globalization and Turkey: Actors, Strategies and Discourses," in P. Berger and S. Huntington, eds., *Many Globalizations* (Oxford: Oxford University Press).

Packenham, Robert A. 1992. *The Dependency Movement—Scholarship and Politics in Development Studies* (Cambridge, MA: Harvard University Press).

Palley, Howard. 1992. "Social Policy and the Elderly in South Korea." *Asian Survey* 32.

Pastore, José. 1998. *O desemprego tem cura?* (São Paulo: Makron Books do Brasil Editora).

Perreira, Luiz Carlos Bresser, José Maria Maravall, and Adam Przeworski. 1993. *Economic Reform in New Democracies: A Social Democratic Approach* (Cambridge: Cambridge University Press).

Pfeffer, Jeffrey, and James N. Baron. 1998. "Taking the Workers Back Out: Recent Trends in the Structuring of Employment." *Research in Organizational Behavior* 10.

Pinto, Álvaro Vieira. 1960. *Consciência e realidade nacional* (Rio de Janeiro: Ministerio da Educação e Cultura, Instituto Superior de Estudos Brasileiros).

Pinto Santa Cruz, Aníbal. 1962. *Un caso de desarrollo frustrado* (Santiago: Editorial Universitaria S.A.).

Pogge, T. 2001. "Priorities of Global Justice." *Metaphilosophy* 32, no. 1.

Poswell, Laura. 2002. *The Post-Apartheid Labour Market: A Status Report.* Development Policy Research Unit, University of Cape Town, February.

Prado Júnior, Caio. 1967. *The Colonial Background of Modern Brazil.* Translated by S. Macedo (Berkeley: University of California Press).

Przeworski, Adam. 1987. *Capitalism and Social Democracy* (Cambridge: Cambridge University Press).

————. 1995. *Sustainable Democracy* (Cambridge: Cambridge University Press).

Racelis, Mary, and Judy Celine Ick, eds. 2001. *Bearers of Benevolence: The Thomasites and Public Education in the Philippines* (Metro Manila: Anvil Publishing Inc.).

Rapoo, Thabo. 1996. *Making the Means Justify the Ends? The Theory and Practice of the RDP* (Johannesburg: Centre for Policy Studies).

————. 2001. "In Poor Voice: NCOP's Weakness Flows from the Westminster System." Johannesburg, Centre for Policy Studies Policy Brief No. 22, April.

Regini, Marino. 2000. "The Dilemmas of Labor Market Regulation," in Gøsta Esping-Andersen and Marino Regini, eds., *Why Deregulate Labor Markets?* (New York: Oxford University Press).

Reis, Elisa Maria Pereira.1990. "Brazil: One Hundred Years of the Agrarian Question." *International Social Sciences Journal* 42, no. 2.

Rios-Neto, Eduardo Luiz G., and Ana Maria C. H. Oliveira. 2000. "Políticas voltadas para a pobreza: O caso da formação Professional," in R. Henriques, ed., *Desigualdade e pobreza no Brasil* (Rio de Janeiro: IPEA).

Rivera Ríos, Miguel Ángel. 2001. "México en la economía global: Reinserción, aprendizaje y coordinación," *Problemas del desarrollo,* IIE, UNAM 32, no. 127 (October–December).

Rocha, Sonia. 2000. "Estimação de linhas de indigencia e de pobreza: Opcões metodológicas no Brasil," in R. Henriques, ed., *Desigualdade e pobreza no Brasil* (Rio de Janeiro: IPEA).

———. 2003. "Pobreza no Brasil: Afinal, de que se trata?" (Rio de Janeiro: Editora FGV).

Rodrik, Dani. 1997. "Trade, Social Insurance, and the Limits to Globalization." Working paper no. 5905 (Cambridge: National Bureau of Economic Research).

———. 1999. *The New Global Economy and Developing Countries: Making Openness Work* (Washington, DC: Overseas Development Council).

———. 2002a. "Feasible Globalizations." Working paper no. 9129 (Cambridge: National Bureau of Economic Research, July).

———. 2002b. "Institutions Rule: The Primacy of Institutions over Geography and Integration in Economic Development" (with Arvind Subramanian and Francesco Trebbi). Working paper no. 9305 (Cambridge: National Bureau of Economic Research, November).

Rodrik, Dani, and Roberto Rigobon. 2004. "Rule of Law, Democracy, Openness, and Income: Estimating the Interrelationships." Unpublished manuscript.

Romero, J. 2004. "El milagro mexicano: Surgimiento, desarrollo y desaparición," in Ilán Bizberg and Lorenzo Meyer, eds., *Una Historia Contemporánea de México.* Vol. 1: *Transformaciones y permanencias* (México: Océano).

Ross Schneider, B. 1990. "La política de privatización en Brasil y México: Variaciones sobre un tema estatal." *Foro Internacional* (México: El Colegio de México), no. 121 (June–September).

Rossi Júnior, José Luiz, and Pedro Cavalcanti Ferreira. 1999. "Evolução da produtividade industrial brasileira e abertura comercial." *Texto Para Discussão* (Brasília: IPEA).

Roux, Edward. 1964. *Time Longer Than Rope: A History of the Black Man's Struggle for Freedom in South Africa* (Madison: University of Wisconsin Press).

Rudra, Nita. 2002. "Globalization and Decline of the Welfare State in Less Developing Countries." *International Organization* 56, no. 2.

Rueschemeyer, D., E. H. Stephens, and J. D. Stephens. 1992. *Capitalist Development and Democracy* (Chicago: University of Chicago).

Sabel, Charles. 1997. "Constitutional Orders," in J. Rogers Hollingsworth and Robert Boyer, *Contemporary Capitalism: The Embeddedness of Institutions* (Cambridge: Cambridge University Press).

Sachs, Jeffrey. 2003. "Institutions Don't Rule: Direct Effects of Geography on Per Capita Income." National Bureau of Economic Research Working Paper No. 9490, February.

Schmitter, Philippe C. 1999. "The Future of Democracy: Could It Be a Matter of Scale?" *Social Research* 66, no 3 (fall).

Schmitz, Tobias. 2000. "The Land Never Bought, the Land Never Sold." *Synopsis* 4, no. 1 (June), Johannesburg, Centre for Policy Studies.

Schwartzman, Simon. 1988. *Bases do autoritarismo brasileiro,* 3rd ed. *Contribuições em ciências sociais; 10.* (Rio de Janeiro: Editora Campus). Online at: http://www.schwartzman.org.br/simon/bases/bases.htm.

———. 1997. *A redescoberta da cultura, Ensaios de cultura; 10.* (São Paulo: Edusp FAPESP). Online at: http://www.schwartzman.org.br/simon/redesc/ sumario.htm.

———. 1999. "Fora de foco: Diversidade e identidades étnicas no Brasil." *Novos Estudos CEBRAP* 55. Online at: http://www.schwartzman.org.br/simon/ pdfs/origem.pdf.

———. 2000. "Brasil: The Social Agenda." *Daedalus (Proceedings of the American Academy of Arts and Sciences)* 129, no. 2. Online at: http://www. schwartzman.org.br/simon/daedalus.htm.

———. 2001. *Trabalho Infantil no Brasil* (Brasília: Organização Internacional do Trabalho). Online at: http://www.schwartzman.org.br/simon/oit.htm.

———. 2002. "Higher Education and the Demands of the New Economy in Latin America." Background paper for the LAC Flagship Report (Washington, DC: World Bank). Online at: http://www.schwartzman.org.br/simon/flagship.pdf.

Scott, James. 1998. *Seeing Like a State: How Certain Schemes to Improve the Human Condition Have Failed* (New Haven, CT: Yale University Press).

Sechuwi. 1998. *Segyehwa Baeksuh.* White Paper on Segyehwa (in Korean) (Seoul: Segyehwa Chujin Wiwonhoi).

Sen, Amartya. 2002. "How to Judge Globalism." *The American Prospect, Globalism and Poverty* (winter).

Senses, F. 2003. "Economic Crisis as an Instigator of Distributional Conflict: The Turkish Case in 2001." *Turkish Studies* 4, no. 2.

Shin, D.-M. 2000. "Financial Crisis and Social Security: The Paradox of the Republic Korea." *International Social Security Review* 53, no. 3.

Shubane, Khehla. 1997. *Yesterday's Remedies: Political Parties, Liberation Politics, and South African Democracy* (Johannesburg: Centre for Policy Studies).

Silliman, G. Sidney, and Lela Garner Noble, eds. 1998. *Organizing for Democracy: NGOs, Civil Society and the Philippine State* (Manila: Ateneo de Manila University Press).

Simkins, Charles. 1988. *The Prisoners of Tradition and the Politics of Nation Building* (Johannesburg: Institute of Race Relations).

———. 1996. "A South African Welfare State?" in Steven Friedman and Riaan de Villiers, eds., *Comparing Brazil and South Africa: Transitional States in Political and Economic Perspective* (Johannesburg: Centre for Policy Studies, FGD, IDESP).

Simone, Abdou Maliq. 1995. "Urban Societies in Africa," in Richard Humphries and Maxine Reitzes, eds., *Civil Society After Apartheid* (Johannesburg: Centre for Policy Studies, December).

Sirowy, L., and A. Inkeles. 1990. "The Effect of Democracy on Economic Growth and Inequality." *Studies in Comparative International Development* 25, no. 1.

Smeeding, T. M., and P. Gottschalk. 1995. "The International Evidence on Income Distribution in Modern Economies: Where Do We Stand?" Working Paper 137, Luxembourg Income Study, CEP/INSTEAD.

Sönmez, M. 2001. *Gelir Uçurumu* (Istanbul: Om).

Soskice, David. 1999. "Divergent Production Regimes: Coordinated and

Uncoordinated Market Economies in the 1980s and 1990s," in Herbert Kitschelt et al., eds., *Continuity and Change in Contemporary Capitalism* (Cambridge: Cambridge University Press).

South African Labour and Development Research Unit. 1994. *South Africans Rich and Poor: Baseline Household Statistics* (Cape Town: University of Cape Town School of Economics).

South African Reserve Bank. 2003. "Statistical Tables," *Quarterly Bulletin,* no. 229 (September) (Pretoria: South Africa).

South African Revenue Service. 2001. *Annual Report 2000/2001* (Pretoria: Government Printer).

Stallings, Bárbara, and Jürgen Weller. 2001. "El empleo en América latina, base fundamental de la política social." *Revista de la CEPAL,* no. 75, pp. 191–210.

Starr, Pamela. 1999. "Capital Flows, Fixed Exchange Rates, and Political Survival: Mexico and Argentina, 1994–1995," in Philip Oxhorn and Pamela K. Starr, eds., *Markets and Democracy in Latin America* (London and Boulder, CO: Lynne Rienner Publishers).

Statistics South Africa. 2000. *Measuring Poverty,* 7 September. Online at http://www.statsa.gov.za.

Stiglitz, Joseph. 2002. "Development Policies in a World of Globalization." Paper read at "New Paths of Development," 12–13 September, Rio de Janeiro.

———. 2004. "Capital-Market Liberalization, Globalization and the IMF." *Oxford Review of Economic Policy* 20, no. 1: 57–71.

Strange, Susan. 1996. *The Retreat of the State: The Diffusion of Power in the World Economy* (Cambridge: Cambridge University Press).

Streeck, Wolfgang. 1997. "Beneficial Constraints: On the Economic Limits of Rational Voluntarism," in J. Rogers Hollingsworth and Robert Boyer, eds., *Contemporary Capitalism: The Embeddedness of Institutions* (Cambridge: Cambridge University Press).

Sung, Myung-Jae. 2002. *A Study of the Redistributive Effect of Tax Policy* (Seoul: Korea Institute of Public Finance).

Suplicy, Eduardo Matarazzo. 2002. *Renda de Cidadania. A saída é pela porta* (São Paulo: Fundação Perseu Abramo).

Suttner, Raymond, and Jeremy Cronin. 1985. *Thirty Years of the Freedom Charter* (Johannesburg: Ravan).

Tavares, Maria da Conceição. 1972. *Da substituição de importações ao capitalismo financeiro ensaios sobre economia brasileira,* 11th ed. *Biblioteca de ciências sociais. Economia Biblioteca de ci ncias socias* (Rio de Janeiro: Zahar Editores).

Theret, Bruno. 2001. "La mondialisation : Phenomene subi ou strategie d'Etat," in Marie-Cecile Naves and Charles Patou, eds., *La mondialisation comme concept opératoire* (Paris: L'Harmattan Cahiers Politiques).

Thompson, M., Richard Ellis, and Aaron B. Wildavsky. 1990. *Cultural Theory, Political Culture.* (Boulder, CO: Westview Press).

Tomlinson, Mary. 1996. *From Rejection to Resignation: Beneficiaries' Views on the Government's Housing Subsidy Scheme* (Johannesburg: Centre for Policy Studies).

———. 1997. *Mortgage Bondage? Financial Institutions and Low-Cost Housing Delivery* (Johannesburg: Centre for Policy Studies).

Tonelson, Alan. 2003. "False Promises on Globalization from Oxfam." *American Economic Alert,* 16 April 2002. Online at: http://www.americaneconomic alert.org.

Tulchin, Joseph S., and Ralph H. Espach, eds. 2004. *America Latina en el Nuevo sistema internacinal* (Barcelona: Edicions Bellaterra).
Tulchin, Joseph S., and Andrew D. Selee, eds. 2003. *Mexico's Politics and Society in Transition* (Boulder, CO: Lynne Rienner Publishers).
United Nations Development Program (UNDP). 2002. *Human Development Report 2002—Deepening Democracy in a Fragmented World* (New York: Oxford University Press). Online at: http://hdr.undp.org/reports/global/2002/en/.
———. 2003. "Human Development Report 2003—Millennium Development Goals: A Compact Among Nations to End Human Poverty" (New York: Oxford University Press).
Urani, André. 2002. "Desenvolvimento e distribuição de renda," in A. C. Castro, ed., *Desenvolvimento em debate: Painéis do desenvolvimento brasileiro* (Rio de Janeiro: Mauad; BNDES).
Uriel, E., et al. 1997. *Las cuentas de la Educación en España: 1980–1992* (Madrid: Fundación Argentaria).
Urquidi, Victor L. 1999. "El gran desafío del Siglo XXI: El desarrollo sustentable. Alcances y Riesgos para México." *Mercado de Valores, Mexico,* Nacional Financiera, 12 December.
U.S. Government, Central Intelligence Agency. 2002. *The World Factbook 2002.* Online at: http://www.cia.gov/cia/publications/factbook/index.html.
U.S. Social Security Administration. 1999. *Social Security Programs Throughout the World.* (Washington, DC: Social Security Administration, Office of Policy, Office of Research, Evaluation, and Statistics).
van den Bergh, Servaas, and Haroon Bhorat. 1999. *The Present as a Legacy of the Past: The Labour Market, Inequality and Poverty in South Africa.* Cape Town, Development Policy Research Unit, University of Cape Town, DPRU Working Paper 99/29.
Van Oorschot, Wim. 2001. "Flexicurity for Dutch Workers—Trends, Policies and Outcomes." Paper presented at the EU COST Action 13 meeting, Ljubljana University, Slovenia, 8–10 June.
Vega, Gustavo. 2004. "La política comercial de México desde la Segunda Guerra Mundial y el nuevo modelo de promoción de importaciones: Logros y retos para el futuro," in Ilán Bizberg and Lorenzo Meyer, eds., *Una Historia Contemporánea de México.* Vol. 1: *Transformaciones y permanencias* (México: Océano).
Vekemans, Roger, Ismael Silva Fuenzalida, and Jorge Giusti B. 1970. *La marginalidad en América Latina: un ensayo de conceptualización* (Santiago: Centro para el Desarrollo Económico y Social de América Latina).
Venter, Lester. 1997. *When Mandela Goes: The Coming of South Africa's Second Revolution* (Cape Town: Doubleday).
Villegas, Daniel Cosio. 1959. *Historia Moderna de México* (México: Editorial Hermes).
Villiers, Riaan de, ed. 1994. *Forums and the Future* (Johannesburg: Centre for Policy Studies, December).
Viola, Eduardo.1996. "A multidimensionalidade da globalização, as novas forças sociais transnacionais e seu impacto na política ambiental do Brasil, 1989–1995," in L. Ferreira and E. Viola, eds., *Incerteza de Sustentabilidade na Globalização* (Campinas, Brazil: Editora da UNICAMP).
Visser, Jelle, and Anton Hemerijck. 1997. *A Dutch Miracle* (Amsterdam: Amsterdam University Press).
von Amsberg, Joachim, Peter Lanjuow, and Kimberly Nead. 2000. "A Focalização

do gasto social sobre a pobreza no Brasil," in R. Henriques, ed., *Desigualdade e pobreza no Brazil* (Rio de Janeiro: IPEA).

Wade, R. H. 2001. "The Rising Inequality of World Income Distribution." *Finance and Development* 38, no. 4.

Waisman, Carlos. 1999. "State Capacity and the Conflicting Logics of Economic and Political Change," in Philip Oxhorn and Pamela K. Starr, eds., *Markets and Democracy in Latin America* (London and Boulder, CO: Lynne Rienner Publishers).

Waters, M. 1995. *Globalization* (London: Routledge).

Watkins, Kevin. 2004. *Rigged Rules and Double Standards: Trade, Globalization, and the Fight Against Poverty* (Oxford: Oxfam).

Weiss, Linda. 1997. "Confronting Globalization: The Myth of the Powerless State." *New Left Review,* no. 225.

Werneck, Rogério L. Furquim. 2002. "Reforma tributária: urgência, desafios e descaminhos," in A. C. Castro, ed., *Desenvolvimento em Debate: Painéis do desenvolvimento brasileiro* (Rio de Janeiro: Mauad; Banco Nacional de Desenvolvimento Econômico e Social [BNDES]).

White, Caroline. 1993. *Makhulu Padroni? Patron-Clientelism in Shack Areas and Some Italian Lessons for South Africa* (Johannesburg: Centre for Policy Studies).

White, Caroline, et al. 2000. "The Social Determinants of Energy Use: Synthesis Report." Unpublished report submitted to the South African Department of Mineral and Energy Affairs, January.

Williamson, J. 1993. "Democracy and Washington Consensus." *World Development* 21, no. 8.

Winters, L. Alan, Neil McCulloch, and Andrew McKay. 2004. "Trade Liberalization and Poverty: The Evidence So Far." *Journal of Economic Literature* XLII (March): 72–115.

World Bank. 1995. *World Development Report: Workers in a Developing World* (New York: Oxford University Press).

———. 2001. *2000 World Development Indicators* (Washington, DC: World Bank).

———. 2003. *Turkey: Poverty and Coping After Crisis.* World Bank Report no. 24185-TR.

Yang, Jae-jin. 2000. "The 1999 Pension Reform and a New Social Contract in South Korea." Ph.D. dissertation, political science, Rutgers University.

———. 2003. "Labor Market Flexibility and the Korean Welfare State: Coping with the Mismatch Between the Labor Market and the Social Welfare System" (in Korean). *Korean Political Science Review* 37, no. 3.

Zaidi, M. A., and K. de Vos. 1998. "Trends in Consumption-based Poverty and Inequality in the Member States of the European Union During the 1980s," Discussion Paper, Economics Institute, Tilburg.

# The Contributors

**Joseph S. Tulchin** is director of the Latin American Program at the Woodrow Wilson Center for International Scholars. He has taught or lectured in nearly every country in the hemisphere and has published over 100 scholarly articles and more than seventy books. His areas of expertise are U.S. foreign policy, inter-American relations, contemporary Latin America, strategic planning, and social science research methodology.

**Gary Bland** is director of the Center for Democratic Governance at RTI International. He has written extensively on decentralization and local governance as well as the legislative process, electoral systems, and democratic transitions. His most recent publication addresses local elections and authoritarian remnants of the Pinochet regime in Chile.

**Ilán Bizberg** is a professor and researcher at the Center for International Studies at the Colegio de México. He has worked on trade unionism in Mexico and on transitions to democracy from a comparative perspective. He obtained his Ph.D. at the EHESS in Paris, France. He has been public policy scholar at the Wilson Center and Humboldt Scholar at the University of Bilefeld. Most recently he has served as editor for *Democracia y Globalización en México y Brasil* (with Carlos Alba) and *Una Historia Contemporánea de México* (with Lorenzo Meyer).

**Steven Friedman** is senior research fellow at the Centre for Policy Studies, Johannesburg, and visiting professor of political studies at Rhodes University, South Africa. His chief research interest is democratization, with a particular interest in the relationship between democracy and inequality. He is the author of a study of the South African trade union movement and editor of two books on South Africa's negotiated transition to democracy, as well as numerous journal articles and monographs.

**E. Fuat Keyman** is professor of international relations at the Koç University in Istanbul, Turkey. His research focuses on international relations, globalization, democratic theory, and Turkish politics. He has authored many articles and books on Turkey and globalization, including *Globalization, State, and Identity/Difference: A Critical Social Theory of International Relations* (1997), "Globalization, Civil Society and Citizenship in Turkey" (2003), and "Globalization, Alternative Modernities and the Political Economy of Turkey" (2004).

**Aprodicio A. Laquian** is professor emeritus of community and regional planning at the University of British Columbia, in Vancouver, Canada. He is a member of the Advisory Council of the Comparative Urban Studies Project, Woodrow Wilson International Center for Scholars, and was a WWICS fellow in 2002–2003. He has written or edited 18 books, the latest of which is, *Beyond Metropolis: The Planning and Governance of Asia's Mega-Urban Regions* (Woodrow Wilson Center Press and Johns Hopkins University Press).

**Chung-in Moon** is professor of political science at Yonsei University and chairman of the Presidential Committee on Northeast Asian Cooperation Initiative of the Republic of Korea.

**Josep Oliver-Alonso** is a native of Girona, Spain. He is currently a professor of economics at the Universitat Autónoma de Barcelona. He is author of books and articles about Catalan and Spanish poverty, and its relation with human capital. He has also written articles on labor market and households behavior in Catalonia and Spain.

**Simon Schwartzman** is the president of the Institute for Studies of Labor and Society (IETS) in Rio de Janeiro. In the late nineties, he was the head of Brazil's National Statistical Office (IBGE) and taught at the University of São Paulo, among other places. He has published extensively on issues of social policy, particularly in the area of poverty and education, and also on science, technology, and innovation policies. He holds a Ph.D. in political science from the University of California, Berkeley.

**Josep M. Vallés** is professor of political science at the Universitat Autònoma de Barcelona. He is author of books and articles about electoral systems, electoral behavior, and local government. He has been president of the Spanish Political Science Association (AECPA). He has been on university leave since 2003, as minister of justice for the government of Catalonia.

**Jae-jin Yang** is an assistant professor of public administration at Yonsei University. His areas of expertise are social policy, comparative public policy, and politics-administration relations. Recently, he has written extensively on structural adjustments and social policies, with publications including "The Rise of the Korean Welfare State Amid Economic Crisis, 1997–1999" and "Democratic Governance and Bureaucratic Politics: The Case of Pension Reform in Korea."

# Index

# About the Book

*Getting Globalization Right* explores political and economic changes in seven new democracies that have in common both a movement toward greater integration with the world economy and the challenges posed by persistent or even increasing domestic economic inequalities.

The authors argue that, without effective national policies to dampen the effects of globalization, the short-term impact of opening the economy has a negative effect on levels of poverty and inequality. In a more positive vein, however, and without minimizing the difficulties involved, they identify the types of social policies that can blunt or counter these negative effects. They also suggest that international governance will have a growing influence on how globalization affects individual nations.

The up-to-date, empirically rich case studies in the book cover the experiences of Brazil, Mexico, the Philippines, South Africa, South Korea, Spain, and Turkey.

**Joseph S. Tulchin** is director of the Latin American Program at the Woodrow Wilson International Center for Scholars. **Gary Bland** is senior public policy and governance specialist at the Research Triangle Institute.